Planning an Appropriate Curriculum in the Early Years

Now in its third edition, *Planning an Appropriate Curriculum in the Early Years* offers a comprehensive guide for early years practitioners and students on how to plan and implement a suitable curriculum for the children in an early years setting. It examines the key roles and responsibilities of practitioners working in early years settings and those with responsibility for leading and managing provision for the Early Years Foundation Stage in primary schools.

Completely revised and updated in line with the review of the EYFS and the latest research evidence, this book covers all aspects of the curriculum including:

- the areas of learning and development;
- assessment procedures and record keeping;
- leadership and management in the early years;
- the role played by parents and carers in children's learning and development;
- planning for child-initiated learning and adult-led activities.

With case studies of good practice and questions for reflective practice and group work, this fully updated best-seller will be welcomed by students and practitioners looking to provide high quality and effective learning experiences for the under fives.

Rosemary Rodger is an early years consultant and trainer. She works with schools, nurseries and children's centres in the UK and is involved in launching the Urban Leadership Centre's Children's Centres leadership model. She was previously Senior Lecturer in Early Years Education at Edge Hill University and Manchester Metropolitan University before becoming an Additional Inspector of primary and nursery schools.

Planning an Appropriate Curriculum in the Early Years

A guide for early years practitioners and leaders, students and parents

Third edition

Rosemary Rodger

Routledge
Taylor & Francis Group

LONDON AND NEW YORK

First edition published 1999
by David Fulton Publishers

This third edition published 2012
by Routledge
2 Park Square, Milton Park, Abingdon, Oxon OX14 4RN

Simultaneously published in the USA and Canada
by Routledge
711 Third Avenue, New York, NY 10017

Routledge is an imprint of the Taylor & Francis Group, an informa business

© 2012 Rosemary Rodger

British Library Cataloguing in Publication Data
A catalogue record for this book is available from the British Library

Library of Congress Cataloging in Publication Data
  Rodger, Rosemary, 1946–
  Planning an appropriate curriculum in the early years : a guide for
early years practitioners and leaders, students and parents/ by Rosemary
Rodger. – 3rd ed.
  p.cm.
  Rev. ed. of Planning an appropriate curriculum for the under fives, 1999.
  Includes bibliographical references and index.
  1. Education, Preschool – Curricula – Great Britain. 2. Curriculum planning – Great Britain. I. Title.
  LB1140.4.R63 2012
  372.190941–dc23
  2011027026

ISBN: 978–0–415–58303–9 (hbk)
ISBN: 978–0–415–58304–6 (pbk)
ISBN: 978–0–203–14801–3 (ebk)

Typeset in Bembo
by Swales & Willis Ltd, Exeter, Devon

MIX
Paper from
responsible sources
FSC   FSC® C004839
www.fsc.org

Printed and bound in Great Britain by
TJ International Ltd, Padstow, Cornwall

To Adam, Alex, Kirsty, Jake and Ethan

Contents

Figures

Tables

Boxes

Case studies

Acknowledgements

To have spent the past twenty-five years working in the early years sector and being involved with trainee and experienced early years practitioners in many ways, it is a testament to their inspiration, professionalism, creativity, ingenuity and commitment that the third edition of this book is now complete. My thanks go to all the practitioners I have worked with. I am particularly grateful to:

- Judy Donnelly, Pennywell Early Years Centre, Sunderland
- Julie Heron, Oxclose Nursery School, Sunderland
- Christine Collins, Hylton Red House Nursery School, Sunderland
- Jinny Fisher, Montpelier Primary School, Plymouth
- Catherine Parkin, Burnside Primary School, County Durham
- Catherine Worton, Trimdon Grange Nursery and Infant School, County Durham
- Valerie Vayro, Laurel Avenue Primary School, County Durham
- Vicky Masters, Pangbourne Children's Centre, West Berkshire
- Nadine Parker, Beech Hill Primary School, Newcastle
- Kayleigh Farnham, Walbottle Village Primary School, Newcastle
- Early Years Team, Washingwell Primary, Gateshead.

For reminders of childhood and how children learn through their play, I thank Ethan Alexander, my second grandchild, for providing me with endless pleasure and the opportunity to carry out uninterrupted observational assessments. Finally my loving thanks to Iain for his support.

1

Introduction

The first five years of a child's life, the foundation years, are absolutely critical. We want a system where every child can thrive, regardless of their social background. If we are to tackle the attainment gap and raise life chances, we must start in the earliest years.

(DfE, 2011a)

This edition is a complete rewrite from previous editions of this book. While its main focus is on the English statutory curriculum for the early years, there are references to early years curricular models across the world, especially those that have influenced practices in England. Amid changes to government and the constant cry of cuts and more cuts in the public sector, it is with some trepidation that this edition has reached completion. The colossal amount of support and training, funding and guidance provided to early years practitioners under the previous government and the statutory legislation should have ensured an almost idyllic, educational start for most of the young children across the country. Sure Start centres proliferated and outreach programmes strove to get to the neediest of children and families in society with, as it turns out, still some way to go to reach those 'hard to reach' families. Feeling somewhat dispirited that all this progress might be slowed down, the publication very recently of *Early Intervention: The Next Steps* (Allen, 2011) is giving me hope that all is not as bleak as it seems. The executive summary makes many recommendations, but the one that is firmly embedded and very dear to my heart is number 16:

> I recommend that we improve workforce capability of those working with the 0–5s. We should: increase graduate-led, or even postgraduate pre-school leadership, ensure that all early years settings employ someone with Early Years Professional Status (EYPS) on site and establish a Workforce Development strategy led by the Department for Education and Health with input from across government, to ensure that we are developing for the future enough suitably qualified candidates who wish to work with the 0–5s.
>
> (Allen, 2011: xix)

The review of the Early Years Foundation Stage (EYFS) was promised when the EYFS was introduced. It was recognised then that, after a period of bedding in, the impact of the EYFS on children's outcomes and on those working in the early years should be evaluated. The review report by Clare Tickell (March 2011) recommends that early years practitioners are to have at least a level 3 qualification (which is equivalent to A level) and the government should consider applying the 'teaching schools' model to the early years. I am further heartened by the publication of *The Early Years Review: Foundations for Life, Health and Learning* (DfE, 2011a). This is an independent report on the EYFS to the government. Some of the key names on the co-production steering group further reinforce the strong feeling of confidence in the review. Therein, we see the names of great early years researchers such as Kathy Sylva, Christine Pascal and an experienced nursery head teacher, Bernadette Duffy. *The Early Years Review* (DfE, 2011a) endorses the EYFS as a framework which could deliver 'consistent and high quality environments for all children in pre-school settings'. There is well-deserved praise for the high priority given to children's learning and development in the past two years.

The evaluation of the EYFS was anticipated. An evidence-led review has taken place to identify what works well and what might need to be improved. This publication, while holding strongly to the existing EYFS, identifies those areas that have to be improved. The report states that 70 per cent of the people responding to calls for evidence thought that the EYFS was successful. The views of parents and practitioners supported the focus on personal, social and emotional development (PSED) (89 per cent of practitioners and 81 per cent of parents) and communication skills (85 per cent of practitioners and 68 per cent of parents) as the bedrock on which everything else is built (DfE, 2011a: 92). Physical development was cited as the third most important assessment area after PSED and communication and language (CL). EYFS is popular because it is based on the very best approaches of skilled practitioners working with young children from birth to 5. There is a simpler presentation of the areas of learning and development. There are reduced requirements for assessment because there are fewer demands for the early learning goals and parents are to have clearer guidance. The report recommends that the approach to assessment is effectively managed and should be compatible with and be valuable to primary teachers so that a child's transition into Key Stage 1 is a smooth process. The tenor of the review is that it is simpler and easier for practitioners to implement the EYFS curriculum. There is likely to be less support provided than in previous years for early years practitioners, so there is an imperative to provide an accessible framework that is relevant to current and future situations. The comments of Chris Pascal, Director of the Centre for Research in Early Childhood, that the EYFS review, 'refocuses attention to those aspects of practice that really shapes children's lives and frees practitioners from many of the perceived burdens they felt were preventing progress' (Chandiramani, 2011) are welcomed.

The Early Years Foundation Stage Framework (DfE, 2011a)

The Tickell review was accepted by the government in July 2011 with implementation expected in September 2012. Making sure that children start school ready and able to learn is a key aim. Children's Minister Sarah Teather said:

> The first five years of a child's life, the foundation years, are absolutely critical. We want a system where every child can thrive, regardless of their social background. If we are to tackle the attainment gap and raise life chances, we must start in the earliest years.
>
> (Chandiramani, 2011)

Government have accepted all the major revisions recommended by Clare Tickell (DfE, 2011a). The new framework radically reduces the number of early learning goals from 69 to

17. It focuses on three prime areas of learning critical to making sure that children develop healthily and happily. Parents will also get much clearer information on how their children are doing with the introduction of a new progress check for every 2-year-old in early education. This is an amendment to the review in which the progress check would take place for every 2-year-old child wherever they were. It is also recommended that parents have more flexibility in the free entitlement of 15 hours of early learning and childcare. It is likely this will be any time between 7am and 7pm.

Implications for Children's Centres

The government have identified a new core purpose for Children's Centres, with a stronger focus on school readiness and supporting families. It clearly sets out the outcomes which Children's Centres should be supporting. The proposals are that the Children's Centres will need to find new ways of running, such as mutuals and cooperative approaches, so parents and communities can be more involved in local decision-making and services. There will be new requirements on all local authorities to publish data on how much they are spending on Children's Centres in their area to improve local accountability.

Statutory requirements

The Childcare Act (DCSF, 2006b) ensures high-quality early learning and care and better access to early childhood services for all children under 5. This is achieved by: the free offer of care and learning, which will increase and become more flexible for parents of 3- and 4-year-olds that want it; the new Early Years Foundation Stage, which will establish a framework to support children's development and learning from birth to 5; and a duty on local authorities to improve the outcomes of young children by providing better joined up and accessible early childhood services through Children's Centres.

Also important in improving outcomes for all, the Act requires local authorities to reduce inequalities between those at risk of the poorest outcomes and the rest. It aims to provide working parents a choice of a wide range of childcare where they can be confident that their children will thrive and be well cared for, enabling them to have greater choices about balancing work and family life. The Act places a duty on local authorities to secure – in partnership with the private and voluntary sector – sufficient childcare for all parents who choose to work or are in training in preparation for work and a duty to provide information and advice to parents on childcare and other services to support parents. It also reforms and simplifies the regulatory arrangements by the Office for Standards in Education (Ofsted). These will provide parents with greater confidence about the childcare they choose.

Local authorities (LAs) will work in partnership with the private and voluntary sector to ensure a diverse and sustained childcare market.

While the statutory requirements remain, the ring fencing of funding for Sure Start centres is removed and responsibility is placed on local authorities. There's the rub, as LAs are faced with needing to make swingeing cuts. At this stage it is not clear how many Sure Start centres may close because of the changes to funding. A recent survey (March 2011) has revealed that up to 7 per cent of Sure Start centres could close within the year, while thousands will be forced to cut back on services because of decreased budgets. Some staff have had issues with 'at risk' redundancy notices. The Chief Executive of the Daycare Trust said, 'behind every

Children's Centre facing closure is a community of families devastated at losing one of their most valued services' (Chandiramani, 2011).

Arrangements for the provision of Children's Centres are outlined in the *Sure Start Children's Centres Statutory Guidance* (DfE, 2010a). However, the government are committed to eradicating disadvantage (Marmot, 2010; Allen and Duncan Smith, 2009; Allen, 2011). These three reports to the government lay claim to the social and economic benefits of intervening early. There is a pledge to provide childcare for disadvantaged 2-year-olds. Clare Tickell (DfE 2011a: 3) also emphasises how children who have specific needs, or come from particularly disadvantaged backgrounds, are identified and supported as early as possible given the overwhelming evidence of the positive impact this has had.

The Early Years: Foundations for Life, Health and Learning (DfE, 2011a)

A brief overview of the recommendations by Clare Tickell in her independent report on the Early Years Foundation Stage follows. Each chapter takes account of the new EYFS framework and retains reference to the themes of 'A Unique Child', 'Positive Relationships', 'Enabling Environments' and 'Learning and Development'. Tickell pays tribute to the current EYFS for the way in which it has emphasised children's learning and development and improvements to outcomes for young children. A clear remit to gather evidence from the early years sector to identify and build on what works well in the current EYFS and to improve those areas that are causing problems has taken place. Forty-six recommendations were made to the government. The key role of parents as educators and steps to increase the partnership between parents and practitioners is a major theme throughout the review. Specific guidance as to the information provided to parents and to creating a clear link between EYFS provision and the health-visitor-led health and development review for 2-year-olds is one aspect (see Chapter 7).

Evidence shows that personal, social and emotional development, communication and language, and physical development are essential foundations for children's life, learning and success. As a result, Tickell recommends that these are to be 'prime' areas of learning in the EYFS. The areas of learning in which the 'prime' areas are applied are literacy, mathematics, understanding of the world and expressive arts and design. Areas of Learning chapters and the Learning and Curriculum chapters provide further information on this recommendation.

A fundamental recommendation that the EYFS be slimmed down and a reduction made in the bureaucracy associated with assessments is to be welcomed. Greater account of the needs of summer-born children and those children who are fast developers is recommended in the introduction of a simple three-part assessment scale which sets out what working towards, what achieving and what exceeding each early learning goal looks like. All aspects of safety and welfare in general are to be renamed as safeguarding and welfare requirements.

Early years evidence pack (DfE, 2011b)

The evidence base for the 46 recommendations in the EYFS review is impressive. A major finding is the widespread agreement about the importance of the early years. What I have found particularly reassuring is the joined-up thinking and combining of the views of politicians, healthcare staff, educational practitioners, researchers, children and parents. The evidence pack that has contributed to the findings makes the following statements in the introduction:

■ We have found overwhelming evidence that children's life chances are most heavily predicated on their development in the first five years of life. It is family background, parental education, good parenting and the opportunities for learning and development in those crucial years that together matter more to children than money in determining whether their potential is realised in adult life (Field, 2010).

■ Even greater priority must be given to ensuring expenditure early in the developmental life cycle (that is, on children below the age of 5) and that more is invested in interventions that have proved to be effective (Marmot, 2010).

■ These early years are absolutely central to the developmental fate of a child, yet until recently they have received virtually no attention. A huge cultural shift must take place. Resources must be invested in the early years of children, concentrating on those most at risk, whose parents/carers are least able to provide what the child needs (Kennedy, 2010).

■ The Sure Start programme as a whole is one of the most innovative and ambitious government initiatives of the past two decades … in many areas it has cut through the silos that so often bedevil public service delivery. Children's Centres are a substantial investment with a sound rationale, and it is vital that this investment is allowed to bear fruit over the long term (DfE, 2010a).

The evidence pack cites many examples of research that demonstrates influences on achievement. The evidence from the national data for achievement in the EYFS shows that, based on the Foundation Stage Profile (FSP) scores, achievement has risen over the past five years. There is a close correlation between achievement on the FSP and at Key Stage 1. Put quite simply, children who achieve a good level of development at age 5 go on to achieve the expected levels of reading at Key Stage 1, and they are five times more likely to achieve the highest level. The Effective Provision of Pre-School Education (EPPE) study (Sylva *et al.*, 2004) found that there is no single factor that determines attainment, but that good quality early years provision is important alongside a good early years home environment and an effective primary school as well as the pre-school situation. The outcomes of this study have influenced the close relationships fostered between Sure Start and Children's Centres in the past ten years. The final project report for EPPE made claims that high quality and longer time in provision has the clearest effect, although the length of time in pre-school may wash out over time, the quality effect remains strong. High quality provision is a result of the qualifications and training staff receive. The presence of a highly qualified practitioner can have a positive impact of less-well-qualified practitioners (Siraj-Blatchford, 2002). A key to influencing current policy with regard to disadvantaged 2-year-olds is the findings of the *Early Education Pilot for Two Year Old Children Evaluation* (DCSF, 2009e), which found that where children attended higher quality settings there was a positive impact on language ability and on their parents-child relationship. As a result, parents *felt* that the setting had positively affected their ability to parent and their physical health and mental well-being, and provided them with opportunities for self-improvement. Recent news coverage over threatened closures of Children's Centres in some local authorities confirms so well how the centres are valued by parents as they plead their case by citing how they have helped with many aspects of health and mental well-being. Undoubtedly practitioners leading Children's Centres, private nurseries, nursery schools and nursery units attached to primary schools do, at times, feel under pressure. The Tickell report suggests this is, in part, due to the differing expectations of Ofsted. It is suggested that Ofsted and the local authorities (LAs) work together to produce clear, consistent advice on the things early years settings have to do, and do not create unnecessary burdens by asking for things that are not specified in the EYFS.

The Early Years Foundation Stage (DCSF, 2008f)

I make no apologies for reminding practitioners of the current EYFS framework and its associated support material, all of which is available on the Department for Education (DfE) website, www.education.gov.uk. Many publications are referred to throughout this book and will continue to provide helpful guidelines to those working in the early years sector at all levels. What has remained from the original EYFS framework are the themes and commitments statements that provide the underlying philosophy, with particular emphasis on the Unique Child and the play-based approach to the EYFS. The principles which guide the work of all early years practitioners are grouped into four themes:

1   A Unique Child – every child is a competent learner from birth who can be resilient, capable, confident and self-assured.
2   Positive Relationships – children learn to be strong and independent from a base of loving and secure relationships with parents and/or a key person.
3   Enabling Environments – the environment plays a key role in supporting and extending children's development and learning.
4   Learning and Development – children learn and develop in different ways and at different rates and all areas of learning and development are equally important and interconnected (revised in the new EYFS framework).

There is more detail as to the elements of each theme in Chapter 2, 'A Curriculum for the Twenty-First Century'. The EYFS Review provides very clear guidance on how to interpret self-initiated learning and the role of the adult in supporting and extending children's learning that will, at last, lay some myths to rest. There is further information about this in Chapter 6, 'Learning and Development', which has a particular focus on the role of the practitioner.

Research

The *Early Years Learning and Development Literature Review* (Evangelou *et al.*, 2009) provided a major part of the evidence base for the EYFS review. The research findings are referred to throughout this book with particular attention to key situations, such as types of interaction and communications that a child experiences and who these people are (family, friends, early years practitioners, peers and neighbours). Practitioners wishing to further their professional development will find the references to the most recent research and theories supported by examples of practice in a range of settings helpful. The aim of the research review was to focus on research findings since 2000 with the purpose to consider the original sources on children's development as well as the critical reviews of these. A principle focus was to identify and review evidence in respect of the process of development for children from birth to age 5. Studies of cognitive, social, emotional and brain development took place. Other objectives focused on findings linked to children's development at the end of the academic year in which they are 5 years old. The review sought out the evidence that identifies the best supportive contexts for children's early learning and development.

The review took a 'constructivist approach' to development (Rogoff, 2003). New research from neuropsychology that informs understanding of brain development and supportive environments to nurture it was included (Blackmore and Firth, 2005). The report recognises recent conceptualisations of development in which various domains of development are interconnected and influence one another. A further research focus was the 'interactionist' tradition, meaning that development is located within nested contexts (Bronfenbrenner, 1979). The work of Vygotsky (1978), which stresses the role of the social and cultural context in children's development, is very evident. For example, in discussion about what supporting a child's learning and development might look like in practice, Tickell quotes directly from Vygotsky as she describes what the support might look like, 'A definition I found very helpful describes this support as the difference between what a child can do on their own, and what they can do when guided by someone else – either an adult or a more able child' (DfE, 2011a: 29).

Conclusion

This book is for aspiring practitioners, whatever their route, to assist with their attainment of the necessary qualifications to work in the early years sector. Practitioners are likely to be: those nearly qualified, newly qualified, coming into the EYFS sector from other careers; experienced practitioners; or leaders wishing to add to their existing qualifications. I hope parents, too, will find the book provides a useful overview of the EYFS world their children meet as they take their first steps into learning away from home. They will also see very strong justification for their role as the child's first and most important educator.

Each chapter stands alone and includes the newly created areas of learning with many examples taken from current practices. As in previous editions, there are also chapters covering: The Curriculum, Assessment, Planning, and Leadership and Management. 'Involving Parents and Carers' and 'Learning and Development' are additional chapters in this edition. The Leadership and Management chapter covers the mandatory safeguarding and welfare requirements that are essential for children's basic safety, security and health as recommended in the EYFS review (DfE, 2011a).

2

A curriculum for the twenty-first century

The touchstone of an excellent curriculum is that it instils in children a love of learning for its own sake.

(DCSF, 2009d)

Introduction

This chapter aims to share various curricular models, but is predominantly, along with the rest of the book, about the Framework for the Early Years Foundation Stage (DCSF, 2008f and DfE, 2011a). Various curricular models from around the world, including the Scottish Early Years Curriculum, the Early Years curriculum in Sweden and the Reggio Emilia curriculum, are outlined also. The revised English early years curriculum for the twenty-first century comprises more than what young children learn in whatever educational and/or care setting they attend. The revisions to the Early Years Foundation Stage Curriculum (DfE, 2011a) leave the themes, principles and commitments to the EYFS as they were in the original curriculum. There are many revisions, including the 'Learning and Development' theme which comprises each area of learning. There is also importance given to ensuring that there is a high priority given to the needs of the most disadvantaged children and their families. The recognition of the strong partnership with parents and carers is paramount in the latest review of EYFS provision. The recommendations of the Tickell report (2011) are that there should be 'prime' areas of learning: personal, social and emotional development; communication and language; and physical development. These three areas of learning are essential foundations for children's life, learning and success. The 'specific' areas of learning are literacy, mathematics, understanding of the world and expressive arts and design. These are areas of learning in which the 'prime' skills are applied. Practitioners fully endorse the four themes and principles in the existing framework. The Unique Child principle and the play-based approach to EYFS are highly valued by practitioners too. The well-being of children, a reduction in the inequalities between young children and the central role of the family are crucial to children's overall learning and development. These requirements became statutory in England as a result of the Childcare Act (DCSF, 2006b) which has taken forward the key commitments of the Ten Year Childcare Strategy (DfES, 2004). Greater investment in the early years and the World Wide Web in the past ten years has enabled practitioners to learn about, and visit, other countries and adapt aspects of differing curricular models into their own settings. The knowledge and understanding gained from practices in other countries are influencing provision in English early years settings. For example, the well-known early years curriculum from New Zealand, Te Whāriki, comprises the sum total of experiences, activities and events with four overarching principles. They are: empowerment, family and community, holistic development, and relationships, with five strands running through each of well-being, belonging, contribution, communication and exploration. The increasing priority given to the key role of outdoor learning links to practices in Scandinavian countries and the outcomes of recent research into the impact of outdoor learning, particularly on boys' behaviour and attitudes to learning. This chapter aims to provide a flavour of a variety of curricular models without promoting any one model over another. However, what is shown is the high priority early years provision is given in many countries and how there are distinct commonalities across the world. The EYFS framework (DfE, 2011a) for children up to the age of 5 is an example that compares very favourably with curricula in other countries. The time is right for celebration and sharing of the EYFS (DfE, 2011a) worldwide. An example of exceptional EYFS practice demonstrates just some of the impact of the EYFS curriculum (see Case Study 2.1).

CASE STUDY 2.1 Washingwell Primary School EYFS provision

Provision in the Early Years Foundation Stage (EYFS) is outstanding. This is most evident in the rapid progress children make in knowing the sounds and letters and writing captions for displays around the indoor classroom. Children start in the EYFS with skills in line with age-related expectations. Children achieve very well and make excellent progress. Standards when they leave Reception are above average. Exceptionally high levels of independence, curiosity and concentration are evident in their indoor and outdoor learning. Children's personal development and well-being are outstanding. They persevere with tasks and take part in innovative play in a harmonious and enjoyable way. Adults are skilled in supporting learning and ensure that children are challenged because of the exemplary planning. Detailed observations provide information for individual progress folders that serve to provide a comprehensive record for parents. The children's welfare is well promoted; staff are fully trained and up-to-date with the latest developments in EYFS. The inspirational leadership of EYFS has transformed the outdoor provision recently to enable children to enjoy their learning inside and outside to the highest level. A common sense of purpose pervades the exciting range of learning. For example, the activities arising from the 'Elves and the Shoemaker' topic are endless and always have at their heart inspirational ways of learning basic skills. This was seen when a group of children paired shoes and demonstrated their ability to count in twos and other children designed and painted different kinds of shoes. Displays fully reflect the whole school priority given to improving writing. Links with the pre-school on site help to ensure a smooth transition from pre-school to the Reception class.

A definition of curriculum for the early years

It is probably useful at this early stage to consider the word 'curriculum' within an early years context. Is it an appropriate term to use? Are we familiar with what a curriculum includes? Is it intentional that the practice guidance for the English EYFS (DCSF, 2008f) uses the word

'Framework' to describe the legal requirements relating to learning and development (the early learning goals; the educational programme and the assessment arrangements)? In addition, there are specific legal requirements relating to welfare; safeguarding and promoting children's welfare; suitable people; suitable premises, environment and equipment; organisation and documentation. There is some discussion of the relative merits or otherwise of the English early years curricular model compared to those in other countries and consideration of the impact a top-down model could have on practitioners. Is this a desirable state of affairs, or something of deep concern for those practitioners with philosophies that are at odds with this model? In the current political climate there are many changes taking place across the early years sector. Because use of the word 'curriculum' is so widespread and familiar, for example, as in *Scottish Curriculum for Excellence* (COSLA, 2008), *High Scope Curriculum* and Australia and New Zealand's curricula, it is felt to be appropriate to continue using the term because of the connotations it has to learning and practical activities. The EYFS (DfE, 2011a) encompasses the early years principles, particularly the Unique Child, Enabling Environments and Learning and Development that are featured too in early years curricula across the world. A definition that appears to fit most models describes the curriculum as a cultural construct derived from what we as a nation value most highly for all our children. What is valued most highly? The appropriateness of the experiences provided to help children learn and develop in situations that are most suitable goes some way towards answering this question. Steadfast attention to the physical, social, emotional, personal, communication and linguistic needs are the areas of learning and development that are highlighted for priority in England currently. Of course, there is sometimes disagreement amongst those who determine what those priorities should be. I am thinking about the tensions there are in defining what exactly the role of the adult is in a setting as to the extent they should be involved in learning or to allow children to take responsibility for what they choose to do. Tickell makes very clear her views based on the evidence gathered for the review that, 'the EYFS requirement relating to delivery through play is clarified, including emphasis that this does not preclude more adult direction or teaching, and by setting out what playful adult-directed learning looks like' (DfE, 2011a: 35). There's the rub, and where disagreements abound, especially in relation to the opposing practices and views on when young children are taught to read and write in England, but more of that in Chapter 9, Communication, Language and Literacy.

In the recent past, amid concern about the welfare of very young children in their homes, attention to welfare arrangements and safeguarding of children in their childcare setting has escalated and is now central to provision and practices (see Chapter 5). This priority is reinforced in the review (DfE, 2011a: 37). In the English system many young children are cared for and educated in a Children's Centre or nursery class attached to a primary school, leading to the inevitable result that practices suitable for older pupils have had an impact on provision for younger children in nursery and Reception classes. Fortunately, this is less common as a result of the introduction of the statutory EYFS curriculum. Indeed, EYFS is beginning to make an impact on the early stages of the primary curriculum. Tickell (DfE, 2011a) too makes a strong point about the preparation needed for children towards the end of EYFS so they are ready to make the transition to Key Stage 1.

The English Early Years Foundation Stage (DCSF, 2008f and DfE, 2011a)

The revised EYFS

Currently, early years practitioners are preparing to adapt their ways of planning and implementing the EYFS framework to reflect the new Framework. The changes are relatively minimal as Clare Tickell says in her review:

> Two years on there is much to be proud of. The emphasis in the EYFS on children's learning and development in the early years has played a crucial part in contributing to a system that has indeed received international recognition and plaudits.
>
> (DfE, 2011a: 2)

The suggested changes are welcomed and serve to make implementation less stressful, more straightforward and much simpler overall for practitioners to get their heads around. A key reason for the changes relate to creating learning and development priorities and simplifying the *Development Matters* statements that practitioners are using to support their planning and assessment. The overarching new framework is robustly based on what is known from research evidence. A key to one of the major changes is that despite all that is currently in place, there are still 44 per cent of children not reaching a good level of development by the end of the year in which they turn five. A new recommendation is that the EYFS curriculum should continue to be a framework that applies to all providers working with children in the early years. The revised EYFS curriculum has three prime areas of learning which are: personal, social and emotional development; communication and language; and physical development. The rationale behind the selection of these prime areas is that they provide the essential foundations for healthy development, for positive attitudes to relationships and learning, and for progress in key skills such as reading and writing. The justification for these areas is that they also inform the work of health visitors as part of the health and development review for all children when they reach 2 years of age. This is an interesting recommendation that is worthy of further debate. There is a wealth of research evidence used to validate the decision to focus on these as the prime areas of learning that is referred to in the appropriate chapters. There is a strong emphasis on healthy development in the review and the prime areas of learning being the ones that are most important for the youngest children and the ones most likely to promote healthy development, positive attitudes to relationships and learning, and for progress in key skills such as reading and writing. These prime areas also inform the work of health visitors as part of the health and development review for 2-year-olds in the Healthy Child Programme. Hence, we may have a short written early years summary for parents of their children's development in the prime areas (see Table 2.1). The summary is based only on the three prime areas of development to be provided to parents at some point between the ages of 24–36 months. It is suggested that practitioners should be relaxed as to when this summary is completed and not be expected to work to deadlines.

EYFS themes and principles

There are four overarching principles which guide the implementation of the curriculum. These are grouped into four themes (see Table 2.2). The EYFS guidance material includes

TABLE 2.1 Prime areas of learning and development

Personal, Social and Emotional Development (PSED)
■ Self-confidence and self-awareness ■ Managing feelings and behaviour ■ Making relationships
Communication and Language
■ Listening and attention ■ Understanding ■ Speaking
Physical Development
■ Moving and handling ■ Health and self-care

TABLE 2.2 EYFS principles (DCFS, 2008f)

A UNIQUE CHILD	POSITIVE RELATIONSHIPS	ENABLING ENVIRONMENTS	LEARNING AND DEVELOPMENT
Every child is a competent learner from birth who can be resilient, capable, self-confident and self-assured.	Children learn to be strong and independent from a base of loving and secure relationships with parents and/or a key person.	The environment plays a key role in supporting and extending children's development and learning.	Children learn and develop in different ways and at different rates and all areas of learning and development are equally important and inter-connected.

Principles into Practice cards to assist practitioners to plan appropriate activities based on the needs and interests of individual children. There are clear expectations relating to welfare requirements for all children and a high priority is placed on the safeguarding arrangements to ensure children are safe from risk of any kind.

Well-researched principles, as described in this book's first edition (Rodger, 1999: 28), provided the basis for the *Statutory Framework for the Early Years Foundation Stage* (DCSF, 2008f) and remain as the core of the revised framework. The four principles are described below.

Principle 1: a unique child

Babies and children develop in individual ways and at varying rates. Every area of development – physical, cognitive, linguistic, spiritual, social and emotional – is equally important. This is the first commitment of this principle. It is followed by the commitment to 'inclusive practice', stating that the diversity of individuals and communities is valued and respected. There is no discrimination against any child or family. Third, there is the commitment to 'keeping safe', which states that young children are vulnerable and develop resilience when adults protect their physical and psychological well-being. The 'health and well-being' commitment states that children's health is an integral part of their emotional, mental, social, environmental and spiritual well-being and is supported by attention to these aspects. This last commitment resonates very strongly with the Tickell review, which calls for a renewed emphasis on healthy development for all children, with better and earlier identification of developmental needs, delivered by closer working with parents, carers and professionals – including health professionals.

Principle 2: positive relationships

The first commitment, 'respecting each other', states that every interaction is based on caring professional relationships and respectful acknowledgement of the feelings of children and their families. The 'parents as partners' commitment is also given a high priority in the review. Parents are children's first and most enduring educators. When parents and practitioners work together in early years settings, the results have a positive impact on children's development and learning. Children learn to be strong and independent from a base of loving and secure relationships with parents and/or a key person. The commitment of 'supporting learning' is crucial. Warm, trusting relationships with knowledgeable adults support children's learning more effectively than any amount of resources. Within this principle is the commitment to a 'key person'. This is someone who has key responsibilities working with a small number of children, giving them reassurance to feel safe and well cared for, and building relationships with parents.

Principle 3: enabling environments

A key commitment to 'observation, assessment and planning' spells out how the schedules and routines should flow from the children's needs, as babies and young children are individuals first, each with a unique profile of abilities. It suggests that all planning starts with observing children in order to understand and consider their current interests, development and learning. The second commitment states that the environment supports every child's learning through planned experiences and activities which are challenging but achievable. This is followed by a commitment related to the learning environment. A rich and varied environment supports children's learning and development. It gives them the confidence to explore and learn in secure and safe, yet challenging, indoor and outdoor spaces. Settings need also to have a commitment to working in partnership with other settings, other professionals and with individuals and groups in the community.

Principle 4: learning and development

This book has the 'learning and development' commitment very firmly as its aim. In their play children learn at their highest level. Play with peers is important for children's development. The commitment to 'active learning' states that children learn best through physical and mental challenges. Active learning involves other people, objects, ideas and events that engage and involve children for sustained periods. The commitment to 'creativity and critical thinking' means that when children have opportunities to play with ideas in different situations and with a variety of resources they discover connections and come to new and better understandings and ways of doing things. Adult support in this process enhances their ability to think critically and ask questions. Finally, we come to the commitment to the 'areas of learning and development'. The EYFS review has changed these to place greater emphasis on personal, social and emotional development, communication and language, and physical development, which are the prime areas of learning. The specific areas of learning are literacy, mathematics, understanding the world and expressive arts and design. For 2-year-olds the prime areas of learning will form the basis of the two-year developmental assessment.

Before I leave Learning and Development it might be helpful to provide some contextual information as to the reasons for the amendments to the areas of learning. Partly, this is a result of evidence that some practitioners have found the requirements of EYFS 'unwieldy and more elaborate than it needs to be'. Also, because it is proposed there should be a renewed emphasis on healthy development for all children, with better and earlier identification of developmental needs, delivered by closer working between parents, carers, practitioners and providers. Tickell has identified a need to increase 'the prominence of the most important areas of children's development' (p. 6).

★ ★ ★

The reviews of the implementation of the EYFS are generally very favourable. The British Association of Early Childhood Education (Early Education) are pleased, having found that practitioners are rising to the challenge of implementing EYFS and that the framework has provided opportunities to be flexible and creative in meeting the needs of young children and their parents. As a result of the responses given during the consultation, completed at the end of the first year of implementation, *Early Education* found that practitioners praised 'the sound principles that enable practitioners to provide education with an emphasis on learning through play, observing the child and planning from and for children's interests in partnership with parents and other professionals' (Megan Pacey, Chief Executive of Early Education).

The Scottish early years curriculum

In Scotland, the Early Years Framework (COSLA, 2008) recognises that the earliest years of life are crucial to a child's development. The EYF seeks to break the cycle of disadvantage through prevention and early intervention and give every child in Scotland the best start in life. The definition of the early years and early intervention framework is pre-birth to 8 years old. This reflects a general picture worldwide. The approach recognises the right of the young child to high quality relationships, environments and services which offer a holistic approach to meeting their needs. Needs are interpreted to encompass play, learning, social relationships and emotional and physical well-being. This approach is planned to be of particular benefit to those children and families requiring higher levels of support.

There are four principles of early intervention:

1. We want all the children to have the same outcomes and the same interventions.
2. We identify those at risk of not achieving those outcomes and take steps to present that risk materialising.
3. Where the risk has materialised we take effective action.
4. We work to help parents, families and communities to develop their own solutions, using accessible, high-quality public services as required.

The vision

The vision establishes a new conceptualisation of early years – that children should be valued and provided for within communities; the importance of strong, sensitive relationships with parents and carers; the right to a high quality of life and access to play; the need to put children at the centre of service delivery; that children should be able to achieve positive outcomes irrespective of race, disability or social background. The rationale behind the Scottish Framework is closely linked to the United Nations Convention of the Rights of the Child and findings of a Nobel-prize-winning economist, James Heckman, who set out the case to show the rate of economic return on early years investment is significantly higher than for any other stage of the education system. UK research highlights the home learning environment in the early years as the largest factor in attainment and achievement at 10 years old.

Curriculum for excellence: principles for curriculum design

To be used as a basis for planning:

- challenge and enjoyment
- breadth
- progression
- depth
- personalisation and choice
- coherence
- relevance.

Practitioners have access to exemplar material via a series of DVDs demonstrating effective early learning, such as children telling an adult what they want to learn, celebrating children and families as individuals, focus on outdoor learning and encouragement for children to become confident. A celebration of the developments came together in June 2009 in a conference entitled, 'Putting Vision into Action'.

The International Primary Curriculum (IPC)

'At the very heart of IPC Early Years is clarity about what children should learn.' Geared to meet the needs of 4- and 5-year-olds in primary schools, this curricular model describes four strands:

1. independence and interdependence
2. communicating
3. exploring
4. healthy living.

The programme consists of 16 units of work, each based on a theme to appeal to young children, for example 'sand and water'. The units of work give teachers the framework to design classroom activities that allow children to achieve the learning outcomes. Well embedded into this scheme is the expectation that parents will be well-informed.

The Swedish early years curriculum

Before sharing how the Swedish early years curriculum compares to EYFS it is important to describe the very different context in Sweden. Funding for EYFS in Sweden is three times that of England. Children may start their early learning shortly after birth and they will stay in the same family group until they leave the nursery at 5 or 6. It is likely the children will leave unable to read or write, because their curriculum is play-based with relaxation being paramount. It is interesting to note that an Australian international review of early years curricula (Victorian Curriculum and Assessment Authority, 2008) found language and language development are areas that are given the highest priority in the Swedish pre-school review. This is reflected in Swedish children's lead in the European literacy table. Children experience a long day in their highly valued family groups which aim to recreate a home-like ethos where there are no anxieties surrounding transfer from one phase to another. The government do not regulate the provision by testing or inspection. The processes in settings are evaluated to ensure core values of challenge, discovery and adventure are promoted. Children are encouraged to sleep and play outside in all weathers. Play provides the context for language development. The revised EYFS curriculum priorities replicate some aspects of this curriculum.

At every level, this sounds an ideal set-up. Small group work increases for rising 6s, who play literacy games, and if the children show an interest in letters this is responded to, but they are not taught to read and write systematically. Video footage of how this takes place would suggest they are well-prepared to start reading. Perhaps there is a strong culture of sharing books in the home that arouses the children's interest. What is of paramount importance, however, is attention to the individual needs of each child, encouraging risk-taking by climbing trees, bonding and building trust. Children have generous space to play and are reported to communicate more readily than their English peers. Positive first learning experiences determine children's attitudes later in life. However, it was reported in *The Guardian* (Shepherd, February 10, 2010) that Per Thulberg, the director general of the Swedish National Agency for Education, said that the introduction of 'free schools' had not led to better results. As hinted earlier, where schools had improved it was because the schools took pupils with better backgrounds than those who attended the institutions they replaced. The concept of the 'free school' was set up in Sweden to help children from deprived backgrounds. International studies show that England ranks higher for mathematics and science. In the 2007 *Trends in International Mathematics and Science Study*, Sweden's science ranking fell further than any other country. It is suggested that Sweden's education standards have slipped because of a lack of accountability and the absence of externally marked exams for older children, not those of EYFS age. *Save the Children* warn that countries are not always being compared 'like for like', noting that Sweden is a comparatively wealthy country.

Reggio Emilia curriculum

The Reggio Emilia approach is reputed to be one of the best educational programmes in the world. Many early years practitioners are implementing aspects of the curriculum in their settings. Schools involved with international projects through Comenius may be able to take part in exchange experiences to further develop their understanding of the Reggio Emilia approach. The approach is based around core beliefs about how children learn. However, it has been evolving in Italy for the past fifty years. The former founder, Loris Malaguzzi, was the guiding genius of Reggio. The programme, or curriculum, gives a high priority to the cultivation and guidance of children's intellectual, emotional, social and moral development. The educational vehicles for this are the long-term projects in which practitioners work alongside children, encouraging initiative, listening to children's views and guiding them appropriately (Gardener, 1998: xvii). The curriculum has a strong child-directed leaning with teachers following children's interests and not providing focused instruction in reading and writing. The outdoor environment plays a key role. Consequently, there are various references to the Reggio Emilia approach throughout the book. Learning Journeys are attributed to this approach. There is some overlap with the Montessori curriculum. Already, I can imagine the conflict that some of you may confront as you sit planning yet more *Letters and Sounds* sessions to meet the statutory requirements of the English EYFS framework (DCSF, 2008f). Experience of observing children in many diverse settings urges a word of caution because not all practitioners understand how to extend children's learning. How do you exploit a playful activity and turn it into a valuable learning experience? Of course, play is valuable for its own sake, but certainly in English settings there are goals to be met that require some adult input. Tickell raises the issue of the role of the adult in play in her review. She supports the view in England that play-based approaches are supported with instructional yet playful teaching. Case Study 2.2 below may give you food for thought. Activities need to make sense to children and ideally need to stem from their interest and involvement. The planned adult-led activity certainly did not meet the interests of the children, whereas the baking activity was familiar and purposeful.

CASE STUDY 2.2 Adult-directed or child-led?

One morning, children in a small early years setting went about their daily activities. One group were making birthday buns for Josh, and another group in a different room were learning about heavy and light. The bakers carefully spooned out ingredients and, guided by the practitioner, they counted the spoonfuls needed. The empty mixing bowls got heavier as the ingredients were added. Discussion with the adult present led to the children themselves making comparisons between the bowls and how heavy/light they were. More counting continued and children picked up the eggs and the bag of flour and compared the two. Which was the heaviest? Which was heavier or lighter? A wealth of learning took place as the children enthusiastically spooned out the mixture and continued to compare the amount of mixture in each bun tin. The children sitting in the next room listened as a bag of flour was held up by the practitioner. One or two children held the bag and were told it was heavy. The children then set off to find objects to be compared with the weight of the flour bag. The objects included a chair, a plank of wood and some paper, to name but a few. Some were able to use the language 'heavy' or 'heavier' but whether they understood what this meant is debateable as items were judged to be heavy when they were lighter than the object they were holding.

Montessori theory

Maria Montessori was one of the most important early years educators of the twentieth century, the innovator of classroom practices and ideas which have had a profound influence on the education of children the world over. She established schools for the disadvantaged children of working parents in Rome and approached their education as a scientist, using the classroom as her laboratory for observing children and helping them to achieve their full potential. There are more than 22,000 Montessori schools globally and 600 in the UK. The Montessori method is a curriculum of learning that comes from the child's own natural inner guidance and expresses itself in outward behaviour as the child's various individual interests are at work. Supporting this inner plan of nature, the method provides a range of materials to stimulate the child's interest through self-directed activity. The materials provided are organised into five basic categories: practical life, sensorial, maths, language and culture. The conceptual understanding of Montessori's methods places a much higher reliance on the child leading their learning than the EYFS, although there are several comparisons with self-directed learning and observational assessment. It is essentially based on the child's natural developmental stages, although children may work in mixed aged groups and are provided with everything they need in their natural environment. Montessori said, 'Never help a child with a task at which he [sic] feels he can succeed'. The goal of the educator in the classroom is to make the child independent and be able to do things themselves. This, it is said, can be achieved by giving children opportunities to move, to dress themselves, to choose what they want to do and to help the adult with tasks. This is in the belief that when children do things for themselves there is an increase in their self-belief and even self-confidence and self-esteem that may carry on throughout life.

What is research telling us about an early years curriculum?

The recent EYFS review is based on an extensive research base, so it is with this in mind that this section builds on an earlier one in this chapter where the use of the word 'curriculum' was discussed.

The next stage is to examine the characteristics of an effective curriculum from a research perspective to identify the common strands that have informed the EYFS in 2008 and also the more recent review. The EPPE Project (Sylva *et al.*, 2004) was the first major European longitudinal study of a national sample of young children's development between the ages of 3 and 7. You may have gathered so far that the separating of the six areas of learning into 'prime' and 'specific' areas gives a clue as to what research has found. It is interesting to note that one of the main findings of the EPPE research was that educational and social development are complementary and equal in importance in settings where children make the best all-round progress. Integrating care and education was associated with good quality. It was also found that settings which put particular emphasis on literacy, mathematics and science/environment promoted better outcomes for children in their subsequent academic attainment, especially in reading and mathematics at the age of 6. Strength in intellectual aspects of the curriculum matched strength in the social and behavioural areas, too. However, what is essential for the early years curriculum is that children have the chance to freely choose play activities, as they provide the best opportunities for adults to extend children's thinking.

A recent visit to a nursery that was developing a magic topic based entirely on the interests of the children reminded me of the powerful imaginations of children and the talents of practitioners in being able to provide resources to extend imaginative experiences. Children learned about magic carpets and where they travelled, played tricks on each other and listened to magic stories (see planning example Table 13.4, p. 197). Staff continually extended learning through the high quality provision and inspirational activities provided.

Throughout the EPPE survey it was found that local authority provision generally made use of curricular guidance to influence their planning. At this time it was the DLOs (desirable learning outcomes) which were broadly similar to the six areas of learning as we know them today. Recent research shows how strong the overlap between each of the areas of learning is with creativity, children's language being singled out as an area which crosses several areas of learning. The DCSF commissioned research into early learning (Evangelou *et al.*, 2009) and suggested that the early years curriculum needed to provide opportunities for problem-solving and for social and emotional aspects of learning, all of which benefit young children.

Of course, the transfer from early years to Year 1 influences what children experience in their curriculum. This is noted by Tickell, who makes a clear distinction between the older children in Reception classes and the under-4s in other settings in terms of what they need to experience. She says, 'children's experiences in Reception class should help prepare them for the move to Year 1' (2011a: 35). This is a change of emphasis that you may wish to discuss.

Discussion points

1. Describe your priorities for the curriculum in your setting.
2. As a Reception class teacher, what do you do to prepare your children for Year 1?

3

Developing effective assessment procedures

Skilled practitioners should spend most of their time interacting directly with children to guide their learning rather than writing things down.

(DfE, 2011a: 30)

Introduction

It is intentional to put this chapter ahead of the planning chapter because assessment is the starting point at which to plan experiences. This chapter covers the suggested revisions of EYFS and provides guidance on how to approach the revised assessment requirements, as well as sharing examples of assessment practices from practitioners and from the wealth of information provided by the early years national strategy pre-2010. The research evidence for the EYFS review concluded that, 'formative assessment will lie at the heart of providing a supporting and stimulating environment for every child' (Evangelou *et al.*, 2009: 5). Basic assessment principles are shared and discussed. At one level, one can be heartened at the reduction in assessment requirements, but on closer examination this may not seem as reduced as Tickell suggests. I have no doubt that those practitioners I work with will keep me abreast of their views in due course. Nonetheless, what I want to have emboldened on every page is the following statement. I urge practitioners to heed this statement at all costs:

> It is the interaction between practitioners and children that helps promote the rich learning environment the EYFS is seeking to create. This cannot be achieved if practitioners are making notes, instead of talking and playing with children.
>
> (DfE, 2011a: 30)

Revised EYFS assessment arrangements

Tickell reiterates the role of formative assessment as the means by which practitioners are expected to guide children's learning in the way they identify the next steps for a particular child. However, she expresses concern about the amount of time that is spent recording achievements. Essentially, assessment needs to be used to guide the next steps in children's learning. A weekly staff meeting is an effective way of discussing what has worked, what particular children have achieved and, importantly, what the next steps are in children's learning. How to record this? The best example I have seen is where this information is added to a weekly plan and subsequent activities are outlined to extend learning and respond to the interests of a small group. A key recommendation of the Tickell report (2011: 19) is that there should be a sharper focus on the early identification of additional needs and some mechanism that essentially differentiates between the needs of under-3s and those children in Reception class (my interpretation). This is clear from the suggested layout of the content of the 24–36-month assessment and that of the early learning goals (ELGs) at the end of the Foundation Stage. The prime areas of learning are those identified as essential for healthy development (see Table 2.1). The evidence shows that areas of personal, social and emotional development, communication and language, and physical development are the essential foundations for healthy development, for positive attitudes to relationships and learning, and for progress in key skills such as reading and writing. They also cover the early development of physical dexterity and movement, as well as healthy eating and exercise. Monitoring progress in these areas is the key to identifying special educational needs and disability (SEND). There is a link between these areas and the assessments carried out by health visitors as part of the health and development review for 2-year-olds as part of the Healthy Child Programme. There are many examples of ways to support and extend learning for the under-3s later in the chapter. This recommendation is a key to identifying those disadvantaged 2-year-olds who may be eligible for the government's free offer. Children not in any form of daycare will be known to the health services and will not miss the assessment because they are not attending any drop-in events etc. in their local Sure Start centres. Children starting pre-school at 3 will also have a baseline starting review to share with the setting. It is recommended that this early years summary would be a signpost, by focusing on those areas in which children excel or where they are in need of extra help. Each area of learning chapter contains the statements of what typical development looks like for 24–36 months in personal, social and emotional development, physical development, and communication and language. The Tickell report (2011) also recommends that the early learning goals are reduced and simplified and made more sensitive to the needs of summer-born children and to those children who are fast developers. The recommendation is that the goals are reduced in number from 69 to 17, with each goal having a simple three-part scale which sets out what working towards, what achieving, and what exceeding each goal looks like (see Tables 3.1, 3.2 and 3.3) As far as the level of development reached by children aged 5, as shown on the EYFS Profile, which is the assessment competed at the end of Reception, there is the recommendation that this is simplified and reduced from 117 pieces of information to 20 that capture the child's development. It is also recommended that the approach to assessment should be compatible with, and valuable to, primary teachers, so that a child's transition into Key Stage 1 is managed effectively and well. There is also the recommendation that there is some leeway for those practitioners working with children for shorter periods of time or during holiday periods. To uphold the principle of the Unique Child, there needs to be recognition that the child's needs are paramount without the pressure on practitioners to cover all learning and development requirements.

TABLE 3.2 Example of format to support summary of development at 24–36 months

PERSONAL, SOCIAL AND EMOTIONAL DEVELOPMENT			
ASPECT	24–36 MONTHS	36–48 MONTHS	EARLY LEARNING GOALS
Self-confidence and self-awareness			
Managing feelings and behaviour			
Making relationships			

TABLE 3.3 EYFS Profile learning characteristics (DfE, 2011a)

LEARNING CHARACTERISTICS	HOW (NAME OF CHILD) LEARNS
By playing and exploring ■ Finding out and exploring. ■ Using what they know in their play. ■ Be willing to have a go.	
Through active learning ■ Being involved and concentrating. ■ Keeping on trying. ■ Enjoying achieving what they set out to do.	
By creating and thinking critically ■ Having their own ideas. ■ Using what they already know to learn new things. ■ Choosing ways to do things and finding new ways.	

Types of assessment

Observational assessment

Observational assessments are paramount in working with very young children, when listening and watching are essential before you can talk with a child. This is supported wholly by the EYFS review, 'observational assessment is integral to effective early years provision' (Tickell,

2011a: 30). Assessments also serve to provide a means of tracking the progress children are making towards the statutory early learning goals (ELGs).

The publication, *Progress Matters: Reviewing and Enhancing Young Children's Development* (DCSF, 2009a), aims to provide examples of successful assessment practices in a range of settings. Although the EYFS Framework is common for all children in early years and child-care provision from birth to 5 years, there are differences in assessment practices. Assessment practices are modified to engage with very young babies in a one-to-one situation, whereas assessment of a 4-year-old may be most effectively achieved via non-participant observation. Recent research is used to provide a more general overview of practices nationally and in other countries.

Some of your children may have additional needs that require involvement of other agencies. As a key worker for a child with additional needs you may be involved in contributing to the Common Assessment Framework (CAF). This is a standardised assessment which gives a full picture of a child's additional needs at any stage. Information from parents is included and it covers all aspects of the child's development, including health, education and social development. It is important that children are seen as individuals and every child's journey is 'unique' to them. Actively listening to children and giving them time to express themselves, monitoring their progress and sharing the findings with children and parents, and planning next steps that will engage and motivate them are at the heart of effective planning for learning and development. Someone needs to analyse the progress children make and respond to the findings in terms of planning, resourcing and teaching. Generally, leaders and managers have a key role to play in improving quality through assessment by establishing systems, supporting staff, and analysing information to:

- track progress of individual children, and use that progress summary to identify next steps and communicate with others;
- involve parents and partner professionals in understanding and supporting children's progress;
- ensure the accuracy of evaluations of children's progress;
- use the information to support transitions as children move on to other settings;
- plan and implement changes to meet identified needs.

(DCSF, 2009a)

However, the reality is that Foundation Stage leaders in primary schools may have to do this themselves and also train their staff to be involved in the process too. The burdensome nature of EYFS assessment is recognised in the EYFS review. Comments from practitioners saying they are overwhelmed by the amount of paperwork they are required to keep have resonated with Clare Tickell. She states quite categorically that, 'skilled practitioners should spend most of their time interacting directly with children to guide their learning rather than writing things down' (2011: 30).

Since the previous two editions of this book, the understanding of the purpose of assessment of young children and how it is integral to informing learning and development has become second nature to practitioners in a very wide range of settings, from child minders to Children's Centres for children from birth to 5. This is due largely to the introduction of the EYFS, the guidance for practitioners and the rapid increase in self-help groups via the internet. Two key points are emphasised by Ruth Pimentel, National Director of the

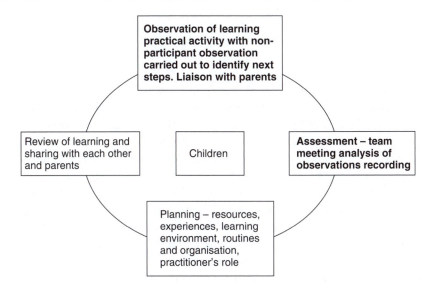

FIGURE 3.1 The assessment and learning cycle

Foundation Stage in the Primary Strategy team. Firstly, working in partnership with other providers and with parents will depend on effective observations and assessments. She was reluctant to prescribe an assessment system, deciding instead to use examples of practice to meet the diversity of care and learning provided for children (Mickleburgh, 2008). Also mentioned was the importance of the future of ICT in early years education and hopes that this would attract significant funding, 'I want to see early years practitioners leading the way in the use of ICT as a powerful tool for communication with parents and with each other.' (Mickleburgh, 2010). The *Statutory Framework for the Early Years Foundation Stage* (DCSF, 2008f: 16) states that ongoing assessment, 'is an integral part of the learning and development process'. It is quite emphatic about the form of assessment. The use of the word 'must' reinforces the expectation that practitioners will observe children and respond appropriately to making progress towards the early learning goals (see Figure 3.1). It further supports this by saying, 'Assessments should be based on practitioners' observation of what children are doing in their day-to day activities.' However, what appears to have hindered the application of this guidance in the past were the 117 items that were required to be assessed by the end of the Foundation Stage. Observational assessments of children and the recording of progress towards the ELGs is rife, but is enough time being given to supporting and extending children's learning? Tickell (2011) thinks not. There is continued emphasis in the review of the time taken away from interaction between practitioners and children by the endless recordkeeping that takes place.

The Montessori method

Maria Montessori used observation without any preconceived ideas that helped her develop materials that children needed and were interested in. For example, if a child starts banging on objects, they have a need for that gross–motor activity, then give them a drum.

Follow the child, they will show you what they need to do, what they need to develop in themselves and the areas they need to be challenged.

(Montessori, 1986)

Local authorities have devised, in some cases, fairly sophisticated systems to measure progress from entry to nursery to exit into Reception classes (Table 3.4 is an illustration of this). Access to exemplars of excellent practice via various websites has helped practitioners to develop their understanding. There are also compulsory summative assessment profiles (DCSF, 2008d) for all children in their final year of EYFS. This will normally be the Reception year or, as is becoming more common, Foundation Stage 2. The revised EYFS framework makes this a much more manageable task with considerable reduction in the number of assessment items.

It is helpful to distinguish between record keeping and assessment, the former sometimes being mistaken for the latter. Assessment is the recorded outcome of an assessment that may have taken place during an adult-directed activity or be the result of an observational assessment of children learning together. The terminology of assessment is varied and can be confusing. I hope the following definitions help to clarify understanding. Formative assessment (observational assessment) is essentially what Montessori suggests and is firmly based on observing the child or children in a self-initiated activity. It is expected that 80 per cent of observational assessments will be of this nature in early years settings. This time split is likely to change as the EYFS review suggests that too much time is being spent assessing children and not supporting and extending their learning. This is linked closely to planning the next steps in learning as you make notes and record what children know, understand and can do. This is a central aspect of planning in EYFS, most frequently referred to in settings for young children as 'observational assessment'. It is important to develop an efficient system of monitoring. From experience, there are various ways that observational assessments are completed. Initially, a discussion with parents or notes from home-visiting may be used to identify any children who may have triggered a concern and need to be closely observed in different contexts (in groups or in solitary play, perhaps). So what happens to the information and how do you gather it? On a post-it or jotted in a notebook, focusing on an aspect of learning or of whatever children in your key worker group are doing. It is likely that with older groups of children discussions are held with one member of staff and another is recording the responses from either all of the children or only a few. Weekly staff meetings may be used to share views and consider the next steps in children's learning to inform planning and activities for the following week. This is a common

TABLE 3.4 Example of summative assessment

Nursery progress

All children (boys and girls)

		NURSERY ENTRY AVERAGES	NURSERY EXIT AVERAGES	NURSERY PROGRESS	LA ENTRY AVERAGES	LA EXIT AVERAGES	LA PROGRESS
Personal, social and emotional development	Disposition and attitudes	3.7	10.8	7.2	3.5	9.3	5.8
	Social development	3.0	10.2	7.2	3.0	8.8	5.8
	Emotional development	3.1	9.7	6.6	3.3	8.5	5.2

strategy. It is important to check the quiet children who may not only be shy, but could have a language delay, or not even communicate much at all. Such children will need to be your focus group for the following week. A recent Ofsted survey (2011: 7) found that involving parents in the ongoing assessment of their children is difficult. They suggested, too, that there are two groups of children who make slower rates of improvement in outcomes than others. These are traveller children and those with special educational needs and/or disabilities.

Using the *Development Matters* statements

The *Development Matters* statements should be used to check whether children are broadly in the age-appropriate development band. I know these age bands are not sequential, but they do provide a useful steer to ensure children lagging behind can be given individual time or to convene a meeting with a parent to check there are no underlying problems. Information can be recorded numerically on the entry profile. Tickell is aware that the support of the *Development Matters* statements is appreciated by practitioners and suggests they continue to do so.

Summative assessments

Summative assessments are based on the judgements you make on a child's achievement at one point in time so that their progress can be tracked. It is likely you will give each child a numerical score (see Table 3.4). This enables comparisons with the local authority and national scores which can help to provide an overall picture of the quality of provision in this particular Children's Centre and in different areas of learning, and, importantly, to provide an evaluation of teaching as well as children's learning. How can this be? This may be where following a Montessori approach to learning will reveal gaps in children's learning because there has not been a focus or priority given to, for example, *Letters and Sounds Phase One* (DCSF, 2007c: 8) as a national solution to young children's lack of reading ability. Of course the assessment data is useful information for the LA, but may be less useful for understanding the development of particular children for a whole range of reasons – absence, trauma in their lives or staffing problems. An interesting discussion point emerges here because it may be useful to a setting to compare their rates of progress in specific areas of learning in which the cohort of children have scored lower than the nationally expected figure. There may be a resource or teaching issue that can explain, for example, the fact that the whole cohort scored much lower than nationally expected in aspects of shape, space and measures. I am mindful of Pimentel's comments reinforcing the importance of observational records for telling the practitioner about the progress of an individual child. I feel I have skirted the issue of recording progress, and this is because I feel that the learning journey record is as fulsome a record of progress, both visually and in the stories and descriptions of activities by professionals and parents. The next section is much more specific about different assessment strategies and how outcomes are used.

Assessing very young children from birth to 3

The early years summary

There has been brief mention of the early years summary earlier in this chapter, but I want to give more detail on this from the Tickell review. Essentially, the early years summary can be seen as a means of getting closer working relationships between professionals in the early years sector. Tickell was prompted to address this relatively weak assessment area in the previous EYFS and the marked impact made on children in school by ECAT (Every Child a Talker) programmes for children with delayed speech and language development. However, she suggests that the identification of children not making typical progress needs to be made earlier. The overlap between the areas of the health and development review for 2-year-olds and the prime areas of learning is strong and provides an opportunity for parents to be offered guidance on their child's health and development through the review. She further suggests that earlier intervention should help those children who are 'school unready'. Also, the information could be used to guide children's ongoing development and support the transition between early years settings. The EYFS should not prescribe the point at which this early years summary should be produced, or the exact content – this should be left to the judgment of early years practitioners, working in partnership with parents and carers to agree the most useful information. I am aware that such reviews and joint working already takes place for children already in early years provision. Essentially, what needs to happen is the creation of a universal system that covers all 2-year-olds. There is concern that information does not always pass between professionals, which has led the Tickell review to recommend that an insert is added to the early childhood health record, known as the Red Book, to encourage parents and carers, or their nominee, to enter information arising from this early years summary and from children's interaction with other professionals, for example, speech and language therapists. Time and politics will tell if this recommendation comes to fruition as it requires an increase in the numbers of health visitors to fully implement the Healthy Child Programme health and development review for 2-year-olds.

Observational assessments

Observational assessment is integral to effective early years provision and evidence shows that this type of assessment lies at the heart of providing a supportive and stimulating environment for every child (Evangelou *et al.*, 2009). Tickell has broached what has always been a major concern of my own when inspecting Reception classes. This is the 80:20 rule. The reliability of the judgement on whether a child achieves as a result of a child-initiated activity or an adult-directed activity is much debated. This has caused dilemmas for practitioners and undermines their professionalism, so to read that Tickell does not think the 80:20 rule is helpful in practice and recommends that assessment should be based primarily on the observations of daily activities that illustrate children's embedded learning is reassuring. The 'Look, listen and note' section in the current Practice Guidance (DCSF, 2008f: 11) provides useful guidance for practitioners to help them decide where children are in their learning and development. While this is due to be revised, there are useful pointers provided for current practices. For example:

- getting to know a child better and developing positive relationships with children and their parents/carers;
- planning appropriate play and learning experiences based on the children's interests and needs, and identifying any concerns about a child's development;
- developing your understanding of a child's development;
- developing a systematic and routine approach to using observations;
- making use of assessments to plan the next steps in a child's developmental progress and regularly reviewing this approach.

Annex A of *Using the Early Years Evaluation Schedule* (Ofsted, 2010: 46) provides a helpful overview of the possible outcomes inspectors may look for when observing very young babies or those with verbal communication difficulties. As an example, inspectors are asked to consider the following when judging how well babies are achieving and enjoying their learning, suggesting that they should:

- develop confidence in exploring their surroundings;
- respond positively to the words, songs and gestures of adults;
- begin to make choices about the resources they play with and where they explore;
- begin to vocalise and imitate adults;
- respond to music, rhymes and stories;
- investigate things repeatedly, such as opening and closing a button on a toy, pushing and pulling a toy, working out that one action has an effect on others;
- written comments by parents, child minders, key workers;
- photographs of the child in the setting and at home;
- photographs of a child engaged in an activity;
- dated examples of children's first mark-making activities;
- evidence of progress towards all areas of learning.

(Ofsted, 2010: 46)

Practitioners use different methods to record what the babies are learning. It is debatable whether examples of what children can do are called 'assessment' or 'planning'. They are, in fact, both and are the next steps to inform learning as well as an assessment of what children

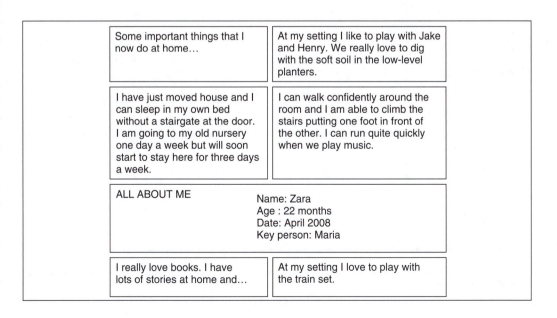

FIGURE 3.2 First assessments

can currently do. Parents may be the ones who provide the first assessment, as the examples shown in Figure 3.2 demonstrate.

The key person plays a central role in collecting information/observations about their key children. It is suggested (DCSF, 2008f) that the key person spend some one-to-one time with children working in an area they have identified from their own observations. This information may be recorded as professional notes (see Tables 3.5 and 3.6) or as the child's learning journey.

TABLE 3.5 Professional notes (DCSF, 2008f – CD Rom)

Name:		Photo
Age:		
Context:		

We observed:	
↓	
We thought:	
↓	
We tried:	
↓	
We found out:	
↓	
We changed:	
↓	
Next we will: →	

EYFS references

TABLE 3.6 Example of professional notes (DCSF, 2008 – CD Rom)

Name:	Erin	Photo
Age:	19 months	
Context:	Free exploration in the role-play area	

We observed:	■ Erin really likes to play in the role-play area. She keeps opening and shutting the doors to see what's inside and finding resources from other areas of the room to put in the washing machine.
We thought:	■ We should add some resources, which might encourage Erin's interest in filling and emptying and 'What's inside?'.
We tried:	■ Adding large pasta shapes, real fruit and vegetables, scarves and some bags.
We found out:	■ Erin was fascinated by the addition of the bags and began to place resources carefully inside them, picking up one object at a time. ■ Erin played for extended periods of time. She also transported the bags all around the room, showing practitioners the contents.
We changed:	■ We are going to leave these resources out for a few weeks and observe Erin's play before we change anything.
Next we will:	■ Consider what other areas of the learning environment could be used to support Erin's interest in filling and emptying. Start a learning journey to document Erin's interest in this area more thoroughly.

The learning journey

This is essentially a record of a child's progress during their time in their setting. It is important to bear in mind that it is being written for and with parents, so needs to be accessible to them. Tables 3.7 and 3.8 provide a blank example of this. It is sometimes called a 'learning story' (see Table 13.6 and Case Study 10.1). It can be compiled in a book and contain a range of evidence.

There could be a summative assessment at times to share with parents. In some settings there are learning journey displays to celebrate what children are doing. Team meetings may provide time for discussion about the learning journeys of key children week by week to enable key workers to update their assessment records. This may be rather an obvious statement given the nature of early years practitioners whose chat is usually about the activities of particular children in a very informal way. The potential for formalising some of this chat as an observation of learning is just a step further and may be assisted by referring to the 'look, listen and note' columns in the *Practice guidance for EYFS* (DCSF, 2008f: 26).

Assessing 3- to 5-year-olds

Using the Early Years Foundation Stage profile

Although there are unlikely to be major differences in assessing 3- to 5-year-olds, I have opted to separate this group because many 3- to 4-year-olds are in an early years unit attached

TABLE 3.7 The learning journey

Insert a photograph here

Name	
Age	
Key person	

Observation / notes

Next steps		
Materials and resources	**Activities and experience**	**Adult's role**

Links with EYFS

to a primary school, in a very small school working alongside older children or learning in a separate EYFS unit of 4- and 5-year-olds in a school without a nursery or Children's Centre on the same site. The learning journey record will continue in the year before children move into Foundation 2 (Reception class) and in some settings it will be used continually. There is no reason why this cannot continue until the children leave the EYFS. I realise having written this that following the EYFS review (DfE, 2011a) there are many changes to the content of assessments but the processes will remain the same in early years settings. A great improvement for practitioners will be access to the 2-year-old assessment information. The reduction

TABLE 3.8 Learning story format

Learning story

Name: Date: Activity: Written by:	PHOTO
Learning story	
Analysis	
Possible next steps	

in the number of goals on the Foundation Stage Profile (FSP) is welcome. Tables 3.1 and 3.3 show this. However, there is still a requirement for older children to have the EYFS Profile completed for the year showing their progress towards the early learning goals. This is can be done electronically via the e-Profile, which is most commonly used in most schools. The primary purpose of the EYFS Profile is to provide Year 1 teachers with reliable and accurate information about each child's level of development as they reach the end of the EYFS, enabling teachers to plan an effective, responsive and appropriate curriculum that will meet all children's needs (DCSF, 2008a: 6). There are likely to be fundamental changes in the assessment process as children get older. The profile lists the following assessment principles:

- Assessment must have a purpose.
- Observation of children participating in everyday activities is the most reliable way to build up an accurate picture of what children know, understand, feel, are interested in and can do.
- Observations should be planned. However, practitioners should also be ready to capture spontaneous but important moments.

- Judgement of children's development and learning should be based on skills, knowledge, understanding and behaviour that they demonstrate consistently and independently.
- An effective assessment will take into account all aspects of a child's development and learning.
- Accurate assessments will also take into account contributions from a range of perspectives.
- Parents and other primary carers should be actively engaged in the assessment process.
- Children should be fully involved in their own assessment.

Transfer to Key Stage 1

In the future the assessment information transferred to Year 1 is likely to be much more useful because the categories fit with the National Curriculum levels (see Tables 3.1 and 3.3). A major recommendation of Tickell's review is that for each early learning goal a simple scale is established. This should define what emerging, expecting and exceeding means for each early learning goal, to take account of the summer-born and more able children. She also recommends that the level of exceeding the early learning goals is to be consistent with the expectations of the current National Curriculum, and evolves in a way that is consistent with the expectations to be set out in the new National Curriculum Programmes of Study for Key Stage 1 in the relevant subjects. Arrangements for the collection of assessment data will remain much as they are, although the reduction in the number of goals to be reached is considerable. The goals that are not easily observed or not sufficiently distinct and not unique to age 5 as a particular stage of development are removed. There is an additional assessment proposal to the slimmed down EYFS Profile. This is a short description of how each child demonstrates the three important characteristics of learning (see Table 3.3). The purpose of including these is to give Key Stage 1 teachers some background information and context for each child's level of development.

Analysing the EYFS Profile data for your setting

It is essential to consider the analysis of the end of EYFS Profile for your own setting and to compare it with national figures to help you provide information to the next stage and for your own understanding of what a typical expectation is for children's attainment at the end of EYFS. Too often this data may be analysed in schools but is not shared with staff. It is crucial that you analyse this, compare your outcomes with national data as well as that provided by LAs (see Table 3.9, showing national data for the past three years (2008–2010)). You need to ask yourself and colleagues the following questions:

- Are the results the same or better that last year?
- Where do your children fit in relation to the national expectations?
- If your children achieve below the national expectations, do you have valid reasons for this (very low attainment on entry, many children with speech and language difficulties, staffing issues)?
- In which areas of learning have your children achieved particularly well/not so well?
- Are you transferring actions to address areas of less progress into priorities in your next year's development plan?

TABLE 3.9 EYFS Profile results in England (2008 to 2010) (http//www.education.gov.ukrsgateway/DB/SFR/s000961/index.shtml)

	PERCENTAGE ACHIEVING SIX OR MORE POINTS	PERCENTAGE ACHIEVING SIX OR MORE POINTS	PERCENTAGE ACHIEVING SIX OR MORE POINTS
	2008	2009	2010
PSE: DA	88	89	91
PSE: SD	82	83	86
PSE: ED	77	79	81
CLL: LCT	79	82	84
CLL: LSL	71	74	77
CLL: R	70	72	74
CLL: W	61	62	65

I know that these are questions asked by senior management and also by Ofsted, to which you need to have some answers. It is interesting to note that these aspects need to be a core element of your self-evaluation and, according to Ofsted (2011: 8), self-evaluation is a weakness in some types of provision. Alongside the data to show the age-related expectation (Table 3.10) there is also national data to show the overall percentage of children achieving a good level of development (that is at least 78 points across the EYFS with at least 6 in each of the scales in PSED and CLL) during 2008–2010 (Table 3.11).

Ofsted expectations

Ofsted are going to look at the ways in which the information is used from observation and assessment to plan activities that are tailored to the needs and abilities of individuals. They will also wish to see evidence of achievement because they will make a summative judgement on

TABLE 3.10 The percentage of children achieving a good level of development between 2008 and 2010 in the EYFS Profile (DfE SFR 2009/2010)

	2008	2009	2010
	% ACHIEVING A GOOD LEVEL OF DEVELOPMENT	% ACHIEVING A GOOD LEVEL OF DEVELOPMENT	% ACHIEVING A GOOD LEVEL OF DEVELOPMENT
ENGLAND	49	52	56

TABLE 3.11 Narrowing the gap between the lowest achieving 20% in EYFSP and the rest of England (EYFS Profile full child collection) [1]

	2008	2009	2010
ENGLAND	35.6%	33.9%	32.7%

1. The percentage gap in achievement between the lowest 20% of achieving children in a local authority (mean score), and the score of the median child in the same authority expressed as a percentage of the same median score.

TABLE 3.12 Attainment on entry to nursery and Reception (Ofsted, 2010)

Attainment on entry to nursery at age 3	The age-related expectation at the beginning of nursery: Most[1] children are likely to be working within the development matters bands for 30–50 months, having shown competence in the preceding 22–36 months.
Attainment on entry to Reception at age 4	Most[1] children are likely to demonstrate some of the elements of skill, knowledge and understanding within the development matters band for 40–60 months, in addition to all the elements in the preceding band for 30–50 months. This may be referred to as the age-related expectation at the beginning of Reception.
Attainment at the end of the EYFS/entry to Year 1	Check how many children score 6 in all of the PSED and CLL scales. This indicates the children are working at a good level of development. Results overall very close to the national figures are likely to be described as broadly average. Check with data from the LA for national figure (a score of 6 in each of the assessment scales).

1. Ofsted define most as the majority or nearly all children, most is 80–96 per cent. Attainment on entry is likely to be below age-related expectations where a substantial proportion of children has not demonstrated all of the elements in the 22–36 month band.

the quality of children's learning and their progress towards the early learning goals. They will, for example, judge how well children learn and develop in relation to their starting points and capabilities. Table 3.4 shows a brief set of figures relating to the progress made by a group of children in a local authority Children's Centre. Importantly, and very unusually, there is a score given for attainment on entry to the setting. Settings will have many and varied ways of recording starting points for their children, a more difficult task if children come from many different pre-school settings where assessment information may not have been passed on. An important question for practitioners to consider is, 'How soon should judgement be made on the children's attainment when they start here?' I am aware that practitioners may have conflicting views on this, but it is important that this judgement is made as soon as possible after the children have started in the setting. Half a term is a long time in a child's life and many will make great strides in their learning in that time with the result that a baseline judgement made six or seven weeks into starting the setting will not be an accurate reflection of their level of learning when they started in the setting. Table 3.12 provides guidance on how to assess attainment of your children at different periods in the Foundation Stage.

Ofsted (2008: 19) have provided inspectors with fairly precise guidelines on judging attainment on entry to nursery and on entry to Reception and at the end of EYFS based on the level at which they are working within the *Development Matters* bands. Table 3.12 lays out the guidance very clearly and can also be a guide to newly appointed practitioners.

Discussion points

1. Share your own assessment practices with colleagues from other settings and decide if there are new practices you may wish to trial.

2. Discuss the implications for your setting of Tickell's recommendations for the revision of the 80:20 rule.

4

Planning for learning

All planning starts with observing children in order to understand and consider their current interests, developments and learning.

(DCSF, 2008f)

Introduction

Although this is a chapter about planning, it is important to recognise that the starting points for whatever children are learning are the children themselves, what they are interested in and how skilled practitioners build on those interests to extend learning. This may result in a framework to guide others and to assist assessment of learning. The chapter covers planning for all age groups from birth to the end of the Reception year and into Year 1. It takes as its basis the practice guidance for the Early Years Foundation Stage (EYFS) and the recent review of EYFS (DfE, 2011a) because they are the most comprehensive guides to provision and practice available to practitioners at this time. Importantly, the examples of planning come from the very best practitioners; they are ASTs (Advanced Skills Teachers) and skilled practitioners in nursery schools, Children's Centres and Reception classes. There is discussion of the revised early learning goals and how they contribute to the 'appropriateness' of the curriculum for the early years. Each of the Areas of Learning chapters provides examples of the recommendations for the revisions and reductions in the early learning goals. The opening quotation, which comes from the current EYFS guidance, is a major factor in ensuring that practitioners strive to create the 'enabling environments' that support the experiences that children engage with and those that are planned to extend children's learning. The commitments that place planning in a context in all settings are the key to successful provision.

Enabling environments

Tickell (2011: 27) has reconfigured the model for learning and development to provide a renewed focus on the earliest experiences. She recognises that practitioners need to understand the different ways in which children learn in order to provide effective support. The recommendations of the characteristics of effective teaching and learning are 'playing and exploring', 'active learning' and 'creating and thinking critically'. Importantly, the EYFS curriculum needs to dovetail with the National Curriculum. To return to the commitment for planning contained in *Enabling Environments* there is the commitment that planning can be for the long-, medium- and short-term to show how the EYFS principles are seen in practice. Here I have a dilemma, which is that planning is very time-consuming and to be in place in three tiers may be too many. It may also be that planning should in most respects arise out of the interests of the children. A suggestion that the long-term plan is the early learning goals for each area of learning is commonplace. Next, I would suggest weekly planning follows a pattern of observation, analysis and then building on what you have found out about children's learning so that you can plan for the next steps. You will need to make links with assessment requirements to judge that your children are learning at a level equal to or below their expected level. The assumption is that planning provides the framework for what is learned and that children learn what they are taught. Experienced practitioners know that this is not entirely the case, hence the need to look at the commitments 'the learning environment' and 'the wider context' in evaluating and assessing what your children are learning and experiencing. Practitioners will continue to focus on the learning journey for each child because that journey takes a personal path based on the child's individual interests, experiences and the curriculum on offer. Care needs to be taken to ensure that there are sufficient new and interesting challenges, because some children may not have a great reservoir of these in previous life experiences. This could be where the medium-term planning comes in. Practitioners have brainstormed with children and colleagues to gather ideas for these dynamic challenges that will excite children, encourage exploration and play, challenge and foster concentration and encourage new ideas, applying what they already know. Children are provided with planned experiences and activities that are challenging but achievable.

In the event that practitioners are going to be required to assess and record learning characteristics and how individual children learn by playing and exploring, learning actively and creating and thinking critically, it would seem that environments for learning will need to create opportunities for practitioners to plan and resource challenging environments where children's play can be supported and extended. They can extend and develop children's language and communication through sensitive observation and appropriate intervention.

Planning for children's learning

The EYFS guidance is well supported by recent research (Moyles *et al.*, 2002) and by the National Director of the Foundation Stage (Mickleburgh, 2010). It is beginning to help transform children's learning from birth to 5 years and beyond and to provide those working with young children an all-embracing guide to children's learning and development and welfare. There are key features of successful planning, whether it is for babies or for older children, in this chapter and in the chapters linked to the areas of learning. Samples of the Individual Education Plans (IEPs) for children with additional learning needs are also provided. It is important to view planning in the total context of children's learning as illustrated in Figure 4.1.

It may be appropriate to start with an explanation of what we understand by planning for children's learning. It is vital there is a balance between what children choose to do themselves and what adults generally regard as worthwhile, planned learning that requires the intervention and support of an adult; for example, if older EYFS children are ready to take their mark

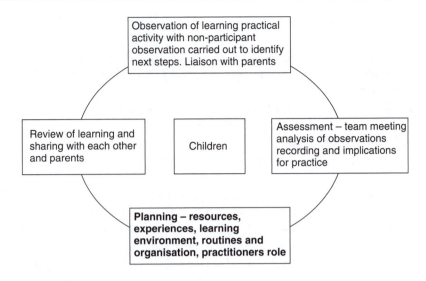

FIGURE 4.1 The planning and learning cycle

making to the next stage. What children can already do is a key starting point. Planning and assessment therefore must been seen to be working 'hand in glove' at all times. The EYFS guidance (DCSF, May 2008f) provided for practitioners is statutory for those settings registered with Ofsted. It is recommended that good planning is the key to making children's learning effective, exciting, varied and progressive because it enables practitioners to build up knowledge about how individual children learn and make progress. It further recommends that the process works best when all practitioners working in the setting are involved. This provides opportunities to think and talk about how to sustain a successful learning environment. By comparing several planning formats I have put together the following list of planning principles as being most useful to early years practitioners:

- Include reference to prior learning (what has happened before, evidence from observations or learning journeys).
- Be flexible in the use of ready-prepared plans to ensure 'magic learning moments' are not missed.
- Identify the next steps based on prior learning.
- Include actions planned in response to children's interests.
- Refer to development statements to highlight differentiation and/or a specific area of learning.
- Include what we want children to learn.
- Vary planning according to its purpose – to support a small group, a class group, an age group or an individual plan for an adult-led activity.
- Provide for the long, medium and short term (see earlier comments).
- For children under 3 the starting point will be the child and his or her interests.

Gateshead LA has also identified four principles for planning. They state that:

1. Planning puts the principles of EYFS into practice and ensures that all children are given a full range of experiences across all six areas of learning.

2. Planning provides an opportunity to clarify thinking for all practitioners within the team and to come to a common understanding about a philosophy and approach to children's learning and development.

3. Planning should be based on observation of what has gone before and finds out how each child's learning and development will or might progress.

4. Planning should be sufficiently flexible to keep a focus on children's individual needs and interests – children also learn from things which have not been planned for.

There are criticisms that there is too much emphasis on aspects of early literacy in EYFS from groups such as Open EYE and concerns that practitioners are not prioritising the quality of their settings in relation to children's real development needs. Possibly, Open EYE claim, the Ofsted agenda may be taking precedence and could have dire consequences for children's development. The debatable issue here depends on your point of view. The inspection regime holds practitioners accountable for the welfare, learning and development of children. Is this a bad thing? A website conversation between the National Director of the Foundation Stage and the Foundation Stage Forum (FSF) states that, 'she understood the concerns among practitioners about Ofsted inspections in the light of the changes made by the EYFS. She was refreshingly clear about the role of the inspectors. "Ofsted have a job to do, which is to regulate. They will take the requirements laid out in the EYFS and turn them into an inspection framework"' (Mickleburgh, 2010). Another concern voiced is that inspection measures what is measurable and may not give enough attention to the heart of a setting. Are matters relating to the care and welfare of children emphasised at the expense of understanding children's learning? There are many issues to discuss, but it may be worth reminding readers that Sweden's lack of a system of inspection or other forms of accountability has resulted in a marked fall in the standards achieved by children as they go through school (see Chapter 2).

Long-term planning for births to 3s

The emphasis for younger children will be on creating a more nurturing environment. The Baby Nest or Cosy Nest are two typical names for this area in Children's Centres. It is likely that this will be a separate area in a Children's Centre or nursery. Alongside the routines mentioned later there are key times of the day, such as the start and end of the session, when babies go from parent to key person, and there will need to be more extensive provision for nappy-changing, washing and preparing food and drinks. Generally the provision should aim to include:

- a cosy area for heuristic play that includes treasure baskets and soft toys;
- sensory exploration providing floor toys and some wheeled walkers;
- doll play with equipment for tea parties;
- messy play;
- singing and music;
- comfortable areas for adults to sit and play with babies;
- sorting play;
- outdoor experiences and visits;

- books and puppets;
- a wheeled toy area.

The starting points are what the babies can do. Children learn by doing things with other people who are more competent, rather than just told what to do. The environment and people they can relate to are crucial. Each child is unique. They are skilful communicators, sociable and curious. Possibly there will be no long-term curriculum plans, but details of resources available and the overarching priority given to recording what happens throughout the day for each child. Medium-term planning can focus on the immediate interests and needs of the younger children. It will be important to gather information about children in your key group which is used to inform planning/focused support for an area of development on a one-to-one basis. The information you gather about your key children can lead to discussions about the resources and experiences provided for continuous provision as well as contributing to

My family	My friends
	My favourite toys

All about me	Name:
	Age:
	Date:

What I like to do	Where I like to go

Areas of learning

PSED

Physical development

Communication and language

Key person:

FIGURE 4.2 All about me

assessment. It will be useful to complete *All about me* sheets as a way to gather your thoughts and knowledge about your key children (Figure 4.2).

Long-term planning for 3- to 5-year olds

The format for planning for older children is likely to include an overview of the year, with events and celebrations, and arrangements for transition to Reception classes or Year 1. It may include a settling-in period as children start into nursery. It is a bit like a calendar for the year. Alongside discussions about the overall experience provided for children you may wish to review how your provision, routines and organisation of learning inside and outside provides opportunities for children to access all six areas of learning and development. This range of provision is sometimes called 'continuous provision', meaning that it is available all the time for children to access independently and where there are no predetermined learning intentions. Although the EYFS framework is for children from 0 to 5 you may need to consider whether you make a distinction between the 0s to 3s in terms of the type of provision available and the 3- to 5-year-olds. This is likely to have implications for planning which may be loosely grouped to take account of the *Development Matters* statements from birth to 24 months for the under 2s and from 24–36 months and 36–48 months for the 3- and 4-year-olds. The revised early learning goals have revised developmental stages which are those mentioned here. Most settings are likely to have the following provision for 3- and 4-year-olds, ideally inside and outside:

- home corner and role-play area;
- sand and water play;
- book area;
- small world area;
- malleable and tactile area;
- construction and block area (not in the book area if possible);
- mark-making and writing area (do not make this an exclusive area for early mark making, which may have more success linked to other areas too);
- digging and planting area;
- large physical apparatus (climbing frame, tunnel, etc.);
- small physical equipment;
- music and sound-making area;
- area for parents and carers.

Medium-term planning for under 3s

The topic approach for under 3s is inappropriate because the learning of younger children tends to be instant and in response to particular interests and experiences. To reflect, the development stage of the under 3s will need to have a key focus on the children themselves, what they do and where they go, and build on their interests at all times. Partnership with parents will also be crucial for under-3s. This may be via a home/nursery journal or the learning journey record. Guidance provided by EYFS (DCSF, 2008f) is very clear about the need to provide 0–3s with high quality continuous provision as a replacement for the medium-term plan. There is likely to be a strong focus on exploring sensory materials or sharing an interest around a visit to a park. The majority of 'planned experiences' should be firmly grounded in everyday routines and the child's need. Table 4.1 is an example of a planning framework that could be used when working with 2-year-old children. There is a completed plan for continuous provision for 3-year-olds (Table 4.2) and a blank planning format for 2-year-olds (Table 4.3) linked closely to assessment. As a result of the revisions to the six areas of learning and the creation of 'prime' areas of learning there are much-reduced expectations for the curriculum of the under 3s. The expectation is that the foundations of early learning have a much higher profile so that those 'prime' areas of development are fully fostered. Personal, social and emotional development, communication and language and physical development are the keys to early development.

Medium-term planning for 3- to 5-year-olds

The premise is that the medium-term plan will include a considerable emphasis on what children have learned in the previous term and how that learning has covered the six areas of learning for 3- to 5-year-olds. A flexible approach to accommodate the outcomes of observational assessments completed by key workers is important. All of this may have a more marked impact on short-term planning. It is for teams to decide where the emphasis is placed when taking account of prior learning. Medium-term planning will tend to give greater priority to the 'prime' areas of learning and also depend on the time of year. For example, in the summer term the focus could be on 'Time', 'Growing' or 'Seaside', linked to planned outings and the natural environment, giving rise to greater learning in understanding of the world and providing a context for learning in the 'prime' areas of learning. The revised EYFS states these as personal, social and emotional development (PSED), physical development (PD), and communication and language (CL). The four 'specific' areas of learning in which the key skills of the prime areas are applied are literacy, mathematics, understanding the world and expressive arts and design. Typically, practices in settings tend to give a greater emphasis to personal, social and emotional development (PSED), communication, language and literacy (CLL), and problem-solving, reasoning and numeracy (PSRN) in FS2 because of the demands of additional strategies provided, such as Letters and Sounds (DCSF, 2007c) and SEAL (DCSF, 2008e). You will need to decide whether you are having a separate medium-term planning

TABLE 4.1 Planning sheet based on children's interests

Name:	Observations/ interests	Links to Look, Listen and Note	*Development Matters* statements for appropriate band	Next steps for development

TABLE 4.2 Planning example based on children's interests

Key points from observations week ending_____

Zara Using the train set and mimicking/verbalising alongside an adult, moving in response to music, using emerging language to communicate

Child B Investigating balls/cylindrical objects, using, exploring dolls and pushchair

Additions to Continuous Provision/The Physical Environment

RESOURCES	ADULT'S ROLE/ EFFECTIVE PRACTICE	ACTIVITIES AND EXPERIENCE	ADULT'S ROLE/ EFFECTIVE PRACTICE
A range of different-sized/ textured balls	Resources related to circles, balls and sphere-shaped objects, introduce a 'Lazy Susan' to the floor space. Introduce circular floor mats – indoors/outdoors.	Support play – rolling balls to and fro, introducing a range of different sizes, textures and noises throughout the week.	Note what it is that Tilly enjoys. Is it the rolling motion, circular objects? What is her response to the addition of bells?
Train set	Introduce bells sealed inside a hamster's ball – indoors outdoors. Support Zara's play/exploration and encourage parallel play with other children to support her development of positive relationships during the first few weeks at a new setting. Engage in imaginative play initiated by the children and model the dolls enjoying a healthy snack and mealtimes to support and encourage.	Building towers with small blocks. Use music of varying pace and rhythm throughout the week for children to move in response to music. In all situations support and encourage children's emerging communication skills both gesture, verbal – babbling and verbal – forming first words.	Involve Jimmy in this much-loved activity, encourage others to participate, note children's ability to stack one item upon another. Observe carefully what styles of music do the children respond to most expressively? Calm, quiet, loud, fast, etc. Note which stage of language development your key children may be at.
Dolls and pushchairs			

sheet for each area of learning, as shown in Table 4.4, or using the format in Table 4.5, which also includes the four key themes.

Short-term planning

This is the planning format that is the most important because it will be based on the outcomes of ongoing observational assessments of children's interests. It is crucial that planning is informed by assessments. The best practice is where there is a planned weekly meeting to share assessments and decide what learning needs to be provided to meet the needs of particular children and what extensions there can be for those who are making rapid progress. The detail of all this is in the assessment folders, learning journey records and from observational

TABLE 4.3 Observation and assessment sheet for 2-year-olds (DCSF, 2008f – CD Rom)

Observational and assessment sheet

Child's name	
Adult observer	
Area of provision	
Date	Time/duration

What happens/happened

Personal, social and emotional development	Physical development	Communication and language

What was learned about the child's interests, abilities or needs?

Child
Parent
Practitioner

Possible lines of development

assessments carried out over a few days. Plans need to be flexible enough to adapt to circumstances (see Tables 4.6 and 4.8). This view is supported by the Principle into Practice cards (DCSF, 2008f) which state:

> Some planning will be short-term – for a week or a day and will show how you will support each child's learning and development. This planning always follows the same pattern – observe, analyse and use what you have found out about the children in your group so that you can plan for the next steps in their learning.
>
> (EYFS, Enabling Environments 3.1)

TABLE 4.4 Sample weekly planning format for FS2

What happened before? Evidence from observations	Next steps planned
(Include Learning Journeys, analysis of baseline data, e.g. numbers of children with a difficulty relating to the learning intention, children's requests, activities the previous week)	*(Teaching strategy – state learning intention. Teacher activity and activities to be provided)*

Activities planned in response to children's interest
What we want children to learn
Adult-directed teaching

Opportunities for children to explore and apply

PSED	KUW	CD	PD
Add age-related Development Matters statements for 30–50 months and example of the activity to meet the statement	*Add age-related Development Matters statements for 30–50 months and example of the activity to meet the statement*	*Add age-related Development Matters statements for 30–50 months and example of the activity to meet the statement*	*Add age-related Development Matters statements for 30–50 months and example of the activity to meet the statement*

CLL	PSRN
As above but relate to each group if a CLL focus to lesson	*Show differentiation here for each group using the age-related statements*

Ongoing: KUW Sand tray *resources* **Water tray** *resources* **Construction 1** *resources*
Construction 2
CD
Outside

Risk assessment

Observations

TABLE 4.5 Medium-term planning for a term (one for each area of learning)

Focus/theme (incorporating children's interests)	Term			FS1/FS2
Personal, social and emotional development				
What has happened before	**What we want children to learn**		**Environment (indoors/outdoors)**	**Resources**
	Unique child Positive relationships Enabling environments Learning and development			

TABLE 4.6 Adult-focused planning format for use with 3- to 4-year-olds

Theme: *Be specific and name book if used*	Session number: *Is this 1/6?*	Date:	Practitioner/s:
What are the children going to learn? *You may only have one learning objective with additional PSED and communication intention. Is it appropriate to have simple success criteria?*	**Early learning goals/NC** *Use the terminology of the* Development Matters *statements and differentiate for age range – are children in the 22–36 month band or 36–48 months?*	**Key vocabulary** *If you list several words here make sure you explain what they mean and use them with the children.*	
Introduction *Always recap prior learning/ refer to observational assessments and make this as practical and first hand as possible so as to use all senses to acknowledge the three main learning styles – auditory, kinesthetic and visual.*	**What are the children going to do?** *Be clear in your expectations and make sure all the resources are readily available, especially when children can make choices – write a list (about what? Paint a picture of ...)*	**What has been successful?** *Refer to children's learning towards the* Development Matters *statements here and below and make a comment to show your own evaluation of your teaching.*	**What needs to be revisited?** *Evaluate your teaching strategy, resource implications.*
Plenary *Encourage children to share their understanding of what they have learned (record if possible). Check children have understood the success criteria again, especially if they formulated these earlier themselves with help.*	**Assessment:** **Most of the children can** *List the children here and identify achievements to be recorded on the profile or as part of their learning journey.*	**Assessment:** **Some of the children can** *You may want to refer to the traffic light system here – green met all the learning objectives, orange met some aspects, red need to revisit – next box.*	**Assessment:** **These children need more help**

Planning for children with additional needs

Meeting the individual needs of all children is at the heart of the EYFS (DCSF, 2008f: 6). It is important that children are not discriminated against, that they are listened to and respected. The range of additional needs children have are extensive, particularly the children for whom English is not their home language or those with speech and language problems linked to physical, developmental or other issues in their lives. Our aim as practitioners is to remove barriers to learning. In the planning stage it will be important that observations and assessment carried out by other agencies are referred to before a programme of activities are provided for children. See Table 4.7 for an example of an individual education plan for a nursery child. The early identification of the signs of need that could lead to later difficulties and being in a position to respond quickly is critical. In line with national recommendations as to the focus needed in any inclusion development programme support for children with speech, language and communication difficulties is the concern of this section.

TABLE 4.7 EYFS Individual Education Plan (IEP)

NAME: D.O.B.::   DATE:

Strengths
Responds well to familiar adult, expresses emotion
Is happy and settled in nursery
Enjoys transport and block play indoors
Enjoys climbing and wheel toys outdoors
Interacts well in 1:1 situation displaying cognitive skills. Begins to initiate
communication with familiar peers and adults

Areas for development
Gross and fine motor skills
Communication
Self-help skills

Long-term targets
To communicate using Makaton signs and picture symbols
To develop cognitive skills
To develop self-help skills
To build peer friendships

Priority targets
To develop fine and gross motor skills
To put on his own coat and wash hands
To use an increasing range of Makaton signs to communicate
To be part of the nursery routine

Parental involvement
Communicates weekly with outreach worker on progress and
works at home with son on shared targets

Outside agency involvement
Speech therapy, educational psychologist
Consultant paediatrician, family health visitor

TARGET	ACTIVITIES AND RESOURCES	MONITORING/ASSESSMENT	OUTCOME HOME AND NURSERY
1. To put his own coat on and wash his hands	Liaise with home	Individual planner with observations	
2. To use an increasing range of Makaton signs to communicate	To support other staff in Makaton use and model an increasing vocabulary repeating as necessary		
3. To be part of the nursery routine	Begin sessions in small room and build up confidence with teddies and join with them for story times and eventually welcome time	Liaise with parents and record progress, barriers and any actions needed	Join in fully
4. To develop fine and gross motor skills	Threading, puzzles, bead frames, etc., low-level climbing to build confidence, playdough and lycra to strengthen fingers		Increased control and coordination

Review date:

Child's view:

Present:

Parent's view:

TABLE 4.8 Weekly planning format for adult-led activity

Area of learning/aspect of area of learning
- Learning intention
- Learning intention

	Monday	Tuesday	Wednesday	Thursday	Friday
Revisit/review					
Teach					
Practise					
Opportunities to apply					

Observations: Emerging .... Expected .... Exceeding ....

Providing for the more able child

DCSF guidance (DCSF, 2010a) claims that very young children often have sophisticated thinking skills and creativity that may not be recognised or valued by adults. They have provided guidance to support practitioners in taking responsibility for creating environments in which all children can discover and gain confidence in their own capacity for learning. It emphasises the importance of *listening carefully to the voice of the child*. It will reveal insights into their learning and development that would never be captured through formal tests or assessments. Narrowing the gap that exists in the achievements and development of some groups of children, including those who are, or who have the potential to be, gifted and talented, was a national priority in 2010. Nationally, 60 per cent of boys were in the lowest-achieving 20 per cent of children. This had implications for practitioners to address barriers to development, provide access to an environment that will engage children and to provide opportunities to extend their learning. Practitioners need to provide rich opportunities for all children to:

- find learning which inspires and engages;
- identify and document evidence of children's interests and abilities;
- plan experiences which can enrich and further develop children's interests.

Girls are more likely to emerge in a supportive environment where children are viewed as active agents in the learning process. It is vital that children are encouraged to find and to solve problems. This approach is evident in the pre-schools of Reggio Emilia. Practitioners may ask: 'how does one recognise children with particular gifts and talents?' There are several suggested responses to this:

- Look for persistence and precision in play activities.
- Look at how children perform in different contexts.
- Look for the ability of the child to perform in different contexts.
- Look for children who interpret the clues and signs in the world about them – street signs, as well as the written word.
- Look out for children who are curious and motivated to find out information or learn new skills for themselves.

Children with particular abilities may sometimes be easily bored, frustrated and may have well-developed social and emotional skills. They may also prefer the company of an adult to other children.

CASE STUDY 4.1 A paraffin moment

Four-year-old Tom shuffled as he sat monotonously chanting out today's new words and applying the appropriate 'sound buttons' to assist with tricky bits. Suddenly he called out 'paraffin' as the next word was turned over. His teacher looked querulously as he beamed with confidence at his success. 'Tom, which sound buttons did you use to help read that word?' A slight pause, before Tom launched into an explanation of the word 'paraffin' and why he knew what it said. He made no use of the sound buttons. This linked to his home experience of camping and the need to have lanterns fuelled by paraffin. Later on when playing outside with an adult nearby he began to explain in great detail the number of tents in the outdoor area and what each one contained and why they needed to have a paraffin lamp.

How many of the responses listed above does Tom show in Case Study 4.1? How, then, can children follow their own lines of inquiry and apply their ideas in their play and learning? There are implications in this for all practitioners as they struggle to meet the needs of the Toms in a group and those of the children who do not have the imaginative, social or intellectual skills to develop basic language and communication skills. Again we need to return to ways of creating problem-solving and finding situations. The notion of 'possibility thinking' lies at the heart of the creative process. For example, when young children are encouraged to think about what 'might be' instead of being asked 'what is?' the sophistication of their thinking is often revealed. As practitioners we need to consider using questions such as:

- What do you think will happen next?
- What do/don't you like about this? Why?
- What would you do?
- Is there another way?
- What might happen if...?

Daily routines

What are the routines over a typical day in a Children's Centre, nursery class or Reception class? Do they need to have the same features? So far, the routines mentioned have prioritised the need for access to outdoor learning on a 'free flow' basis if possible. The EYFS guidance reinforces the need for outdoor/indoor learning along with time for spontaneous play. It suggests a need for practitioners to recognise that learning takes place in boisterous situations, sometimes children will want to sit and discuss and describe what they are doing or they will want to sit quietly and reflect as they play. Small group times may be needed for adult-led activities to encourage discussion of a particular topic. What, then, are the implications of all this for practitioners? My experience has shown that reorganisation of the setting has usually been the first priority for newly appointed EYFS leaders. Below is a list of the provision you should consider having when reviewing what the optimum conditions are for the over-2s' learning. The interests of children need to be paramount. This may require a degree of flexibility in the resources available so that children can follow their own interests by being able to access the resources they need. Collections of outdoor boxes for investigative work can be ready-prepared for different weather conditions and seasons of the year. The list below provides a starting point:

- areas for specific resource-dependent areas of learning – creative area for making things;
- investigational resource area for accessible equipment and information books;
- dedicated book-sharing area including prominently displayed reading material with comfortable chairs and cushions for adults and children;
- cosy corners (under a table, for example) where children can be alone or sit quietly with a friend;
- well-resourced sand and water trays;
- construction area – blocks accessible with selected small-world equipment to enrich play;
- role-play areas – definitely a typical home area and others related to children's interests or the foci for their learning – baby clinic, hospital, veterinary surgery, garden centre, garage, airport, on board a ship – and a store of resources for children to create role play inside and/or outside;
- writing and mark-making areas with pencils, crayons, paper and notepads of different sizes. Clip boards for use in other areas and interactive whiteboards around the setting;
- interest tables for exploration and to encourage talking – teapot collections, cups, mugs, etc., linked to learning rhymes such as 'Polly put the kettle on' and 'I'm a little teapot' (many young children may not know what a teapot is);
- snack-time table for independent snack time;
- key person group areas – these can be in any of the above areas;
- natural material collections for sorting and counting – number lines at child height to help with counting;
- musical instruments, headphones to listen to songs in a dedicated area;
- physical play equipment inside and outside.

I realise the above list is very comprehensive and possibly daunting for the EYFS leader in a small primary school.

Outdoor learning

The challenge for practitioners is how to achieve the balance between child-initiated and self-directed learning with adult-focused planning for whole groups, small groups or individual children. Central to provision is the way in which the outdoor environment contributes to learning. EYFS guidance makes specific reference to learning outdoors that is reiterated in Ofsted's guidance to inspectors:

> Play underpins the delivery of all EYFS. Children must have opportunities to play indoors and outdoors. All early years providers *must* have access to an outdoor play area which can benefit the children. If a setting does not have direct access to an outdoor play area then they must make arrangements for daily opportunities for outdoor play in an appropriate nearby location.
>
> (DCSF, 2008f: 7)

A check of recently published inspection reports of nursery schools and Children's Centres reveals the praise for, 'A highly creative curriculum [that] presents both indoors and in the exciting outdoor environment opportunities to investigate and explore' (Ofsted, February 2010). In outstanding settings there is frequent mention of Forest School principles to help children learn to relate to each other, discover their own identity and appreciate nature. Central always to the high quality of provision is the way outdoor provision matches high-quality indoor provision. Consistently, settings that do not make the best use of the outdoors to develop learning are more than likely to find themselves with an area for improvement such as, 'Improve the opportunities for children to learn outdoors, ensuring that the outdoor activities cover all areas of learning and are accessible to children'.

Forest Schools

The Forest School concept was brought to England by the staff of Bridgwater College, Somerset, following an exchange visit to Denmark in 1993. The rationale for this approach to learning and development chimes well with traditional views of 'good' early childhood education (Maynard, 2007) and the EYFS curriculum framework. The importance of outdoor play cannot be underestimated given the decline in children's freedom to play outdoors safely. It has been given a tremendous boost with the EYFS framework's expectations that indoor and outdoor learning complement one another. Others have written widely of the benefits of outdoor learning (Bilton, 2002; Maynard, 2007). Children have more space to move around, greater opportunities for fantasy play, especially boys. A major finding from Maynard's research is the attention given to small, achievable tasks in which children succeed, become more confident and have a greater level of self-esteem as a result. The Forest School is an outdoor approach to education and play in which the outdoor environment becomes the classroom. This is reputed to increase children's self-confidence and self-esteem. This is particularly true for children who do not do well in a school classroom. The findings of research into changes in 24 children in three case study areas over eight months identified the following impact:

■ Confidence – this was developed by the children having the freedom, time and space to learn and demonstrate independence.

- Social skills – children gained increased awareness of the consequences of their actions on peers through team activities, such as sharing tools and participating in play.
- Communication – language development was prompted by the children's sensory experiences.
- Motivation and concentration – the woodland tended to fascinate the children and they developed a keenness to participate and the ability to concentrate over longer periods of time.
- Physical skills – these improvements were characterised by the development of physical stamina and gross and fine motor skills.
- Knowledge and understanding – the children developed an interest in the natural surroundings and respect for the environment.

(O'Brien and Murray, 2007)

Planning for outdoor learning

As already stated, the critical role played by outdoor learning in promoting children's confidence and overall well-being is well researched. How should this be planned? Does it need to be planned or is it acceptable to let children have the freedom to explore as they wish? The answer lies some way between the two and at times it may be appropriate to allow children to explore and develop their social skills, learning to share equipment and take turns on play equipment. However, this may be no more than many children do in their home environment, so how does the outdoors enrich learning? In *Playing Outside*, Bilton (2004) stresses very emphatically that quality outdoor play is needed for children to become confident, independent and learn a great deal. Planning needs to identify the possible learning outdoors, but of key importance is the way in which practitioners can capitalise on children's interests to develop basic skills. I am reminded of this as I watched a 3-year-old cautiously climb into the tree house, counting the steps one-by-one with a nearby practitioner. Not only was this little boy learning to count, but also to balance, succeed and achieve what to him was a great step in developing his confidence. Other children in the same setting planted vegetable plants and enjoyed camping for their holidays in one of many tents fully equipped to extend learning about the outdoors. Case Study 4.2 illustrates the importance of resources for an 18-month-old as he engaged in a 'gardening activity'.

CASE STUDY 4.2 A gardening experience

Fully equipped with two buckets, a watering can, a pile of stones of various sizes and a supportive adult, Ethan set out to garden. Searching for a pair of gardening gloves he struggled successfully to put these on and set out to sort the stones by size, water the nearby plants and learn how to hold the watering can without spilling the water on himself. The concentration and persistence in completing these tasks lasted for more than 20 minutes as he busied himself outside.

Boys particularly need access to the outdoors to experience freedom to pursue their interests and space to run and climb, which practitioners need to develop to ensure this physical play is channelled into new experiences, such as what happens when you are camping.

What Ofsted expects

The latest inspection framework (Ofsted, 2010) states clearly that there is no requirement to have written plans, but that during an inspection it would be expected that planning is available. What does this really mean? A closer examination of the guidance for inspectors states that they should take account of 'the quality of planning for individuals to ensure that each child is offered an enjoyable and challenging experience across the areas of learning' and 'the extent to which there is planned and purposeful play and exploration, both in and out of doors, with a balance of adult-led and child-led activities that fosters active learning'. Is it feasible for a child minder to have the same level of detail for perhaps one or two children as a nursery teacher with many more children and a much wider age range in their care?

Exemplary planning examples

The planning examples that follow are actual plans devised by a Reception class teacher (Tables 4.9 and 4.10). They are exemplary because they very clearly show how planned activities are based on interests shown by the children the previous week as well as ensuring that there is a good balance between adult-directed activities and child-initiated learning throughout the day. The extensive example supports the recommendation in the Tickell review (2011).

Transition arrangements

It is five years since the DfES first reported on the transition from EYFS to Year 1 (DfES, 2004). The recommendations were very clear and summarised as:

- Transition is to be seen as a process, not an event.
- EYFS staff should meet with Key Stage 1 staff to discuss children's needs.
- Routines, expectations and activities are to be similar in Year 1 to the Foundation Stage.
- Parents are to be involved in the process.
- School managers are to allocate resources to enable Year 1s to experience some play-based activities – sand, water, role play, construction and outdoor play.
- There should be additional support for children with learning difficulties, disabilities, English as an additional language and less able children.
- There should be a reduction in the amount of listening and more encouragement of independent learning and learning through play.

A follow-up HMI survey (HMI, 2005) focused on how children developed social skills, attitudes, knowledge and learning in their transition from Reception to Year 1. Their findings stated that:

- The literacy and numeracy strategies provided continuity.
- There was less continuity between the nursery and Reception classes.
- Less attention was given to improving standards through creative and expressive areas.

TABLE 4.9 Exemplary planning: a foundation stage unit in a primary school – prior learning and next steps

WHAT HAS HAPPENED BEFORE? EVIDENCE FROM OBSERVATIONS	NEXT STEPS PLANNED
– Previous week moved to new classrooms and outdoor area. – Learning journeys – AG and EB completed linking elephant puzzle, unsure in identifying some numerals and during observation did not know a strategy to use to find out. – Baseline observations of counting indicate that many children find it difficult to count a given number of small objects. – Opportunities throughout the week encouraging children to blend sounds in words; lining up saying phonemes in names, writing special helpers names on boards, playing Ink's Gym. Introduced across the river and encouraged children to segment sounds in words. *Letters and Sounds* assessments indicate children beginning to link some letters to sounds. – Class 1 EK asked for ice cream play dough. Class 3 SC and FB took socks to sand tray and chose to fill up talking lots. – Class 2 EP and BC in the book corner, selected space non-fiction, showed an interest in finding out more, asking questions. – Class 1 JB cut black paper and making marks. – Previous week, clay table introduced with adult support. – Children made super models and enjoyed activity. – Children explored building with reclaimed materials and MD3. One third observations made. – Spirals CLL and KUW groups formed on the basis of initial observations and using transfer documents.	– Children settling well and following new routines. Mid-week introduce lunchtime play changes. Foundation children can use foundation area or choose to play in the larger playground. Thursday pm open unit 3.20–4 pm, parents invited to view new classrooms. – Teach strategy so children able to identify numerals independently: I can use a number line. – Introduce number of the week – one and model making one clap, one hop ... Questioning: what will be the last number we say? – Teacher activity – counting a given number of objects found in the caves, encouraging 1:1 counting. Using the number line to find the correct number. Independent bear hunt in classroom. – Begin to introduce Set 1 Phase 2 *Letters and Sounds*. Include many opportunities to support and develop oral blending and segmenting in small groups. – Play dough contents and vanilla essence. – Different sized socks, scoops and spades in the sand. – Space non-fiction box provided. – Black paper and chalks. – Clay table to be used as an opportunity for children to explore and apply ideas independently. – Introduce constructing for a purpose to help the Bear Hunt family cross the mud. – Spiral groups to begin Monday and Tuesday pm.

TABLE 4.10 What we want children to learn and adult-directed teaching

PSED	KUW	CD	PD
PSED *3.1: separates from main carer with support*: encourages children to enter the classroom independently and engage in an activity. *40–60 months: has an awareness of the boundaries set, and of the behavioural expectations of the setting.* Recap rules 1, 2 and 4 and the behaviour system. *30–50 months: shows increasing independence in selecting and carrying out activities.* Rooms 1, 2 and 3: one table to be left empty for children to select their own trays independently.	*30–50 months: knows how to operate simple equipment.* Listening corner – the wheels on the bus. Laptop – black background spray can tool. **KUW** *1.2: observes, selects and manipulates objects and materials.* Feely tray – textured stones and stars. Room 1 pm: tuff spot – black sand and spheres. *30–50 months: investigates various construction materials. Joins construction pieces to build.* Problem-solving table – the rocket is broken. Can you make a new rocket to fly the astronauts home? **KUW** *1.3: constructs in a purposeful way, using simple tools and techniques.* Rooms 1 and 2: freeze frame the family crossing the mud. Show tray with mud. What will happen if they go through? Discuss ideas to help the family cross and the resources needed. *I can help the family cross the mud.* Room 1: exploring collage and reclaimed materials. Children may choose to make a construction to help the family cross the mud or may choose to use the materials for other purposes.	**CD** *1.1: explores different media.* **CD** *1.2: creates simple representations of events, people and objects.* Room 1: table collage resources, rocket template. Room 2 pm: black paper and chalks. Room 3 pm: planet collage, circle paper and materials. Room 1 and 4: replay the story, all join in with repetitive language and retelling. Pause to explore instruments to add sound – *I can use an instrument to tell the story.*	*Shows awareness of own needs with regard to eating, sleeping and hygiene*: introduce lunchtime routine. Using soap to wash hands before eating and knowing why. *40–60 months: explores malleable materials. Handles tools and malleable materials with basic control.* Clay table playdough – vanilla ice cream cones, scoops and tubs. Room 3 pm. Plasticine and black mats **PD** *1.2: moves with confidence in a variety of ways showing some awareness of space.* Outdoor play. **PD** *1.3: uses a range of small and large equipment.* JD/DK general observations. Room 1: bikes, den building box with bear hunt props (see PSRN JD).

TABLE 4.10 (continued)

CLL	PSRN
***CLL** 3.1: developing an interest in books. 30–50 months: handles books carefully. Begins to show an interest in books.* Choosing books to share at home Rooms 1 and 3: Story-telling chair *We're Going on a Bear Hunt* story and props. Room 1 pm: Selection of non-fiction space books and paper *30–50 months: knows information can be relayed in the form of print. Holds books the correct way up and turns pages. 40–60 months: knows that print is read from left to right.* RSS guided reads.	*Says some number names in familiar contexts. Says number names in order.* Register, counting lunches, number of children in the class. Rooms 1 and 3: the bears have all left their caves and Rodney has been asked to put them back. Rodney does not know his numbers and he has the cave numbers to find out how many bears live there. Can we help? Model how to use a number line. Match number and count along the line to find put the number. Count teddies 1 to 1. *I can use a number line.*
***CLL** 3.3: recognises a few familiar words.* Encouraged to find out own name on peg, tray, snack card, behaviour board. *Listens with enjoyment to stories and rhymes, sustains attentive listening, responds to relevant comments, questions or actions.* Story time – *Come to Tea on Planet Zumsee, Here Come the Aliens, Aliens in Underpants Save the World, The Way back Home, The Park in the Dark.* Room 1: Watch DVD *We're Going on a Bear Hunt.* Retell story using flashcards and noting the repetitive language. *I can tell you about the story.* *30–50 months: talks activities through, reflecting on and modifying actions.* Room 1: Home Corner, Room 2 Space Rocket, Room 3 Space World. Role play areas: Room 1 Home Corner, Room 2 Space Rocket, Room 3 Space World. ***CLL** 4.1: experiments with mark making, sometimes ascribing meaning to marks.* ***CLL** 4.2: uses some clearly identifiable letters to communicate meaning.* Room 1: Compares bears hidden around the room. Table – clipboards: children may choose to go to own bear hunt or use clipboards for other purposes. Space HQ role play, continuous provision, observations and risk assessments	Feely box – squidgy shapes. Room 1: Teacher group observation *MD 1.2/3 Counts up to 3 to 6 objects correctly. 40–60 months: select the correct numeral to represent 1 to 5 objects. Extend MD 1.6 Counts up to 10 objects correctly. Recognises numerals 1 to 9.* Children to count number of spiders found in the cave. We need to help the bear match the number to the spiders. Model using the number line to find the correct number. Find the correct number, then food for bear. Can you pack a basket? Children to use number line to identify numeral and then count that number of strawberries for bear. Room 1: JD *MD 1.2/3/6 Counts up to 10 objects correctly. Selects correct numeral to represent objects.* Outside activity. Cave Street, caves labelled 0–9 and groups of bears, children to count the bears and place in the correct cave.

Ongoing:

KUW: sand tray – socks, scoops and spades. Water tray – playdough with stars, astronauts and play paper. Construction 1 – Jungle Duplo. Construction 2 – snowflakes. Construction 3 – 3D shapes.

CD: *sings simple songs from memory:* singing songs as a class. Nursery rhymes and number actions.

PD: *uses a range of small and large equipment. Travels around, under, over and through, balancing and climbing equipment* – outside play equipment, bikes, mini assault course. *Moves with control and coordination* – jigsaws, table top games, tracing threading beads, morning cutting and handwriting activities.

PSED: *works as part of a group taking turns and sharing fairly* – circle games, table top games and snack time.

CLL: *is developing an interest in books. Knows that print conveys meaning.* Rooms 1, 2, 3 book corners.

Observations – planned activities and opportunities to explore and apply:

Rooms 1, 2 and 3: Bear Hunt Teacher Activity – group observation *MD 1.2/3 Counts up to 3/6 objects correctly. 40–60 months: select the correct numeral to represent 1 to 5 objects. Extend MD 1.6: counts up to 10 objects correctly. Recognises numbers 1 to 9.*
Rooms 1, 2 and 3: RSS Learning journey observations – in all rooms (purpose matching provisions to the children's interests and using to inform baseline and next steps).
Rooms 1, 2 and 3 pm: RSS **CLL3** *Reading:* observations to inform baseline.
All practitioners' general observations.

Risk assessment:

Take care by water and sand tray. Foundation outdoor area checked by team. Soap used before snack and lunch. Introduce feely tray/playdough and discuss safety with contents. Awareness of bikes on the playground and bike routine. Parents invited into school Thursday pm to view the new classrooms.

TABLE 4.11 Blank adult-focused plan

THEME:	SESSION NUMBER:	DATE:	PRACTITIONER/S:
What are the children going to learn?	Early learning goals/ NC	Key vocabulary	
Introduction	What are the children going to do?	What has been successful?	What needs to be revisited?
Plenary	Assessment: Most of the children can	Assessment: Some of the children can	Assessment: These children need more help with

- Leaders were not involved in planning for transition.
- Teaching assistants were important.
- Too much assessment was taking place.

Current preparation for transition

The Tickell review signals a new dimension to transition quite strongly. This is the recommendation that when children are in the Reception class, their experience should prepare them for the move to Year 1, both in terms of the level of development most children should have reached and in the knowledge that most children would be expected to have. The recommendation that arises from this is that the:

> EYFS requirement relating to delivery through play is clarified, including emphasising that this does not preclude more adult direction or teaching, and by setting out what playful, adult-directed learning looks like.

> (DfE, 2011a: 35)

The proposed early learning goals have an exceeding column which is a direct match, or will be, to the revised National Curriculum. The implication of this is that there will be a proportion of more-able children in all Reception classes who are working at National Curriculum levels and beyond the early learning goals. So what, then, are the implications of this for expectations, teaching and learning in the Reception class? The EYFS *Practice Guidance* states

TABLE 4.12 Experiences in Year 1

RECOMMENDED	NOT RECOMMENDED
■ Play-based	■ Work-based
■ Active	■ Static
■ Led by adults or children	■ Directed by adults
■ Thematic	■ Subject-based
■ Emphasises a range of skills	■ Emphasises listening and writing

clearly that there should be continuity between settings, with the children's social, emotional and educational needs addressed appropriately. Transition is a process, not an event, and should be planned for and discussed with children and parents. Settings should communicate information which will secure continuity of experience for the child between settings. Effective use should be made of the summative assessment of each child recorded in the EYFS Profile to support planning for learning in Year 1. A case study described by the National Strategies highlights the difficulties faced by children's transition to Year 1. The results being that the teacher spent too much time managing classroom behaviour and the children's learning suffered because they were not engaging in the decontextualised activities provided. Assessment records in the form of learning journals were not referred to. The school reorganised into a lower school comprising the Foundation Stage and Year 1 with continuity in experiences provided in the autumn term and a gradual move towards whole class sessions by the end of the year. The features of effective practices for those 5- and 6-year-old children identified the features of good practice and less effective practice outlined in Table 4.12.

A review of your current practices using the format in Box 4.1 could be a useful starting point. It is all too familiar to hear Year 1 teachers blaming the independence and freedom of their children in EYFS as the reason for their inattention and misbehaviour in Year 1. Tickell is clearly inferring from her review that learning in a Reception class is likely to be different in some ways and needs to prepare children for Key Stage 1. It is important that the whole school review the likely needed changes to some of the long-established routines and organisation in Year 1 classrooms. It is possible to create a lower school comprising EYFS and Year 1 as a unit. This possible finding is favoured following two recently published reports, *The Independent Review of the Primary Curriculum* (Alexander, 2009) and *The Cambridge Primary Review* (University of Cambridge, 2009), both of which challenge the status quo with regard to Year 1. The latter review suggests that EYFS should be renamed and extended to age 6. A report entitled 'Drying the tears of a tricky transition' in the Times Educational Supplement (TES, 2008) is unequivocal, 'More play-based lessons instead of sitting still in class could help end bad experiences for Year 1 pupils and staff'. Also, a gem of a comment by a Year 1 boy who said that being sat on the carpet, 'wastes your life' (Sanders *et al.*, 2005). *The Primary Curriculum Review* (Alexander, 2009) debates this issue in relation to summer-born children. The issue for such very much younger children is that they are disadvantaged in several ways. Lack of free pre-school education, less time in a play-orientated early years environment and continued lower achievement throughout the school system, the latter being most marked in the early stages of education. The summer-born children risk being treated as immature in comparison with their older classmates, giving rise to a lack of confidence and low self-regard and may limit expectations of them and their expectations of themselves. Below is an example of an action plan for transition from EYFS to Year 1.

BOX 4.1 Action plan for transition from EYFS to Key Stage 1

Summer term
1. Review the progress of EYFS children to identify the proportion not likely to meet the ELGs.
2. Meet with Key Stage 1 leader and Year 1 teacher(s) to arrange transition strategies – teacher swap, children familiarised with Year 1.
3. Decide on the reorganisation needed in Year 1 classrooms (more play-based activities and access to outdoor learning if possible).
4. Arrange for Year 1 and EYFS teachers to swap roles to enable Year 1 teachers to see the effectiveness of EYFS practice on children's behaviour and attitudes to learning.
5. Can teaching assistants move to Year 1 with children with EAL or learning difficulties?
6. Arrange a meeting with parents to inform them of the need for some continuation of EYFS practices in Year 1.

Autumn term
1. Monitor the learning, attitudes and behaviour of the Year 1 pupils.
2. Evaluate the impact of all the suggested changes and agree priorities for future practices.
3. Write a transition policy for EYFS to Year 1 to fit alongside transition from pre-school/nursery to Reception (if children are not already in the school's EYFS).*

* There is an assumption made here that nursery and Reception children in one school will already be working together. If not, then apply transition arrangements which are likely to be well established.

Discussion points

1. Discuss your strategies for planning and reviewing learning in your setting.
2. Compare the samples of planning formats with your own and discuss.
3. Discuss how closely you are working with Year 1 and the routines agreed for EYFS to prepare children for Key Stage 1.
4. Audit the activities you provide as a Reception class teacher to prepare your children for Key Stage 1.

5

Leadership and management in the early years

Introduction

This chapter provides examples of exemplary leadership in a range of early years settings. Also outlined are a range of professional development routes for early years professionals wishing to take on a leadership role. The chapter includes the revised EYFS framework section on safeguarding and welfare requirements. Ofsted surveys provide extensive evaluations of the strengths of leaders in early years settings from Children's Centres to nursery schools in some very diverse locations. One of the most challenging leadership roles is that of the EYFS leader in a primary school with children attending a nursery part-time. Nonetheless, the attributes of leaders are fairly consistent whatever the circumstances of their leadership. It is clear from all surveys, especially those of the effectiveness of Sure Start Children's Centres, that there is a strong correlation between the effectiveness of the setting and the quality, drive and vision of the leader.

The key leadership aspects in Sure Start Children's Centres

Sure Start Children's Centres bring together services for children under 5 and their families in new ways. The services they offer integrate health, childcare, education and parental involvement. As a result, staff working in Sure Start Children's Centres generally come from different professional backgrounds and may work in multi-professional teams, often working in partnership with agencies in the private and voluntary sectors. Parents too have a key role in helping to shape and drive the Children's Centre services. Leaders make a difference by:

- Establishing and sustaining an environment of challenge and support where children are safe, can flourish and learn.
- Providing the vision, direction and leadership vital to the creation of integrated and comprehensive services for children, mothers, fathers and families.
- Leading the work of the centre to secure its success, its accountability and its continuous improvement. Central to such success is the quality and level of collaboration with other services and the whole of the community.

- Working with and through others to design and shape flexible, responsive services to meet the changing needs of children and families.
- Ensuring that all staff understand children's developing needs within the context of the family and provide appropriate services that respond to those needs.
- Ensuring that the centre collects and uses all available data to gain a better understanding of the nature and complexity of the local community served by the Children's Centre.
- Using such knowledge and understanding to inform how services are organised and how to offer differentiated services that are responsive to all groups including fathers, children or parents with disabilities or additional needs, and black and minority ethnic communities.

(DfES, 2007)

The *Sure Start Children's Centre Practice Guidance* (DES and DH, 2006) for leaders in Sure Start Centres provides a wealth of guidance covering all aspects of the role. I am providing a summary of this here to outline the extensive roles and responsibilities of centre managers. The key pointers to success are to know the community by gathering as much data as possible about the local community and setting up outreach and home-visiting schemes to encourage families to use the centres. This is a key aspect in the guidance to the centres mentioned above. Managers need to plan the services they can provide for children and families. Alongside this are included the findings of the various evaluations of the Sure Start programme (Melhuish, 2008). At all times the evaluations focus on the outcomes for children and families. The final evaluation concludes how great the gains are in the Children's Centres in the past seven years. The impact is because of the increased quality of service provision and the greater attention paid to hard-to-reach families. To summarise, the overall improvements are:

- greater exposure to children and families;
- inter-agency collaboration essential for good services;
- active engagement with health services.

However, although these findings are fairly helpful they do not really pinpoint the qualities of leadership that ensured the improvements took place. An example of a Sure Start team's view of management is cited in the *Sure Start Practice Guidance* (DfE, 2010). The team said that the secret of their success was the 'style of management – lots of freedom, but lots of responsibility' which enables them to develop their skills and try out their ideas. More recently, Ofsted (2008) in their *Early Years: Leading to Excellence* survey reviewed early years and childcare provision over three years with a focus on organisation and leadership and management. In the best settings children are at the heart of all that happens, there is a robust approach to keeping children safe, inspiring environments enable children to thrive, well supported by knowledgeable adults who keep a close watch over their development and monitor progress and providers further improve on already outstanding practice. Ofsted wrote:

Leaders have a clear sense of purpose, an ambition for excellence, and clear vision for the future of the setting. This is supported by clear plans for its development and improvement for children. The adults are committed to continuous improvement, by further developing their knowledge and skills, reflecting on their practice, and enhancing what they do to promote the best outcomes for children. They test out their own practice against the best that research describes.

(Ofsted, 2008: 50)

Self-evaluation

A self-evaluation system underpins a settings' ability to improve. In the best-organised settings, providers and staff reflect on the quality of their practice, assess what difference it makes to children's welfare, learning and development, and plan accordingly. Weaker areas are recognised and changed or adapted. A large proportion of providers responded to an Ofsted survey by saying they regularly evaluate their service and write down how well they are doing as part of their efforts to improve areas, such as updating policies and procedures, better involvement of staff, parents and children. There are a series of questions at the end of the chapter to help providers use the evidence of this survey to improve their own practice.

Development planning is a key responsibility for centre managers. There is considerable variation in the format of these. Table 5.1 is an example of a very small section of a three-year development plan from a Children's Centre (previously an Early Excellence Centre) in the centre of a very disadvantaged part of Sunderland. The yearly evaluation (Table 5.2) in the next section is from the same setting and illustrates how strengths and areas for further development are identified.

Monitoring and evaluating the quality of your provision

The yearly evaluation of an aspect of the three-year development plan in Table 5.2 very clearly evaluates what has worked and what still needs work in this setting. Next steps are clearly identified, as are those responsible. This is a very effective working document that accurately appraises the work of the Children's Centre. One of the core purposes of Sure Start Children's Centre leaders is to make a difference by leading learning and development. The key standards for this section (Table 5.3) are to show that leaders can, 'review and evaluate learning, teaching and care practice to promote improvement in outcomes for children and families with a particular focus on the most disadvantaged' (DfES, 2007).

The term 'governance' means the system of decision making which determines the services offered through the Children's Centre and applies at all levels at which decisions are made – including local authorities, children's trust partners, providers, advisory boards, school or college governing bodies and centre managers. When evaluating the extent to which ambitious targets drive improvement, provision is integrated and there are high expectations for users and the wider community. The following points are expected to be taken into account:

- the effectiveness of senior leaders in communicating high expectations to all staff and users;
- the effectiveness of the local needs analysis to identify integrated provision that is targeted at narrowing the gap for the most disadvantaged;
- how well the centre delivers early childhood services, including the steps taken to ensure that early years provision either made directly or commissioned by the centre is of good quality;
- the extent to which the centre's development plan sets out the priorities, challenging targets for improvement, how and when they will be delivered and the resources required to deliver them;

TABLE 5.1 An exemplary section from a Children's Centre's development plan and evaluation

Centre Improvement Plan: A 3-Year Forecast
Priority 2 – Leading Learning and Development
To provide improvement in outcomes for child and family through Learning, Teaching and Care Practices

ACTON TO BE TAKEN	PERSONNEL	PLANNED PROGRAMME AND OUTCOME	SUCCESS CRITERIA	MONITORING (Checking that it has happened)	EVALUATION (How effective were actions)	COST/ FINANCE (2008– 2009)
To improve boys' thinking and learning Ask question: Does this early years setting meet the needs and interests of boys?	■ Lead – head and all key workers – x and y.	■ Observe, track and monitor current activity by boys to gain a clearer picture of take up and use of provision. ■ Complete an in-depth study of learning stories and ask question: do we meet the needs/ interests of boys under the remit of the Unique Child? ■ Attend training to support boys' achievements. Share with staff. ■ Develop expertise amongst staff to identify dispositions and how to promote/extend boys PSED.	■ Staff are aware of the needs/interests of boys and reflect this in the learning environment. ■ Tracking and monitoring. Identified AEN/SEN registration and intervention for boys. ■ Raise staff awareness through in-house training and impact on practice. ■ Unique Child needs are met.	■ Planning. ■ Learning stories. ■ Reflections. ■ Through increased identification of need and response. ■ Practice records. ■ Baseline strands. ■ SIO reports.	■ Whole staff review. ■ Gender equality scheme action plan review. ■ Staff competent and confident in supporting the Unique Child. ■ Effective movement through Code of Practice.	None

(This is one of three actions in this priority)

TABLE 5.2 Part of a Children's Centre's development plan evaluation (see Chapter 9)

CENTRE DEVELOPMENT PLAN EVALUATION 2007–2008	
PRIORITY 3: DEVELOPING SUCCESSFUL LEARNERS AND CONFIDENT INDIVIDUALS	
ACTION TO BE TAKEN	EVALUATION
To support the development of the lowest-achieving 20% of children at FSP. CLL focus – Learning and Development	■ Primary Strategy Phase 1 has been introduced to staff and implemented at SGT. It has been enhanced by staff's attendance at Ros Bailey's Phonological Awareness, Communication Matters and I CAN training. ■ Staff who attended reported them to all be important but in different ways: the key focus was to get the child to communicate. Individual training should now be reflected in practice, and supported through SENCO monitoring. How these strategies and resources are used is determined by the needs of the individual groups at SGT: we need a mixed economy of approaches. ■ The sounds and letters packs were found to be easy to follow, very effective and accessible. As part of the intervention programme repeated and SGT activity for the purple group, these resources made a big impact on these children's progress. Baseline data indicates good progress was made. Time is now needed for staff to become familiar with all packs so to make informed choices for next year. ■ Ros Bailey's ideas and strategies rose awareness of the ways to question, gain attention and develop confidence to participate, listen and be more aware of sounds. Listening activities were made more user-friendly and ideas distributed to all staff. They were found to be 'more fun' than Sounds and Letters. The introduction of charts was very popular, particularly with boys. ■ The Rhyme Packs have encouraged an active relationship between home and the centre in learning completed packs 1 and 2. There was very positive feedback from parents. They have definitely supported the children's progress. ■ Singing, music and drama have all become a big part of the nursery day through enhanced provision in the music drama area with the dance studio set etc. Boys' and girls' needs are met through careful resourcing and planning of the environment. ■ The Time for Rhyme activity for child and parent has been poorly attended, but those who did become involved benefited and gained from the experience. It had a direct impact on children's confidence with the Nursery Rhyme Packs. ■ The library has been offered to all children across the centre – the Babynest promotion has been well used and books are regularly borrowed and returned. For other age groups it is very important to continue take-up. We need to be more organised next year, particularly in recruiting and retaining parental volunteers.

TABLE 5.3 Standards for leading, learning and development (DfES 2007)

STANDARDS
THE HEAD OF THE CHILDREN'S CENTRE MUST BE ABLE TO SHOW THEY CAN:

- Review and evaluate learning, teaching and care practices to promote improvement in outcomes for children and families with a particular focus on the most disadvantaged.

- Identify, promote and encourage effective practice.

- Establish a safe environment in which children can develop and learn.

- Develop and foster a learning culture that enables children, families and staff to become, successful, enthusiastic and independent learners.

- Ensure that staff acknowledge the expertise of parents and find ways to share this knowledge and understanding of individual children's learning at home, in order to work together and improve learning opportunities in the centre.

- Help parents to overcome barriers such as lack of confidence or poor basic skills and support them to take decisive action to return to study, training and employment.

- Respect diversity and respond with sensitivity to different cultures and beliefs and ensure equality of access to learning opportunities.

- Regularly review their own practice and take responsibility for their own personal and professional development, seeking support where appropriate.

- Create experiences that will inspire children, their families and staff to raise expectations for their own achievement, enjoyment and economic success and make a positive contribution to the community.

- the extent to which resources are clearly identified, targeted at identified priorities and shifted to meet changing needs;
- the extent to which partners, including users, are clear about the priorities and have been involved in identifying them at both local and strategic levels;
- a judgement will also be made on how efficiently and effectively the centre uses and manages its available resources to meet the needs of users and the wider community to achieve value for money;
- safeguarding and welfare requirements.

Evaluating teaching and learning

A key area that early years leaders have found less easy to evaluate is the day-to-day quality of teaching and learning in their settings. A typical comment is that, because head teachers or managers are working alongside their colleagues on a daily basis, there is 'no need to carry out a formal evaluation of teaching'. There is a statutory requirement linked to performance management that monitoring will be carried out. A review of this has taken place recently to remove the limit to the number of times that a practitioner may be observed. However, that is the least of the reasons why there needs to be a professional dialogue between colleagues about the way they interact and extend children's learning. I have worked with settings that have filmed aspects of teaching and learning in their own setting and used it as a basis for staff development. Informal discussions as to the key learning taking place leads naturally into evaluative comments about teaching. This paves the way to creating a trusting atmosphere between colleagues as they work together to provide the best for the children in their care. Examples of a format for leaders to evaluate teaching and learning are included in Tables 5.4 and 5.5. These are taken from the a national strategies publication, *Challenging Practice to Further Improve Learning, Playing and Interacting in the Early Years Foundation Stage* (DCSF, 2010b). The standards for the early years professional status award also provide useful guidance on evaluating teaching and learning. The following list combines some of the professional standards for all qualified teachers and the standard for Early Years Professional Status (EYPS):

- professional knowledge and understanding. As already mentioned, this relates to the practitioner's familiarity with the principles and content of EYFS. This is manifest in practice through reference to *Development Matters* statements in planning;
- an understanding of observational assessment techniques;
- how the safe and imaginative use of new technology supports learning;
- an understanding of how to monitor progress and share this information with parents;
- how to create an environment of challenge and support where children can flourish and learn;
- professional qualities and skills;
- demonstrating personal enthusiasm for and commitment to learning by, for example, participating in research, analysis and debate about effective learning and how to improve achievement;
- actively seeking to engage parents and help them to adopt practices that will promote their children's health and development;
- identifying and challenging discrimination that obstructs access to and engagement with learning.

However, I believe that the Tickell review has accurately identified what excellent teaching and learning looks like as a result of the findings in the extensive research review (DfE 2011b). The crucial factor in excellent settings is the encouragement of more 'sustained shared thinking' (Sylva *et al.*, 2004). This is defined as 'an episode in which two or more individuals "work together" in an intellectual way to solve a problem, clarify a concept, evaluate activities, extend narrative, etc.' A child and an adult are expected to contribute to the child's thinking and must help to develop and extend that thinking. The EPPE research project found that generally this did not happen very frequently. In excellent settings there was more attention to encouraging children to extend their thinking than in good settings. This led the research team to conclude that periods of 'sustained shared thinking' are a necessary prerequisite for excellent early years practice, especially where this is encouraged in the home through parent support. The evidence suggests that 'adult modelling' is often combined with periods of sustained shared thinking, and that open-ended questioning is also associated with better cognitive development. The research found that open-ended questions made up only 5.1 per cent of the questioning used in even the excellent settings. Another crucial finding is that there is an equal balance between who initiates activities, staff or a child, in the excellent settings. Staff in excellent settings regularly extend child-initiated activities but do not dominate them. The balance in Reception classes changes, with much greater emphasis on adult initiated episodes. Children spend much of their time in small groups. However, episodes of sustained shared thinking were most likely to occur when children were interacting one-to-one with an adult or a single peer partner. Freely chosen play activities provide the best opportunities for adults to extend children's thinking. Adults have to create opportunities to extend child-initiated play as well as teacher-initiated group work as both have been found to be important for promoting learning. The monitoring examples taken from the national strategies in Tables 5.4 and 5.5 capture the need for balance in the role of the adult in a setting or in the home.

TABLE 5.4 Observation of learning, playing and interacting (adult-directed) (DCSF, 2010b)

Practitioner observed......................... Observer ....

Date........................... Context........................... Purpose.....................

POSSIBLE PROMPTS	OBSERVATIONS	REFLECTION: IMPACT ON LEARNING
Close, caring and respectful relationships.		
Encourage and support children to relate to others.		
Support children to resolve conflicts through problem-solving.		
Observe children as a natural part of all normal activity.		
Interpret children's actions and words to try to understand the child's thinking and learning.		
Scaffold children's learning through, talk, discuss strategies and ideas, suggest possibilities and model approaches.		
Provide brief, well-planned, focused learning opportunities in response to observed interests, learning and development.		
Use daily events within the routine to provide worthwhile real-life experiences.		
Vary experiences, using fresh, creative and playful approaches.		
Provide first-hand experiences to explore and discover.		
Directly teach through demonstrating or explaining.		
Support children to persevere through difficulties, to take risks, to ask questions and problem-solve.		
Use the language of learning to focus children on themselves as learners.		
Identify and support the next steps in learning.		

TABLE 5.4 (continued)

Observation evaluation/discussion notes

Strengths:	
Areas for development:	
Agreed actions by:	**Timescales:**
Leader/manager:	
Practitioner:	

The key person

Each child in a group setting must be assigned a key person. In child minding settings the child minder is the key worker. A key person has special responsibilities for working with a small number of children, giving them the reassurance to feel safe and cared for, and building relationships with their parents. They are also likely to be the first point of contact for a parent. The relationship between a baby and key person in an out-of-home setting is especially significant. There is a growing body of literature (Lindon,1998) which emphasises the importance of a continuing attachment relationship which links between key persons who care for, play and educate children in settings outside their homes in close association with children's significant attachment figures from the home.

TABLE 5.5 Observation of learning, playing and interacting in the EYFS (child-initiated)

Practitioner observed..................... Observer ....

Date........................ Context........................ Purpose....................

POSSIBLE PROMPTS	OBSERVATIONS	REFLECTION: IMPACT ON LEARNING
Close, caring and respectful relationships. Encourage and support children to relate to others.		
Support children to resolve conflicts through problem-solving.		
Ensure sustained time to develop child-initiated activities.		
Arrange, resource, and make time for children to freely use rich indoor and outdoor spaces.		
Observe children as a natural part of all activity.		
Interpret children's actions and words to try and understand the child's thinking and learning.		
Use sensitivity when deciding when to interact.		
Join in play and child-initiated activity following children's agendas.		
Scaffold children's learning through talk, discuss strategies and ideas, suggest possibilities and model approaches.		
Use daily events within the routines to provide worthwhile real-life experiences.		
Directly teach, demonstrating or explaining.		
Support children to persevere through difficulties, to take risks, to ask questions and problem-solve.		
Use the language of learning to focus children on themselves as learners.		
Identify and support the next steps in learning.		

What research tells us

Several research projects were commissioned to explore the impact of pre-school on children's intellectual and social development. One example of this was *The Effective Provision of Pre-School Education* (EPPE) *Project* (Sylva *et al.*, 2004). The impact of EPPE's findings may have been a contributory factor in later legislation requiring there to be a practitioner in each setting awarded Early Years Professional Status (EYPS). In relation to Children's Centres, a key finding was that children who had an earlier start (under age 3) related to better intellectual development and that quality was higher overall in settings integrating care and education. This research also found that settings that had staff with higher qualifications had higher quality scores and their children made more progress. Other quality indicators included warm interactive relationships with children, having a trained teacher as manager and a good proportion of trained teachers on the staff.

A much later, small-scale report by Ofsted (July 2009) evaluated the impact of integrated services on children and their families in Sure Start Children's Centres. Outstanding centres demonstrated that feeder schools reported children's improving attitudes to learning and social development were easing their transition to school. Also, children with special educational needs and those with developmental delays gained much from working in close partnership with professionals from several services, and parents particularly appreciated being able to access a range of professional support under one roof. Examples of excellence where all three services worked together cited the work of speech and language therapists working effectively between health, education and care. However, at this time, Ofsted reported that half of the centres were finding it problematic to reach out to the most vulnerable families who may not ask for support, but where the need is greatest. From April 2010, a revised inspection framework for Sure Start Children's Centres was in place. As far as leadership and management were concerned the expectations were that arrangements regarding the quality of safeguarding, equality and diversity would be significant and have an overall impact on the quality of leadership and management. As a consequence of these key priorities I am including the inspection criteria from Ofsted (2010) in Table 5.6.

Safeguarding and welfare requirements

> Young children are vulnerable. They develop resilience when their physical and psychological well-being is protected by adults.
>
> (A Unique Child, 1.3 Keeping Safe)

Tickell (2011: 37) has reported on the key improvements that need to be made in ensuring that children are safe, happy and healthy. She recognises that safeguarding is everyone's responsibility and must be their first and foremost consideration. This means that everyone needs to be vigilant and know what to do if they have concerns about a child. Nonetheless, the review suggests that there is need to make it very clear what information is for guidance and what is a statutory legal requirement. It is likely, then, that the current requirements are to be redrafted to improve their clarity. There is to be advice and good practice for food nutrition in the early years. The key areas are how inappropriate behaviours are identified in children and also in adults as a result of the recommendations arising from the Plymouth Serious Case Review. A sense of security is essential for safety in settings, but this may result in too many requirements. Tickell is firm in her statement, for example, that there should be no banning of mobile phones in settings. There are other recommendations that are only tentatively covered,

TABLE 5.6 Ofsted inspection criteria for leadership and management of Sure Start Children's Centres

- The extent to which governance, accountability, professional supervision and day-to-day management arrangements are clear and understood.
- The extent to which ambitious targets drive improvement, provision is integrated and there are high expectations for users and the wider community.
- The extent to which resources are used and managed efficiently and effectively to meet the needs of users and the wider community.
- The extent to which equality is promoted and diversity celebrated, illegal or unlawful discrimination is tackled and the centre fulfils its statutory duties.
- The effectiveness of the centre's policy, procedures and work with key agencies in safeguarding children and, where applicable, vulnerable adults.
- The extent to which evaluation is used to shape and improve services and activities.
- The extent to which partnerships with other agencies ensure the integrated delivery of the range of services the centre has been commissioned to provide.
- The extent to which the centre supports and encourages the wider community to engage with services and uses their views to develop the range of provision.

such as ratios of adults to children in Reception classes and ratios during breaks and lunch times. That the review is evidence-based is very apparent in this section where there is the recommendation that too many risk assessments are taking place and are too time-consuming to complete. In my own experience in schools, it would be unheard of for there to be no risk assessment for trips out of school. Generally, schools in the maintained sector follow the LA guidelines for this and regard their completion as an essential element in organising a visit out of the setting. For these reasons the recommendations of the current guidance are included with an example of a priority in a Children's Centre improvement plan (see Case Study 5.1).

In outlining the arrangements to ensure the highest priority is given to children's welfare I will refer to the EYFS statutory guidance to alert leaders and practitioners of their statutory responsibilities. Children's Centres will need to cooperate with all the relevant agencies to safeguard and promote the welfare of children. It is also worth emphasising that, in inspection terms, if a setting is not meeting their statutory duties this should prompt a judgement of 'inadequate' for safeguarding and have a knock-on effect on the overall judgement for leadership and management, which is unlikely to be better than 'satisfactory'. The information inspectors need to take into account is extensive, as shown in the list below. They need to consider:

- how well safeguarding is prioritised (aims of Centre, improvement plan, self-evaluation form, policies);
- how well the Centre discharges its responsibility to work together with key agencies to safeguard children and, where applicable, vulnerable adults (meeting minutes, individual case files);
- the extent to which the centre identifies concerns about possible abuse, records information relevant to safeguarding concerns clearly and accurately and shares it appropriately, both internally and with other agencies (protocols, records);
- the clarity of information sharing protocols and child protection procedures, understanding of thresholds for referral to social care services and effectiveness of communication between all agencies;
- the extent to which the Criminal Records Bureau, vetting and recruitment procedures comply with current government requirements and local protocols;

- the extent to which managers from the agencies working within the centre ensure that practices comply with their agency policy and the centre's policy;
- the extent to which the centre's procedures ensure that all staff working on site have the appropriate checks, including the suitability of any other adults looking after children or having unsupervised access to them;
- the effectiveness of the systems to ensure the physical safety, health and well-being of children and vulnerable adults, including the effectiveness of risk assessments and actions taken to manage or eliminate risks;
- how well parents and other users are made aware of safeguarding issues and understand the importance of ensuring that children in the centre are kept safe;
- parents' views on how they are helped to keep their children safe and to support their emotional health and well-being, for example through information, courses, parenting classes or access to support;
- the extent to which all staff receive appropriate and up-to-date, high-quality safeguarding training, especially those working with more vulnerable children and adults, for example those with learning difficulties and/or disabilities;
- how well children and vulnerable adults are supported in making concerns known and whether action is taken as a result.

The above reflect the EYFS statutory guidance in all respects. An issue for leaders is how much of the above statutory requirements can be delegated to others as they so often appear to be where there are issues with non-compliance. As stated above, the centre leader has ulti-mate responsibility for ensuring that all protocols and procedures are in place. Case Study 5.1 provides an example of how one early years centre tackled addressing the most recent require-ments to revise their safeguarding policy and practice in the centre improvement plan.

Equality and diversity

> The diversity of individuals and communities is valued and respected. No child or family is discriminated against.
>
> (A Unique Child, 1.2 Inclusive Practice)

Meeting the individual needs of all children lies at the heart of the EYFS. The government introduced the *Inclusion Development Programme* (IDP) (DCSF, 2008a) to provide support for leadership teams in schools and early years settings. It is of particular relevance to EYFS because of the support provided to help identify children with speech, language and communication difficulties. All early years providers must have and implement an effective policy for ensuring equality of opportunities and for supporting children with learning difficulties and disabilities. This does not mean that all children should be treated the same, but that the unique skills and abilities of each child should be recognised and developed. It is an area in which settings have legal responsibilities. The following questions provide a guide to practitioners as to their role and responsibilities if they lead on this area of the setting. Do you as a leader or manager:

- Make the development of children's speech, language and communication skills a priority?
- Have a thorough knowledge of this area yourself?

CASE STUDY 5.1 Safeguarding improvement plan

Priority 1 – Stronger families and stronger learning communities

Action to be taken	Personnel	Planned programme and outcome	Success criteria	Monitoring (checking that it happened)	Evaluation (how effective were actions)	Cost, finance
1.2 To revise Safeguarding Policy and Practice	Designated and nominated personnel SMT	▪ Use safeguarding audit to identify gaps and create an action plan ▪ Agree and adopt the safer working practices document for staff ▪ Use template for CRB, identification and vetting purposes of all staff, visitors, professionals and students on site	▪ All staff trained in agreement and signed document ▪ Knowledge and understanding of LADO ▪ Robust systems in place to keep children safe	▪ Head and SENCO monitoring to check that working practices are followed ▪ Spreadsheets have no gaps and no 'yes' entries	▪ Ofsted regulations and standards met ▪ Training increased skill in working practices and the identification of 'significant' harm ▪ Comply with Section 175 of Education Act 2002 and Safer Recruitment 2007	▪ In house costs for one-day training – September 2009
		▪ Designated and nominated staff attend CP training (and then every two years). Whole staff aware of procedures and alert officers re concerns, monitoring, observations disclosures ▪ Staff handbook to be completed in light of safeguarding and working practices	▪ Mandatory training attended and up-to-date ▪ All staff act upon information and are confident in procedures and systems ▪ Updated staff handbook	▪ Certificates awarded ▪ Governors informed via HT termly report ▪ Agenda item on weekly staff meeting ▪ Minutes of meeting ▪ CP records and monitoring files ▪ Robust systems used	▪ All staff and CP officers have ability to follow LSCB safeguarding children procedures ▪ Confidence in making referrals and accurate records kept. Attendance and contribution to CP conferences/core group made ▪ Protection plans undertaken by appropriate staff leading to effective safeguarding for all ▪ A whole centre approach to collective responsibility is evident	
		▪ Update policies: ➤ Inclusion ➤ PSHE, including behaviour ➤ Photography ➤ Smoking and drugs ➤ ICT & 'E' learning ➤ Health and safety emergency plan and drills	▪ Policies and Procedures reviewed and in place ▪ Staff and governors aware and adopt ▪ All staff are confident	▪ HT and SENCO report to governors ▪ Evidence through minutes/observation of practice/feedback from link governors and SIO	▪ Codes of behaviour are universal ▪ Policies are adhered to ▪ Parents understand and feedback is positive ▪ Families demonstrate safer, healthier lifestyles ▪ Vulnerability of child/student/staff/adult is reduced	

- Ensure that the training and development plans for the setting include a requirement that all practitioners access training and development on speech, language and communication at a level appropriate to their professional needs and the needs of the setting?
- Plan regular opportunities for practitioners to discuss children's levels of development and to plan support for children?
- Review children's progress, including an analysis of the EYFS Profile results, reflect on that progress and support practitioners in implementing necessary changes in the setting and their own practice?
- Have a policy on the use of dummies that is implemented sensitively, taking into account children's emotional needs?

(DCSF, 2008a: 22)

The implementation of the Tickell recommendation that children are provided with a learning and development assessment at age 2, as well as their health review, is a welcome development for practitioners. The short summary provided by practitioners or health visitors for those not in a childcare setting will be of the child's communication and language, personal, social, emotional and physical development between the ages of 24–36 months. The practice guidance for the Unique Child provides guidance on effective practice when a new family arrives into your setting. How would a family arriving at your setting know that all children are welcomed and valued? They would observe:

- information in pictures, words and signs indicating how to get attention;
- a warm smile and a greeting from the receptionist;
- a welcome board showing children and families from a variety of cultures, saying 'Welcome' in different languages;
- signs, symbols and photographs or objects relating to the lives of families who use the setting;
- displays showing photographs of children's play, development and learning.

For those of you working in schools with a very small number of children from other cultures a welcoming touch would be to have a display depicting aspects of the families' culture to welcome all the family into the community of the setting. *The Inclusion Development Programme* (DCSF, 2008a) has a focus on supporting children with speech, language and communication needs in the early years. There are many examples of ways to work effectively with children and families for whom English is an additional language. The series of questions below can be used with your colleagues to answer questions about your provision.

Do you:

- Record detailed language background and home language use, preferences and skills on admission to the setting?
- Check the spelling and pronunciation of children's and parents' names?
- Reassure parents that use of home languages in the setting will support their child's overall learning and developing use of language, including English?
- Work effectively with bilingual staff, wherever possible, to provide positive role models, raise self-esteem, raise language awareness of all children and support home-school links?
- Seek religious and cultural advice from relevant experts in the community?

- Ensure effective two-way communication of information via interpreter, written translation or the Internet?
- Look closely at your practice and find it to be equitable for all families?
- Genuinely welcome all families and children without prejudice?
- Openly discuss emotive and difficult subjects such as racism or the effects of religious, cultural or economic intolerance in our community?
- Seek training, advice and support in order to improve your provision for children learning English as an additional language where necessary?
- Have policies that include provision for working with children and families learning English?

(DCSF, 2008a: 9)

On a more practical level, while a setting may have all the recommendations suggested above in place, it is the quality of the day-to-day interaction with practitioners that will help to improve spoken English and its meanings. A key resource for this is a rich, play-orientated environment in which children learn to play together, share, discuss ideas, copy and imitate others and set up those social relationships with peers that are so fundamental to language development (Rice and Wilcox, 1995). Research tells us that some children, particularly from low-income homes, do not experience the rich, well-planned communication and language provision in their settings that is necessary to support their development. Children who have limited language experience may choose to spend very little time in pre-school engaging in conversation. Dickinson and Tabors (2001) audio-taped 4-year-olds and found that in their free-play activity time 17 per cent was spent in meaningful conversation with a practitioner, 18 per cent was spent in meaningful conversation with peers and 59 per cent was spent not talking at all. It is important to plan for the development of communication, speaking and listening skills by making sure of all the multi-sensory activities that children enjoy participating in (DfES, 2007b).

Professional development opportunities for leaders in EYFS

The National Professional Qualification in Integrated Centre Leadership (NPQICL) is an equivalent qualification to the National Professional Qualification for Head Teachers (NPQH) of maintained schools. Professionals working in either sector can pursue either qualification to meet the requirement to be a head teacher. The NPQICL qualification prepares participants for a range of roles linked to Children's Centres, whether they are called managers, co-ordinators or directors, or whether they are responsible for one or more centres (see Table 5.7).

The NPQICL programme gives participants the opportunity to reflect in depth on their leadership work. It can be completed as a study programme working with tutors and colleagues or as a research project focusing on your own leadership role. You will be expected to explore the leadership dimensions of your roles and be able to place this in the wider context of developments in integrated service provision. Whichever route you choose, you will engage in some degree of research relating to your own workplace setting. Further information about this can be found at www.nationalcollege.org.uk.

Children's Centre Leadership Model

The Urban Leadership Centre (ULC) has developed a set of competencies which transcends agency divides, enabling greater cross-fertilisation, understanding, movement and cooperation between agencies. The importance of multi-agency cooperation, highlighted by Beverly Hughes in a speech to Sure Start Children's Centre leaders in 2008, states:

> Mark Friedman, in his book *Trying Hard is Not Good Enough*, writes about turning the curve in children's service – an evidenced approach used in many local authorities … but in the end, doing your best is necessary but isn't always sufficient. What matters most of all is the positive impact that the activity actually has on the children, on families and on communities. First, we have to ensure that practice is of a sufficiently and consistently high quality to make a difference, but we will only improve outcomes if the right relationships are in place between Children's Centres and other services. Finally, we must reach out more effectively to draw in those who have the most to gain.

A comparison can be made between the Urban School Leadership Model competencies (2006) and the National Standards for leaders of Sure Start Children's Centres (DfES, 2007) in Table 5.8

The Children's Centre leadership model is designed for leaders of Children's Centres and covers all the leadership skills expected at every level within the early years organisation.

The coordination of Children's Services is undoubtedly complex. The Urban Leadership centre is working towards a coordinated approach to reducing the silo mentality, which clearly militates against a coordinated approach to the needs of children by developing leadership competencies applicable across the entire spectrum of Children's Services. 'What matters most of all is the impact that an activity has on children, families and schools' (Friedman, 2005).

The Competencies Framework comprises twelve competencies grouped into four clusters:

Enabling
- Vision and Belief.
- Courage and Moral Purpose.
- Empowering Culture.

Operating
- Resourcing Creativity.
- Leading Learning Innovation.
- Situational Judgement.

Relating
- Emotional Intelligence.
- Balancing Change and Empathy.
- School and Community Champion.

Sustaining
- Stability and Consistency.
- Maintaining Focus.
- Enduring Resilience.

Embedded in the Children's Centre model is the concept that leadership is relevant to everyone in the organisation. It is only when their individuals are clear about the leadership competencies required of them and given opportunities to develop them that organisations can truly

TABLE 5.7 Key areas of the national standards for NPQICL

LEADERSHIP OF INTEGRATED CHILDREN'S CENTRES	
Leading Learning and Development	
Stronger Families, Stronger Communities	IMPROVED OUTCOMES
Being Accountable and Responsible	FOR
Shaping the Present and Creating the Future	CHILDREN AND FAMILIES
Managing the Organisation	
Building and Strengthening Teams	

fulfil their remit and move from 'good' to 'excellent'. The Framework has a series of Pathways and leadership stages. The Pathway takes the person on a journey that reviews their performance, behaviours and experience. Head teachers are encouraged to develop their leadership behaviours and may use it as part of the settings performance review process.

Discussion points

Keeping children at the heart of all that happens

1. How confident are you that nothing in your policies or procedures hinders you in welcoming children from all backgrounds and children with special educational needs and disabilities?

2. Do all the children you care for have access to all the activities you offer? If not, why not? How could you make them accessible?

3. How clear is your vision for where your provision should be in three years' time, and about the steps you will take to get there?

4. How well do you know each child's current stage of development and plan their next steps?

5. How involved are parents in what you plan and do for children?

6. How well do you respond to any complaints, including any allegations about staff?

Keeping children safe

7. How well do you help children learn about keeping themselves safe?

8. How do you talk to parents about keeping children safe at home?

9. How confident are you in identifying any potential case of child neglect or abuse, and in responding appropriately when you are concerned that the welfare of a child may not be properly protected?

10. How rigorously do you assess and manage the risks to children?

11. How rigorously do you investigate any concerns and complaints, and resolve any issues identified to improve children's safety?

Improving your practice

12. How well do you think about what you do and how good it is?

13. How well do you and those working with you learn new skills, keeping up-to-date with changes and improving your practice for children and families?

14. How well do adults who work with you, parents and children contribute to ongoing improvements in your setting?

15. What external help and resources do you look for and use to help improve the quality of your provision? When you use this help, how do you assess how useful it has been?

Providing a well-organised environment

16. How well does the way you use space and the resources support and extend children's all-round development, in and out of doors?

17. How well do you organise the setting and overcome obstacles to provide a stimulating environment that responds to the particular needs of each child?

TABLE 5.8 ULCCCLM competencies compared to Sure Start

THE URBAN SCHOOL LEADERSHIP MODEL, 2006	NATIONAL STANDARDS FOR LEADERS OF SURE START CHILDREN'S CENTRES, 2007
Competency: Enduring Resilience	**Standard: Managing the Organisation**
Demonstrates passion, stamina, self-sufficiency and perseverance	*Displays resilience and tenacity in the face of difficulties and challenge*
Competency: Vision and Belief	**Standard: Shaping the Present and Creating the Future**
Develops a shared vision of what the school will look like in 5–10 years time	*Creates and communicates a shared vision in a range of compelling ways*
Competency: Leading Learning Innovation	**Standard: Building and Strengthening Teams**
Seeks mentors, coaches and input from within and beyond education, through formal and informal networks	*Seeks and accepts support and advice from others*
Competency: Balancing Challenge and Empathy	**Standard: Stronger Families, Stronger Communities**
Seeks the support of other agencies to address barriers to pupils' well being	*Recognises the importance and mutual benefit of networking, sharing and working with other Children's Centres, schools and other partner agencies*
Competency: Balancing Challenge and Empathy	**Standard: Building and Strengthening Teams**
Mediates and negotiates effectively between staff, pupils parents and other parties	*Mediates and manages conflict*

6

Learning and development

The provision of meaningful interaction between adults and children to guide new learning is an essential element of the EYFS.

(DfE, 2011a: 29)

Introduction

Another new chapter in this edition chosen because Learning and Development reflects one of the four aspects examined as part of the government's review of the EYFS curriculum. It is refreshing to feel justified in including this chapter, possibly as a result of too much pressure on outcomes for learning at the expense of the process of learning in previous years. It is with great pleasure that I can share the findings of the recently published review in the hope that the changes to this will be minimal as it is received so positively. The chapter covers all aspects of early learning, with a particular focus on the EYFS principles which underpin the current EYFS and are set to remain in the revised EYFS, and the learning characteristics taken from the original EYFS framework that now give a higher status as an integral part of assessment at the end of the Foundation Stage.

The role of the practitioner is given some attention as it is in the review where very clear messages are given as to the nature of adult–child interactions. The review of EYFS by Clare Tickell provides practitioners with a wealth of information about the characteristics of children's learning and a very plausible explanation for the creation of the 'prime' areas of learning.

Research about learning

The research review (Evangelou *et al.*, 2009) describes the fundamental development of very young children. Children are primed to encounter their environment through relating to and communicating with others, and engaging physically with their experiences. This is captured well in the learning characteristics added to the end of Foundation Stage assessment requirements. These are:

- playing and exploring;
- active learning;
- creating and thinking critically.

Case Study 6.1 captures the essence of these statements and I am sure will resonate with many practitioners and parents.

CASE STUDY 6.1 Playing in the garden

Seventeen-month-old Ethan set to work investigating and exploring with a bucket and a long stick. He persevered with the logistics of carrying the bucket and the stick together in the bucket for at least ten minutes as he set about systematically walking the length of the garden, stopping every so often to put the bucket down, mixing the imaginary contents with his stick and off again to catch dandelion seeds blowing in the wind. At some point Ethan found a pair of gardening gloves which he put on and modelled what he had seen his mum doing when gardening.

Case Study 6.1 admirably demonstrates the importance of contexts for learning and plenty of space outdoors, which helped Ethan make connections in his environment as he worked out how to mix in his bucket all around the garden. The activities were carried out with total concentration and obvious pleasure shown in the success achieved in managing the task. The impact of the open space, freedom and safety to roam as he investigated added to the perseverance shown. What was he thinking about as he built up his ideas about what could be done with a stick and a bucket in an ideal context for learning? The evidence of him copying what he had seen others do was very strong. He was also showing signs of repeatable behaviours (Athey, 1990: 68) in the evidence of the use of 'space schemas' and early 'motor' level in the way he repeated the actions with the bucket and stick.

The Tickell review is informed by a wide range of evidence, in particular an academic review on child development sources in the past ten years. The review takes a 'constructivist approach to development' (Rogoff, 2003). The crux of this is that when looking at child development it is not carried out in isolation. Various domains of development are interconnected and influence one another. The review also focuses on research within the 'interactionist' tradition that conceives of development as located within nested social contexts (Bronfenbrenner, 1979). This means that development is effected by cultural contexts and by the make-up of the brain. The nested social contexts include the impact of the influences of the close family on child development and the vital role of parents. As covered in an earlier section, Vygotsky's social-constructivist model of learning is evident throughout the review. The review cites evidence from several longitudinal studies. What was particularly striking was the overlap provided by some domains, particularly creative development. The key findings of the review into children's development which have influenced the EYFS review are listed below.

- Children are born without a sense of self; they establish this through interactions with others (adults, siblings and peers) and with their culture.
- Children thrive in warm, positive relationships characterised by contingent responses. The 'warmth' of relationships is not a novel concept but there is new research on the importance of adults responding to the child's initiation, often called contingent responding.

- Play is a prime context for development. Again, this is not new, but there are now studies on different kinds of play, especially the ways it can be enriched by guiding, planning and resourcing on the part of staff in the settings.
- Conversation is another prime context for development of children's language, thinking, but also their emotions … we now know more about the two broad types of conversation; one serves to confirm a child's understanding or feelings, while the other elaborates and extends that understanding.
- Narrative enables children to create a meaningful personal and social world, but it is also a 'tool for thinking'. It is most effective when children are encouraged to form their own accounts, rather than passively accepting those of adults.
- In enhancing children's thinking, it is more important to aim at depth and not breadth. Deep understanding is more important than superficial coverage.
- Early years curriculum needs to provide opportunities for problem-solving to develop logio-mathematical thinking rather than only focusing on context-specific elements.
- Children's phonological skills are important in learning to read but so is vocabulary. Phonological skills at age 5 are better predictors of reading at age 7 than at the age of 11. Vocabulary at age 5 is a better predictor of the more complex tasks of reading at age 11.
- Development theories such as those of Piaget (1983) have been linear, with children following similar paths to adulthood. New theories assume that development proceeds in a web of multiple strands, with different children following different pathways.
- Children's self-regulation requires the development of effortful control which facilitates the internalisation of social rules.
- Cultural niches and repertoires must be important considerations in shaping the context of children's learning.
- The concept of children's voice is not new but has become an increasing focus of research.

(Evangelou *et al.*, 2009: 4)

Key learning characteristics

Placed in the position of needing to revise this edition prior to publication to reflect the revised EYFS framework, it was with a silent cheer that I read that, despite criticisms of the Learning and Development section of the current EYFS guidance by some early years sectors, the review has confirmed that the EYFS captures, in the main, how the best settings support young children's learning and development. The implementation of EYFS has improved the quality of the early years sector. As a result, it is recommended that early years settings must use the EYFS as their curricular framework unless there are specific reasons for not doing so, such as settings following the Waldorf-Steiner or Montessori curricula. The report cites the evidence to show that healthy development depends on high-quality provision. The next sections describe each of the key learning characteristics. These are all assessed at the end of the Foundation Stage.

Play and exploration

- Finding out and exploring.
- Using what they know in their play.
- Being willing to have a go.

There are many facets to play and exploration in the development of very young children. It is through the observation of children's play that practitioners can learn the most about children. There are many dimensions to play. Children may be playing alone, especially toddlers, as they explore the properties of equipment and use it to solve a problem. The range of experiences we provide for children will all enrich their ideas, concepts and skills. Children may play emotionally and physically, alone or with others. Practitioners need to ensure they are on hand to provide support and extend play by providing additional resources, language, encouragement and praise. This is absolutely crucial and because of this, practitioners need to be cautious in their interpretation of the guidance as to the role of play in their settings. The quotation below from the EYFS practice guidance card 4.1 *Play and Exploration* is one that is frequently used to allow children to have total freedom as to what they do in settings.

> Children's play reflects their wide-ranging and varied interests and preoccupations. In their play children learn at their highest level. Play with peers is important for children's development.
>
> (DCSF, 2008f)

Active learning

- Being involved and concentrating.
- Keeping on trying.
- Enjoying achieving what they set out to do.

Effective practice is dependent on staff having time to reflect on what they have observed about individual children and to reach conclusions about what learning occurs. There is the need to achieve a balance between giving the children independence in their learning while retaining control over the curriculum in the guidance for practitioners. However, with 'learning plans' for children and attention to specific *Development Matters* statements, learning can be channelled to the needs of the child. Montpelier primary planning portrays this particularly well (see Chapter 4). Adults provide mental and physical challenges to extend children's thinking. Vygotsky (1978) emphasised how much we all learn from interacting with other people, how much we are helped by what we are taught and by what we see other people doing. Vygotsky's view is that knowledge is social, and what we are able to do is much more a matter of our upbringing and education than of our inborn potential. He believed that we should think of the child as being at two levels of development. One is the 'actual' or 'present level of development', that is what the child can do on its own without the support or instruction of adults. The other is the 'potential level of development', that is what the child can achieve in collaboration with adults or more skilled people giving the optimum help. The gap between the two levels indicates that the child is ready to learn, given adult help. Vygotsky calls this the 'zone of proximal development'. Teaching that is directed towards getting children to do without help what they can at present do only with help is the best way to improve development.

Reggio Emilia approach

One of the prime influences on active learning is the Reggio Emilia approach. It fully embeds all strands of a child's being. The role of the teacher is to foster children's intellectual development through a systematic focus on symbolic representation. The environment is the key to children being able to explore and express themselves through all of their 'expressive, communicative and cognitive languages' (Edwards and Redfern, 1998: 7). Classrooms are organised to support a highly collaborative problem-solving approach to learning. There are small project learning groups led by teachers, who stay with their group for up to three years. The curriculum planning guides experiences of joint, open-ended discovery and constructive posing and solving of problems. The approach is partly drawn from important intellectual traditions of Piagetian and Vygotskian constructivist psychologies. The active learning element of the Learning and Development principle embodies this very well.

Outdoor learning

Although this is a stand-alone section on the outdoor environment, this is not intended to pigeon-hole it in any way. Outdoor learning needs to permeate all aspects of the early years curriculum. As stated earlier the outdoors offers children freedom to explore, use their senses and be physically active and exuberant. Central to EYFS provision is the way in which the outdoor environment contributes to learning. EYFS guidance makes specific reference to learning outdoors that is reiterated in Ofsted guidance to inspectors:

> Play underpins the delivery of all EYFS. Children must have opportunities to play indoors and outdoors. All early years providers *must* have access to an outdoor play area which can benefit the children. If a setting does not have direct access to an outdoor play area then they must make arrangements for daily opportunities for outdoor play in an appropriate nearby location.
>
> (DCSF, 2008f: 7)

A check of recently published inspection reports of nursery schools and Children's Centres reveals the praise for, 'A highly creative curriculum [that] presents both indoors and in the exciting outdoor environment opportunities to investigate and explore' In outstanding settings there is frequent mention of Forest School principles to help children learn to relate to each other, discover their own identity and appreciate nature. Central always to the high quality of provision is the way outdoor provision matches high-quality indoor provision. Consistently, settings that do not make the best use of the outdoors to develop learning are more than likely to find themselves with an area for improvement such as, 'Improve the opportunities for children to learn outdoors, ensuring that the outdoor activities cover all areas of learning and are accessible to children'.

Outdoor learning was not always a feature in pre-school provision (Bilton, 2002). Children with access to a Forest School have enhanced self-confidence because of the small, achievable and progressively more challenging tasks they set themselves (see Case Study 6.1). Children become engrossed in tasks, set themselves goals, try harder, persist for longer and are more resilient in recovering from any failure. Very simply, children need to experience success. Children are given the opportunity to develop a sense of independence and autonomy, thus becoming independent as thinkers and learners.

Creating and thinking critically

- Having their own ideas.
- Using what they already know to learn new things.
- Choosing ways to do things and finding new ways.

The third learning characteristic is creating and thinking critically about children making connections in their learning environment. It is also about practitioners being able to support this process and to enhance children's ability to think critically and ask questions. Creativity provides one of the best opportunities for children to engage in 'sustained shared thinking' (Siraj-Blatchford *et al.*, 2002). Practitioners need to get involved in the thinking process with the children. Sustained shared thinking involves the adult being aware of the children's interests and understandings and the adult and children working together to develop an idea or a skill. For example, I recently observed a nursery practitioner gather a group of children around her as she excitedly shared the materials gathered on a recent trip to the seaside. Questions by the children flew backwards and forwards as she encouraged them to talk about their findings, express their own ideas and learn new things. This episode demonstrated so effectively a trusting relationship between the practitioner and the group of children.

How practitioners support learning

The Tickell review provides practitioners with a very clear steer as to their role in supporting and extending children's learning. It is with relief to know that the extensive developments and progress made in the early years sector in the past ten years are still well protected. Currently, the *Practice Guidance for the Early Years Foundation Stage* (DCSF, 2008f) provides information on the types of activities and experiences that children might be involved in as they make their journey through the early years. Importantly, it also provides a framework for continuous assessment. Essentially, the Learning and Development areas of learning provide the core knowledge required by practitioners to be able to support and extend children's learning and development as they progress towards the early learning goals. Practitioners were least happy about this aspect of the *Learning and Development* principle in the evidence provided for the EYFS Review (DfE, 2011a). Many practitioners provided evidence to the review that they wished to see the early learning goals, which define the level of development most children should have reached by the end of the year in which they are 5, reduced and simplified, and also to be made more sensitive to the needs of summer-born children and to those who are fast developers. Consequently, the recommendation that the early learning goals are reduced in number from 69 to 17 was made. Alongside this is the recommendation that the formal assessment requirements are reduced to 20 pieces of information rather than the current 117 pieces. Table 6.1 provides a sample of the detailed information provided to help you to observe, plan and assess your children based on their individual development from the current EYFS framework. The key for practitioners is the 'look, listen and note' column. Hopefully, the revised guidance will eventually provide the same level of support. Practitioners will see that the phrasing of the new learning goals is less specific and much more user-friendly, which should make assessment less onerous and, importantly, be easily understood by parents.

TABLE 6.1 Example of guidance on development points and associated practices (DCSF, 2008f)

DISPOSITION AND ATTITUDES				
Birth–11 months	Development Matters	*Look, Listen and Note*	*Effective Practice*	*Planning and Resourcing*
	■ Develop an understanding and awareness of themselves. ■ Learn they have influence on and are influenced by others. ■ Learn that experience can be shared.	■ How young babies begin to explore their own movements and the environment in individual ways. ■ How babies respond to adults and children.	■ Say or sing made-up rhymes or songs while stroking or pointing to the babies' hands feet or cheeks. ■ Respond and build on babies' expressions, actions and gestures. ■ Find out what babies like and dislike through talking to their parents.	■ Devote uninterrupted time to babies when you can play with them. Be attentive and fully focused. ■ Plan time to share and reflect with parents on babies' progress and development, ensuring appropriate support is available where parents do not speak English.

As a result of my own beliefs, corroborated to some extent by the findings of the EPPE Project (Sylva *et al.*, 2004) that, 'effective pedagogy includes provision of instructive learning environments and "sustained shared thinking" to extend children's learning', I cannot emphasise strongly enough the key role of the adult in promoting early learning, whatever the age of the child; a view developing from the work of Vygotsky (1978) and the succession of recent reports (Allen, 2011; Allen and Duncan Smith, 2010) that pay tribute to the prime role played by an adult in young children's development and, perhaps more significantly, the dire consequences when developing children do not have an adult to share experiences with, to help children make sense of the world and to aid the social and emotional development that is so pivotal to successful readiness for the challenges of life. Tickell identified there is some confusion about how to interpret the EYFS requirement for planned, purposeful play with some practitioners, stating that they are advised that, 'any element of adult direction or teaching would contravene the requirements of the EYFS' (DfE, 2011a: 29). I can concur with this based on my own work supporting schools in difficulty.

Clarification is needed of what learning through play actually means, and what the implications of this are for the role of adults. The answer lies in the use of play-based approaches combined with instructional yet playful teaching. Practitioners need to have a flexible approach to teaching, based on the level of development of the individual child. Tickell states quite categorically that it is not possible to separate out child-initiated from adult-guided or direct learning. When working with young children, the exchange between adults and children should be fluid, moving interchangeably between activities initiated by children and adult responses helping to build the children's learning and understanding. She further goes on to say that throughout the early years, adults should be modelling, demonstrating and questioning. To exclude elements of teaching from the early years would increase the risk of children not being ready to move to Key Stage 1. The research review supports this view wholeheartedly. The key for practitioners is the quality of their interaction with children to extend their learning. How do we talk to children? The list below gives an indication of all one expects of children as they develop cognition in discussion with a practitioner. The demands are in ascending order from simple to complex.

- What is it? What do we do with it? (Labelling and simple function.)
- What did you see? What was that over there? (Memory.)
- What is happening in the picture? (Description.)
- Feel that. What is it? (Non-verbal demand.)
- Demonstration. Now do what I did. (Imitation.)
- What else was there on the tray? (Incidental memory.)
- Before you build the tower show me the bricks (Delay.)
- Look at this picture. Find me the rabbit (Visual search.)

(Meadows and Cashdan, 1988: 69)

There are many ideas about how children learn that are relevant to early childhood education. A common strategy used by parents in the home may be a model of learning that emphasises passiveness. A small child is surrounded by happenings and has experiences. If two events are close together the child learns to associate them. For example, exploring and touching the television controls triggers an immediate 'No!' from a parent. Thus, the child may learn to associate touching the controls with parental disapproval and stop doing it. However, this does not help the child interpret or work out why. There are lots of examples of things that children learn passively that leads ultimately to knowledge, for example, the names of colours. But do children passively soak up information all the time? I think not! Piaget suggested some of the ways in which children handle information. Assimilation and accommodation are what children do, but what children assimilate is governed by what they already know, and as they become aware of additional information that may then accommodate the concept. However, the drawback of this theory of learning is that children will have limits to what they can assimilate and accommodate. Young children will find some information too strange or too distant from what they already know and will have great difficulty learning it. This is why current thinking about learning emphasises the activity of the learner. Hence we have 'hands-on' experiences and the practical activities that abound in early years settings.

Children learn too from observing others, adults and children alike. They imitate others. They learn that a radiator is hot by observing someone else getting burned by it. Children, as stated earlier, do learn when they are told something. Play has been heavily idealised in much of the educational writing of the past 50 years. It has been said to be spontaneous, absorbing, refreshing, enjoyable, creative and the ideal way of learning. If children are not allowed to play as they choose, it has been claimed, their development will be impaired. It is suggested that adults have evolved so that they need to play in order to learn, to work off their surplus energy and to practise skills they may need in later life. It is questioned that there is no compelling reason to elevate play to *the* way of learning (Meadows and Cashdan, 1988: 47).

I do not propose to go into the Piagetian theories that justify play, although the third concept of 'readiness' is worthy of further explanation. Piaget saw learning as controlled and limited by development: unless children had developed to a point where they were ready, they would not be able to do the thinking, assimilation and accommodation that are necessary for learning. To try to teach might harm the child's own development was the theory. Thus we have the reason for encouraging play as the medium for early childhood education. When one applies this approach to learning to read, it can be seen that 'readiness' is not the issue, but that the practitioner presents the opportunity to learn to read by helping the child to learn to recognise words – labels or the child's name, for example. The next section looks at some of the more recent research on children's learning.

★ ★ ★

What does effective early years teaching look like? Tickell (2011) makes some suggestions that might make early years leaders ponder. Is there a difference in our expectations of children under 4 and those in Reception classes which, to me, is apparent in the review? For example, when phonics teaching is referred to, it is in the 'Reception class'. Ofsted provides some indications in their inspection of Children's Centres in 2004 where they found that teaching overall in the centres was good with the features of the most effective teaching:

- good levels of knowledge about the Foundation Stage;
- well-planned, focused teaching of key skills; and accurate identification of what children already know across the areas of learning and of what they need to learn next;
- teaching has most impact on children's personal, social, emotional and physical development. In these aspects, children are likely to exceed the early learning goals;
- teaching is not as strong in mathematics, early literacy and aspects of creative development, although the majority of children are likely to meet the early learning goals;
- children that are more able are not always challenged sufficiently;
- a third of the centres do not evaluate the quality of teaching and learning enough in the Foundation Stage to identify and act on strengths and weaknesses;
- there is a lack of knowledge about the strategies needed to take prompt action to address the weaknesses. Consequently, some children, especially the more able, are not making as much progress as they could;
- children with complex SEN make particularly good progress. This is because the support programmes and procedures for their development and inclusion into mainstream education are generally very well thought through;
- where it is provided, support for children when, and after, they transfer to Reception classes in primary schools is outstanding.

Guidance for inspectors says the following about teaching and learning and what inspectors should be looking for in all early years settings:

- how well the adults support learning and development;
- the quality of the learning environment both indoors and outdoors;
- the quality of planning for individuals to ensure that each child is offered an enjoyable and challenging experience across the areas of learning;
- how well information from observation and assessment is used to plan activities that are tailored to the needs and abilities of individuals;

- how well additional learning and/or development needs are identified and provided for;
- the extent to which there is planned, purposeful play and exploration, both in and out of doors, with a balance of adult-led and child-led activities that fosters active learning;
- the steps taken by the key people to safeguard and promote the welfare of the children and how well adults teach children about keeping safe;
- how good health and well-being are encouraged and whether necessary steps are taken to prevent the spread of infection, and whether appropriate action is taken when children are ill;
- how effectively children are encouraged to develop the habits and behaviour appropriate to good learners, their own needs, and those of others;
- the suitability and safety of outdoor and indoor spaces, furniture, equipment and toys.

The research carried out by Siraj-Blatchford *et al.* (2002) into *Effective Pedagogy in the Early Years* found that pedagogy in the early years involves both the kind of interaction traditionally associated with the term 'teaching', and the provision of instructive learning environments and routines. In terms of links to good outcomes for children their research found the following:

- Adult–child interaction that involved 'sustained shared thinking' and open-ended questioning to extend children's thinking.
- Practitioners having good curriculum knowledge as well as knowledge and understanding of child development.
- Shared educational aims with parents and carers.
- Formative feedback to children during activities.
- Behaviour policies in which staff support children in being assertive, at the same time as rationalising and talking through their conflicts.

(Siraj-Blatchford *et al.*, 2002)

The research also found that children's cognitive outcomes appeared to be directly related to the quantity and quality of the teacher-/adult-planned and initiated focused group work for supporting children's learning.

There are implications for the professional development of practitioners of these findings and especially the support they are given by the Tickell review. Are there emerging differences in the teaching styles to support learning as children get older?

Discussion points

1. Debate the ways in which you achieve the balance between child-initiated and adult-led learning.
2. Has reading this chapter and the EYFS review encouraged you to review the way in which you engage and extend children's learning?
3. In a group, give examples of the activities your children enjoy and brainstorm the ways in which you have interacted with the children.

7

Involving parents and carers

No child's future should be predetermined by the decisions or mistakes of his or her parents, and I firmly believe every child should have the chance to succeed, regardless of their background. Intervening earlier with troubled families can not only prevent children and their parents falling into a cycle of deprivation, antisocial behaviour and poverty but can save thousands if not millions of pounds in the longer term.

(Sarah Teather, Children's Minister, press release, 2010)

Introduction

A new chapter in this edition is included because of the key role parents play in their children's development and the consistent confirmation of this in research findings, most recently linked to Sure Start, but for many years previously in research by the Oxford preschool research project in their publication *Parents and Preschool* (Smith, 1980). In addition, *At Home in School* (Edwards and Redfern, 1998), and, linked to preparing parents to develop their children's literacy skills, *Preparing for Early Literacy with Parents* (Nutbrown and Hannon, 1997). Currently, a wealth of information is available from government bodies (Allen and Duncan Smith, 2008; Allen, 2011) that improvements in early learning experiences for very young children are most effective if there is a commensurate level of involvement by parents and carers. Very recently the government have published their response to the recommendations from Graham Allen MP, Rt Hon. Frank Field MP and Dame Clare Tickell in *Families in the Foundation Years* (DfE, 2011c). The Tickell report (2011a) includes a recommendation that, 'greater emphasis is given in the EYFS to the role of parents and carers as partners in their children's learning'. An illustration of an example of this is that practitioners are required to provide to parents and carers a short summary of their child's communication and language, personal, social and emotional, and physical development between the ages of 24 and 36 months. This should form part of the health-visitor-led health and development review at 2. The chapter aims to share the findings of key reports and research and to illustrate key recommendations with examples of excellent practices and case studies from a variety of settings. Other chapters refer also to the key role of the parent/carer, particularly those linked to early communication and language and development, and their vital role in supporting children with additional learning needs.

★ ★ ★

Rereading the introduction, there is a suggestion from Teather's comments that the coalition government are keen to innovate with regard to early years provision when in fact for many years the role of parents has been a central factor in effective child development and success in later life. As long ago as 1973, Home-Start: a four-year evaluation (Van Der Eyken, 1982) charted the evaluation of the community-based family support scheme started in Leicester in 1973. Since that time many initiatives have come and gone, until in 2000 Sure Start was launched to operate in disadvantaged areas as part of the government's policy of reducing social exclusion. The programme's aim was to improve the health and well-being of families and their children under 4, so that the children will have a greater opportunity to flourish when they start school. The core services offered by Sure Start Local Programmes (SSLP) are early learning, play and childcare. Recently, Charity4Children described Sure Start Children's Centres as 'one of the greatest achievements of modern government' as the number of centres in England reached 3,500. Anne Longfield, chief executive of 4Children, said Sure Start centres helped thousands of families to 'become stronger and better able to cope with tough times'. Box 7.1 is an example of the kind of information you may wish to give parents.

BOX 7.1 What can I do to support my child?

- Choose a special time and place to share and enjoy books, five to ten minutes each day will make a difference, but be flexible. Young children have a short attention span.
- Choose books that have lots of joining in – farmyard animal noises, counting or actions.
- Catch initial attention: tone of voice; create suspense 'I wonder what this story is about? What can you see at the front? Can you guess what's inside?
- Encourage your child to get involved – turn the pages, lift the flap, etc.
- Take time to let your child look through the pictures and relate it to their own experiences and interests.
- Draw attention to features in the book. Make comments, 'look at that huge dinosaur', or ask questions, 'can you see where the little mouse is hiding?'
- Using props such as a puppet or toy vehicle will encourage your child to retell the story.
- Take an interest in what your child is doing in nursery, you could link stories with themes they are covering in class, e.g. holidays, weather, etc.
- Books can be varied, cloth books, bath books, or even a catalogue.
- Most importantly have fun and enjoy the story together.

Families in the foundation years (DfE, 2011c)

The general drift of the most recent government publications relating to families are that they wish to build on recent improvements in the quality of services for young children to create an environment in which local communities, business and public services work together to help families and parents to be the best they can be. Teather, in her letter to directors of children's services, states that 'families are the cornerstone of our society, and that this government wants the country to be the most family friendly in Europe'. The positive actions taken so far to achieve this aim are:

- extending the free entitlement to early education for 15 hours a week for 3- and 4-year-olds and from 2015 for all disadvantaged 2-year-olds;
- increasing the health-visitor workforce by 4,200 by 2015;
- doubling the number of vulnerable young families who will benefit from the Family Nurse Partnership;
- investing in relationship support;
- consulting on a new flexible system of shared parental leave;
- retaining a network of Sure Start Children's Centres, accessible to all families but focused on those in greatest need.

That all children should have a fair start in life is a commitment of the government, who claim in *Families in the Foundation Years* (DfE, 2011c) to take its obligations under the United Nations Convention on the Rights of the Child very seriously. There is to be less bureaucracy in order to free professionals to do the job they are trained for, so they can spend most of their time in direct contact with children and families rather than on paperwork and form filling. Time will tell as to whether the reality for the future matches the governments' rhetoric given the swingeing cuts being made to local authority budgets. As practitioners reading this you may wish to debate how your setting is coping and taking steps to keep up with the revisions to key early years practices.

Positive relationships

The Early Years Foundation Stage Principles into Practice cards linked to the theme of Positive Relationships states:

> Parents are children's first and most enduring educators. When parents and practitioners work together in early years settings, the results have a positive impact on children's development and learning.
>
> (EYFS: Principles into Practice 2.2)

The key points made from this principle are the importance of communication, respect of diversity and learning together. A welcoming atmosphere with approachable staff helps to create effective communication. Effective communication means that there is a two-way flow of information, knowledge and expertise between parents and practitioners. All communication is important, including gesture, signing and body language. Posters, pictures and other resources on display will show the setting's positive attitudes to disability, and to ethnic, cultural and social diversity. They will help children and families to recognise that they are valued.

Respecting diversity

All families are important and should be welcomed and valued in settings. Families are all different. Children may live with one or both parents, with other relatives or carers, with same-sex parents or in an extended family. Families may speak more than one language at home; they may be travellers, refugees or asylum seekers. All practitioners will benefit from professional development in diversity, equality and anti-discriminatory practice whatever the ethnic, cultural or social make-up of the setting. Parents and practitioners have a lot to learn from each other. This can help them to support and extend children's learning and development. Parents should review their children's progress regularly and contribute to their child's learning and development record. Parents can be helped to understand more about learning and teaching through workshops on important areas such as play, outdoor learning or early reading. See Table 7.1 for an example of activities parents can try with their children. Some parents may go in to access further education at their own level. In true partnerships, parents understand and contribute to the policies.

Effective collaboration with parents and carers

How, then, do these principles translate into effective practice? EYFS offer guidance, stated below. It is valuable also to be able to celebrate the innovative practices present in early years settings across the country, which also follow next. EYFS define effective practice in promoting parents as partners as follows:

- Display lists of words from home languages used by children in the setting and invite parents and practitioners to contribute to them. Seeing their languages reflected in this way will encourage parents to feel involved and valued.
- Find out from parents the greetings they use either in English or in other languages.
- Encourage staff, parents and children to use the greetings.
- Make sure that everyone who enters the setting received a friendly welcome.
- Talk with parents about their children's progress and development, providing appropriate support for those who do not speak or understand English.
- Ask parents for their views on the care and education you provide.

The impact of Sure Start on encouraging parental involvement

One of the key aims of the Sure Start programme is to provide a range of support services to parents from pregnancy onwards. These services are tailored to be attractive to parents.

CASE STUDY 7.1 Information for parents

East Downlands Sure Start Centre, West Berkshire

The vision of the Children's Centre is a commitment to providing families with a supportive and nurturing environment both at the Centre and through outreach opportunities across the area covered. Family support workers facilitate the outreach work. All services are planned around the five *Every Child Matters* themes of being healthy, staying safe, enjoying and achieving, making a positive contribution and achieving economic well-being. Parents are provided with a small glossy booklet, illustrating and listing the full range of activities available for parents, including fathers and children. A photographic record of family case studies linked to *Every Child Matters* also provides compelling celebration of everything achieved in the centre with detailed information about courses and training parents can attend. A termly newsletter outlines in great detail the range of child health and maternity services for the area as well as reviewing the success of visits. It is good to see a weekend 'Dads Stay and Play' session too.

Several evaluations of Sure Start (Melhuish *et al.*, 2008 and 2010) highlight the importance of staff understanding the nature of the local communities and especially the families that are often excluded from services. There are two key actions used by Sure Start Children's Centres to increase involvement: outreach and home visiting. These two key first steps provide a basis for enabling greater access to services for families who are unlikely to visit a centre. Case Study 7.2 is a good example of how to get reluctant dads to work with their children. Managers are expected to track which families are using services and monitor levels of service usage by different groups. Secondly, the increase in actions to increase parental involvement will lead to improvements in children's life chances. This is the ideal, but is this what is happening? Do you do all of the following to maximise contacting as many parents as possible? Or, if a potential early years practitioner, what you will need to consider?

- Publicise what is on offer in a centre, in post offices, GP services and libraries.
- Contact parents in pre-schools, surgeries or cafes.
- Consider a range of ways to engage parents in consultation in a Children's Centre that is comfortable, welcoming and enjoyable.
- Always provide refreshments, offering travel expenses and providing a crèche.
- It is vital to manage the consultation process is in a relaxed and organised fashion.
- Leaders of a consultation might benefit from having a semi-structured interview with key questions to guide the discussions.
- If working with a group of parents it is useful to have a facilitator who is able to keep a written record. This is essential to enable parents to have a record of what discussions took place.

CASE STUDY 7.2 Involving dads in the children's centre

A mixture of centre-based sessions and visits over a half-termly period took place. Five sessions for parents and staff to work together preparing, evaluating previous experiences and documenting significant learning. The key to the involvement of fathers was the technological aspect of it all that included training for them to operate a digital camera and download photographs of their visits and activities with their children. The head of a Children's Centre in another authority spoke with passion of her success in getting a group of fathers from a very disadvantaged area to join the project. It was a case of, 'You will do this … rather than 'Would you like to …' It was intended that four visits were made: one to the coast focusing on rock pools and collections, one to the coast focusing on building and creating with sand or pushes and pullies (moving sand), one to the Sealife Centre, and one to a venue selected and researched by parents. The sequence was to run as listed below over the half-term period.

Week 1
Introduce project and intentions. Introduce equipment and expected usage. Evaluate current knowledge and attitudes through activities to examine possible learning opportunities. Prepare for next week's visit to the coast and learning opportunities.

Week 2
Visit the coast, rocks, examining rock pools, discussing wildlife and environmental issues, collecting natural items. Parents to take some collections home to work with the children creatively and take photos of the process. Staff to do the same in school, use dictaphones for stories.

Week 3
Feedback from the visit and subsequent activities, examining learning opportunities, sharing experiences and initiating documentation took place. Preparation for Sealife Centre visit.

Week 4
Sealife Centre visit to investigate creatures found in the sea, take photos of creatures, draw and record observations.

Week 5
Feedback from Sealife Centre and checking ongoing documentation. Preparation for coast visit, using planned and reclaimed resources to play creatively, solve problems and have fun or build with sand or 'moving sand'.

Weeks 6 and 7
Visit the coast/beach for above purposes and take photographs. Feedback from beach visit and documentation of learning takes place. Planning parents' choice of visit for next week.

Weeks 8, 9 and 10
Parents' choice of visit, feedback from this and working with a technician to create a presentation for a wider audience. Planning a party and a final session of celebration of events involving the wider community and other parents took place culminating in a vibrant display in the centre, including a clear statement of the aims of the project for parents, practitioners and children.

A recent survey (Ofsted, 2008) made the recommendation that more information should be shared with parents. This survey found that generally the quality of information was poorer where there is most deprivation. The Findings from the *National Evaluation of Sure Start* (Melhuish *et al.*, 2008 and 2010) focused on impact of programmes on children and families. Through a series of themed studies, promoting speech and language development, early learning, play and childcare services, family and parent support, outreach and home-visiting, empowering parents and children and parents with special needs, the impact of Sure Start Local Programmes (SSLPs) were evaluated. The findings in 2005 for 3-year-olds revealed that among non-teenage mothers there was greater child social competence, fewer child behaviour problems and less negative parenting. On the other hand, the findings among teenage mothers showed less child social competence, more child behaviour problems and poorer child verbal ability in SSLP areas. The evaluation then set out to find out why some SSLPs were more effective in achieving outcomes than others. Three factors were considered in measuring proficiency. These were governance and management, the informal but professional ethos of the centre and the empowerment of service providers and users. At this time several challenges for Children's Centres and training emerged. They were:

- higher reach needed (especially overcoming barriers for the 'hard-to-reach');
- better multi-agency working;
- sustainable shared systems for monitoring service use/treatments;
- more rigour in measuring the impact of treatments;

- grasp of the cost of effective deployment of specialist/generalist staff;
- coordinating outreach and centre-based services.

A convincing result in the 2008 evaluation comparing the results of 14 outcomes shows a significant difference between SSLP and non-SSLP areas. The beneficial effects were:

- child positive social behaviour (cooperation, sharing, empathy);
- child independence/self-regulation (works things out for self, perseverance, self-control);
- parenting risk indicator (harsh discipline, home chaos);
- home learning environment;
- total service use;
- child immunisations and accidents.

(Melhuish, 2008)

It is interesting to note that there were no differences between the two areas for the fathers' involvement with their child or a child's language development. While it is acknowledged that later findings are more encouraging, it is clearly apparent that the positive results between 2005 and 2008 indicate an increase in the quality of service provision, greater attention to the hard-to-reach, the move to Children's Centres and greater exposure of children and families. A key priority of this evaluation is that there needs to be a focus on child language development. One of the main findings of the EPPE project (2004) was that:

> For all children, the quality of the home learning environment is more important for intellectual and social development than parental occupation, education or income. What parents do is more important than who parents are.
>
> (Key finding over the pre-school period, Sylva *et al.*, 2004)

A more focused research project is the *Supporting Parents in Promoting Early Learning: The Evaluation of the Early Learning Partnership Project* ELPP (Evangelou *et al.*, 2009) which aimed to put in place family-based educational support as a protective factor in the lives of young children aged 1 to 3 who were at risk of learning-delay and to encourage parents to engage with their children's learning. Several intervention strategies employed by the voluntary sector were evaluated and included: Bookstart; Campaign for Learning; Listening to Children; I Can: Newpin's Family Play Programme; One Plus One's Brief Encounters; PAFT; PEAL; PEEP; PICL; SHARE; and Thurrock Community Mothers. Case Study 7.3 describes a nursery based Bookstart meeting. Most of the associations offered associated training. While many of the findings developed understanding and skills in the workplace, the ELPP showed that it is possible to reach and engage with some vulnerable families in disadvantaged areas to support their children as learners. There was also evidence, as in the evaluation of SSLPs of improvements in parents' relationships with their children. Parents also showed improvement in organising the children's environment through better health and safety practices and more opportunities for children to learn from day-to-day activities with their parents outside the home. However, in the short timescale of this research there was no improvement in parenting behaviour that challenged children's thinking or extended their language. Table 7.1 shows how a Children's Centre set about improving their plans to engage with their parent body.

TABLE 7.1 Developing parental involvement

School Improvement Plan
Reference – Further Parental Involvement in Early Years documentation

Context
Where are we now?
The school was invited to join the PPEL project during the last academic year and made successful connections with 5 out of 6 harder-to-reach families. School staff found the PPEL project exciting and would like to continue to use this in an in-house modified form. Parents enjoy reading documentation of learning produced by staff and are beginning to contribute to some particular projects. We would like to consolidate and extend this involvement.

What we want to improve:

■ Parents' awareness of the documentation on view in the Early Years Unit.
■ Parents' skills in participating in documentation, particularly at home.
■ Parents' awareness of the learning potential in everyday experiences.

How are we going to improve?

Key tasks for managers

■ Devise and promote projects to break down boundaries between home and school e.g. Water Bottle Project, Secret Reading Places Project, Shoe Box Project, Tree of Wishes Project.
■ Head and Assistant Head to attend training.
■ Support parent participations in the execution of the programme.

Key tasks for teachers

■ IT coordinator to provide technical support.
■ Class teachers in Year R and N to provide informal support for parent participants and model documentation to share with children.

Key tasks for others
HLTAS to display home documentation in consultation with parents and to provide encouragement and advice on request.

Key resources
Six digital cameras to lend to parents on request.

How will we check our progress?
Termly 'learning-walk' by SMT and Early Years Staff to ensure that parental contributions to learning and to learning stories are recognised and celebrated in the learning environment. Use a questionnaire or interview parents about the importance of documentation and their confidence in participating in the documentation process.

How will we evaluate our achievement?
The participation and views of at least 75% of parents are recognised in the learning environment.

Linking home and school

CASE STUDY 7.3 Using Bookstart with families

As one of several actions to enrich early literacy development following evidence that children in a nursery made very little progress in the reading strand of CLL, an early years family liaison officer met with a group of parents and grandparents in the nursery to find out about how to support and help children enjoy reading at home. It was clear from the provision in

---

the nursery that sharing books and displaying books extensively in the nursery had not been typical of their provision until very recently. The family liaison officer skilfully engaged the parents and encouraged them to share their own book experiences and favourite stories as she read snippets of some favourites. 'What can I do to support my child?' and 'Activities that promote children's development' handouts were passed around as the parents enjoyed a cup of tea or coffee. Finally, they all left with a book treasure chest containing information about Bookstart and two firm favourites for 3-year-olds, *You Choose* by Nick Sharrat and *Each Peach Pear Plum* by Janet and Allan Ahlberg. Suggestions for how to support your child can be seen in Box 7.1.

Heads of centres and practitioners have a vast range of creative and innovative ideas to encourage parental involvement in their children's learning. In discussions with a head teacher of a nursery school in the north east it was apparent that they were not attracting the interest of fathers. To tackle this they set about putting together a bid to get additional resources and expertise to launch the Parents as Partners in Early Learning Project which was to use the local and coastal environment for children and their families. I am very confident in citing this as a successful enterprise as its attraction to fathers became evident as the project spread across several early years centres and nursery schools in several local authorities in the north east. Case Study 7.2 outlines the activities provided for all the fathers. Head teachers are vigilant when it comes to working with hard-to-reach families. An effective example from a small village infant school demonstrates this in their school improvement plan.

Involving parents with birth to 3-year-olds

A cross-party survey carried out for the Centre for Social Justice by Graham Allen MP and Rt Hon. Iain Duncan Smith MP in 2008 (Allen and Duncan Smith, 2008) cries out for attention to, and the importance of, 0- to 3-year-olds and parental intervention. Unusually this is not an educational report but that of lay persons presenting a considerable body of medical evidence to highlight the importance of years 0–3 in human development and the vital influence on years 0–3 of their primary caregivers. The human brain has developed to 85 per cent of its potential at age 3 (and 90 per cent at age 4). Evidence from the US WAVE trust shows the very young brain's enormous capability for change. They cite two simple conclusions:

1. What parents do at this very early age appears to be absolutely decisive in terms of child outcomes.

2. What we do to prepare at-risk parents and potential parents to be effective is the most important social policy issue for modern society.

Intervention programmes in Sure Start Children's Centres are geared up to support the children in families with some level of dysfunction, although research does suggest that they do not reach the most disadvantaged families. However, great strides are made in many settings to forge strong communication with parents. A very common link between home and setting is the 'All about Me' record provided by the setting and completed at home by parents/carers (see Figure 4.2 on p.41). Discussions about children's development is a key strength because managers and key staff take time to gather information from parents about their children and set in place systems to inform working parents of their child's progress (Ofsted, 2008:18). In some centres, a minibus service is run by the providers that ensures parents, children and staff in rural areas can attend, a parent's forum enables parents to put issues to the provider collectively and a translation service is available for parents.

I cannot leave this chapter without sharing with you the view of one of those disadvantaged parents that are so crucial to your success in promoting successful parental involvement. The account of the parent, written below, sums up the wide-reaching impact that your work can have for those 'hard-to-reach' parents.

My time here at the Nursery

I like it here at the nursery it is good to get herd it is good to no your wanted at the nursery and the children are so good and they care in there own way I like to see how mrs corns controles the children when they are nortey it gives me some help when mine are nortey so Don't think I am getting fedup here as I am not I like being here I've always wanted to be with children some way when I was small I wanted to be with children so I am doing somethink Ive always wanted to do I hoped some day I wood been able to worke full time with children but I am not very clever so I nevere tried so I wood like to thank you for given me the chance to be with them

Love from
PS it as helped me alote I feel much better in myself now.

Discussion points

1.   Brainstorm the strategies used in your setting to encourage involvement of parents and then discuss how these strategies help them understand how they are helping their children learn.

2.   Discuss arrangements for making your first contact with parents and list the key information you need and the most effective ways of beginning to gain the trust of parents.

3.   Discuss the implications for your setting of the increased hours for 3- and 4-year-olds and how you are planning to work with disadvantaged 2-year-olds.

8

Personal, social and emotional development (PSED)

Introduction

This chapter shares a range of ways in which practitioners provide opportunities to support the personal, social and emotional development of the children in their care. Central to this will be a consideration of the role of a supportive adult, the impact of the quality of the relationships children have with parents in the home and how different settings plan to ensure children's social and emotional development progresses. An interesting question to ponder as the chapter develops is how adults assist children to become personally and socially competent in a planned way. Are social and communicative skills taught in a systematic way? Do they need to be? Another important thread of the chapter is the relationship between the context in which personal, social and emotional development (PSED) occurs and other areas of learning. Can attitudes to learning be taught? Is it possible to work with the child in isolation from his or her family to create effective relationships in a nursery setting? How is successful behaviour management achieved? How does the PSED of birth to 3-year-olds differ from that of older children? Answers to those questions from a wide range of research evidence and practical examples from early years settings are provided. The recent elevation of the PSED area of learning to a 'prime' area of learning is to be welcomed. As stated in other chapters PSED is at the heart of learning whatever the title of an activity. For very young children it is the foundation of learning. The poem below reminds us of the important role model offered by adults to the children in their care.

Children Learn What They Live

If children live with criticism,
They learn to condemn.

If children live with hostility,
They learn to fight.
If children live with ridicule,
They learn to be shy.
If children live with shame,
They learn to feel guilty.
If children live with encouragement,
They learn confidence.
If children live with praise,
They learn to appreciate.
If children live with fairness,
They learn justice.
If children live with security,
They learn to have faith.
If children live with approval,
They learn to like themselves.
If children live with acceptance and friendship,
They learn to find love in the world.

(Excerpt from *Children Learn What
They Live 1972, 1998* by Dorothy Law Nolte.
Reproduced by permission of Workman
Publishing Co. Inc., New York
(all rights reserved))

There are several ways in which early educators may define personal, social and emotional development. The DCSF (2008f) defined PSED in the following six strands. These are: dispositions and attitudes, self-confidence and self-esteem, making relationships, behaviour, self-control, self-care and a sense of community. The recently revised EYFS has changed these to reduce the pressure on practitioners to three areas, self-confidence and self-awareness, managing feelings and behaviour and making relationships. Table 8.1 shows the framework to support the summary of development at 24–36 months.

The revised definition of personal, social and emotional development covers every facet of children's relationships with others and with themselves. For all 5-year-olds to have acquired this level of relationship and attitudes is a great achievement, and, when in place, lays a firm foundation for their future lives. Do we as educators in England give enough attention to this area of learning in our day-to-day work? Is the attention intuitive? We comfort children, who are upset, encourage cooperation and collaboration. Do we need to contrive situations in which children feel secure and so help to develop their confidence? The need for security in a small boy whose basic need for stability and familiarity is met in a nursery domestic play area is described in Case Study 8.1.

TABLE 8.1 Framework to support summary of PSED development at 24–36 months

PERSONAL, SOCIAL AND EMOTIONAL DEVELOPMENT			
ASPECT	24–36 MONTHS	36–48 MONTHS	EARLY LEARNING GOALS
Self-confidence and self-awareness	Children separate from their main carer with support and encouragement from a familiar adult. They begin to recognise danger and know who to turn to for help. They seek to do things for themselves knowing that an adult is close by, ready to support if needed.	Children can select and use activities and resources with help. They talk about their own needs and feelings in simple ways. They are confident to talk to other children when playing together and will talk freely about their home and community.	Children are confident to try out new activities and can say why they prefer some. They talk about their ideas, choose the resources they need to plan and carry out activities they have decided to do and can say when they do or don't need help.
Managing feelings and behaviour	Children are aware that some actions can hurt or harm others. They seek the comfort with familiar adults in the setting when needed. They respond to the feelings and wishes of others, and their own needs and feelings.	Children are aware that some actions can hurt others' feelings. They begin to accept the needs of others, taking turns and sharing resources with support. They can adapt their behaviour to different events, social situations and changes in routine, and their own needs and feelings.	Children can talk about how they and others show feelings and manage their feelings. They can talk about their own and others behaviour and its consequences. They can work as part of a group or class and understand and follow the rules. They can adjust their behaviour to different situations and to changes in the routine.
Making relationships	Children seek out others to share experiences. They play alongside others and can be caring towards each other.	Children can play in a group. They demonstrate friendly behaviour, initiate conversation and form good relationships with peers and familiar adults.	Children can play cooperatively, taking turns when playing. They can take account of one another's ideas about how to organise their activity. They can show sensitivity to the needs and feelings of others and form positive relationships with adults and other children.

Research findings

2-year-old children

'The 0–3 age range is a vital period when the right social and emotional inputs must be made to build the human foundations of a healthy, functioning society. The key agents to provide these inputs for 0–3 children are parents' (Allen and Duncan Smith, 2008: 4). An

---

CASE STUDY 8.1 Jamie's home corner

Jamie enjoyed nursery school. He loved the home corner, setting the table, putting the plates out and putting them away. He liked it best when he was on his own, because he could set the dolls and teddies out as he wanted. He talked to them all the time. Jamie had just returned following a long period of absence from the nursery school. His home was destroyed in a house fire some months earlier, along with the death of his two younger sisters and his mother. In his time away from the nursery Jamie was with a foster parent, but he was now back in the area living with his aunt. He spoke very little on his return but enjoyed the security and stability of the home corner as often as he could.

Can you as practitioners know how to cope with such grief and sadness in a young child's life? The home corner was the turning point for Jamie. Slowly, he began to regain his confidence as he welcomed playmates into his substitute home.

---

early education pilot (DCSF, 2009e) for disadvantaged 2-year-old children that provided free early years education to over 13,500 disadvantaged 2-year-olds between 2006 and 2009 confirms this view. The key findings from this evaluation were that the pilot did not significantly improve children's social development, the parent-child relationship or the home learning environment relative to the matched comparison group. However, where children attended higher quality settings, there was a positive impact on language ability and the parent-child relationship. Parents were the ones who benefitted from involvement in the pilot study because they felt that the setting had positively affected their ability to parent, their physical health and mental well-being. An outcome of the pilot was a recommendation that 2-year-olds should only be able to access free provision in 'good' settings based on Ofsted judgements. The report published by the Centre for Social Justice (Allen and Duncan Smith, 2008) made a case for there to be early intervention for the 0–3s, quoting figures from the US WAVE TRUST research that highlights the very young brain's enormous capability for change, and how this rapidly diminishes well before children start school. There is absolute support for the claim that 'children's experiences in their earliest years of life are laying the foundations for their futures – for good or ill' (p. 46). This leads to two very simple conclusions:

1. What parents do at this very early stage appears to be absolutely decisive in terms of child outcomes.
2. What we do to prepare at-risk parents and potential parents to be effective is the most important social policy issue for modern society.

A further truism in this report is the claim that very young children need a high level of emotional responsiveness and engagement to ensure the reduction in the statistic that 30 to 40 per cent of abused or neglected children go on to abuse or neglect their own children. The report recommends SEAL (Social and Emotional Aspects of Learning, DCSF, 2008e) and Roots of Empathy (Gordon, 1996). The latter Canadian programme helps children to learn compassion and caring. Emotional intelligence skills are learned by showing children how to learn from the bond between babies and parents. This is achieved through parents with very young babies spending time in the setting on a weekly basis. The programme claims that this develops empathy in the children observing the mother–child relationship and enables them to engage in more pro-social behaviour, such as helping, sharing and including.

Children also learn about empathy by being treated in an empathetic, caring way by their parents at home. This approach is seen to have a hitherto unforeseen effect on bullying. It is used extensively in New Zealand, the United States and the Isle of Man. A further study in New Zealand, known as the Dunedin study (1972), monitored the development of 1,000 children from birth. When the children were 3, nurses assessed them by watching them play for 90 minutes to identify those they judged to be at risk. At follow-up at age 21, it was found that the 'at-risk' boys had two and a half times as many criminal convictions as the group deemed not to be at risk.

The Effective Provision of Pre-School Education (EPPE) Project (Sylva *et al.*, 2004) in England found that high-quality pre-schooling was related to better social/behavioural development and in line with evidence from the WAVE trust. The quality of the home learning environment is more important for social development than parental occupation, education or income. What parents do is more important than who parents are. There is also research that has impacted on the organisation of staffing to provide maximum benefit for children. The key person system, with a small number of individually designated practitioners relating to particular children, enables responsiveness and sensitivity to individual children (Elfer *et al.*, 2002). The government recognised the need to provide 15 hours of nursery education for disadvantaged 2-year-olds in the 2010 spending review, as stated in Chapter 1.

The key person

As mentioned earlier, the key person is paramount for the all children in the birth to 5 age range, but particularly for babies who need to develop an attachment to a significant person to feel that personal relationship developing through smiles, gurgles, long stares and pre-verbal exchanges of sound (Lindon, 1998). Although not applicable now, the National Standards describe key persons as 'providing a link with parents and carers and crucial in settling children into the setting . However, checking the *Principles into Practice* cards (DCSF, 2008f: 2.4), the same definition remains in their description of a key person as someone who has 'special responsibilities' for working with a small number of children, giving them the reassurance to feel 'safe' and cared for and building relationships with their parents. The requirement for this is in group settings. I know from experience that this does not take place in many Reception classes because there is a different ratio of staff to children required for Reception-aged children.

The fundamental role of the key person ensures children and their families feel secure and trusting in the care of their child. Ideally, each family has a key person who gets to know them well, and this helps everyone feel safe. A baby knows that this key person is special and will do the same things as a parent will do. Peace of mind for a mother as she leaves her baby in day care is paramount to give her confidence in sharing worries with a familiar face each time she brings her child into the setting.

★ ★ ★

It is important to distinguish between the term 'key person' and 'key worker'. These two terms are often used interchangeably in nurseries. There is a clear distinction between the two terms. A 'key worker' is often used to describe the role that is about liaison or coordinating between different professionals or between different disciplines, making sure that services work in a coordinated way. This is very different from the 'key person' as defined earlier. The term 'key worker' is also used to describe how staff work strategically in nurseries to enhance smooth organisation and record keeping. This is part of the 'key person' role but it is also an emotional relationship as well as an organisational one (Elfer, Goldschmied and Selleck, 2002).

Personalised learning

Already, we can see from the research mentioned above that parents have a vital role in securing emotional stability for their very young children. It may be useful to practitioners to look at the seminal work of Daniel Goleman (1999) in defining the key elements of schemes designed to develop one's emotional intelligence. The framework of skills he outlines in identifying and managing emotions sit well alongside the strands of PSED in the EYFS framework. These are shown in Table 8.2.

TABLE 8.2 A framework for emotional intelligence (Goleman, 1995, 1998) outlines a framework of skills involved in identifying, understanding and managing emotions

PERSONAL COMPETENCE: THESE COMPETENCIES DETERMINE HOW WE MANAGE OURSELVES
1. Self-awareness – *Knowing one's internal states, preferences, resources and intuitions*   Emotional awareness: recognising one's emotions and their effects   Accurate self-assessment: knowing one's strengths and limits   Self-confidence: a strong sense of one's self-worth and capabilities
2. Self-regulation – *Managing one's internal state, impulses and resources*   Self-control: keeping disruptive emotions and impulses in check   Trustworthiness: maintaining standards of honesty and integrity   Conscientiousness: taking responsibility for personal performance   Adaptability: flexibility in handling change   Innovation: being comfortable with novel ideas, approaches and new information
3. Motivation – *Emotional tendencies that guide or facilitate reaching goals*   Achievement/drive: striving to improve or meet a standard of excellence   Commitment: aligning with the goals of the group or organisation   Initiative: readiness to act on opportunities   Optimism: persistence in pursuing goals obstacles and setbacks   Social competence: these competencies determine how we handle relationships
4. Empathy – *Awareness of others' feelings, needs and concerns*   Understanding and sensing: others' feelings and perspectives and taking an active interest in their concerns   Developing/sensing: others' development needs and bolstering their abilities   Service orientation: anticipating, recognising, and meeting customers' needs   Leveraging diversity: cultivating opportunities through different kinds of people   Political awareness: reading a group's emotional currents and power relationships
5. Social skills – *Adeptness at inducing desirable responses in others*   Influence: wielding effective tactics for persuasion   Communication: listening openly and sending convincing messages   Conflict management: negotiating and resolving disagreement   Leadership: inspiring and guiding individuals and groups   Change catalyst: initiating or managing change   Building bonds: nurturing instrumental relationships   Collaboration and cooperation: working with others towards shared goals   Team capabilities: creating group synergy in pursuing collective goals

Practitioners working with very young children are likely to be aware that there are some basic emotions such as happiness, sadness and anger that children acquire in infancy before emotions such as empathy, guilt or shame, according to research by Denham *et al.* (2003). There are key triggers to help children develop emotionally, such as:

- encouraging children to communicate and to discuss emotions;
- using stories and puppets to help develop understanding of various situations;
- ensuring that children forge an attachment with one key worker to foster the trusting and open relationship needed to share emotive issues;
- the use of appropriate language to share cultural messages.

An excellent way to promote almost all aspects of PSED during child-initiated learning time is to have a free-flowing snack time, as described in Case Study 8.2.

CASE STUDY 8.2 Starting nursery

On entry to the pre-school each child searches for their name and sticks it on the registration board. A table is laid in the corner of the room next to a jug of orange juice and a collection of differently coloured mugs. In the kitchen an adult and three children are buttering bread and spreading jam prior to cutting the squares of bread into four triangles. As the session progresses the children wander to their self-registration board, collect their name card and go to have their drink and snack, sometimes in pairs but very often on their own, secure in the knowledge that there will be someone sitting at the table eating their snack to talk to. Above the table, displayed on the wall is a menu illustrated with snack-time foods and labels. The children's eyes wander to the notice and some of the children discuss the list and point to familiar letters. On finishing their snack the children return to their play. Some days an elderly pensioner sits with the children during snack time to share their talk and to help where needed. The older children encourage the younger ones to go for their snack some time during the morning. Josh went twice one morning because he missed his breakfast but generally the children know they only have their snack once during the session.

Boys and girls

It may seem an obvious statement to make, but boys and girls are different, and just as we respect children's similarities, we need to be aware of their differences. There is sufficient research evidence to suggest that young boys underachieve (DCSF, 2007a; Marmot, 2011). The crux of the matter may be linked to perceptions held of what is valued in settings. Boys tend to be exuberant, energetic and like to explore. Do we stereotype boys? Check how much attention you give to boys in their free-choice activities. Is it more satisfying to sit with a group of girls keen to 'write' and draw quietly rather than round up a group of boys intent on putting out all the imaginary fires with a collection of improvised hoses and alarm sounds coming from the ring leader? Is it good enough to accept the view that 'it's the boys at it again' without intervening and deconstructing what is going on in terms of their learning. Recent newspaper headlines say it all.

Almost half of 5-year-old boys are failing in their development by their first year in school. In some parts of the country, as many as six out of 10 boys are lagging behind the levels of behaviour and understanding they should have achieved.

(*Daily Mail*, February 11, 2011)

The Guardian newspaper (Ramesh, 2011) at the same time linked this to behaviour and quoted the percentage of boys from disadvantaged backgrounds in less affluent areas failing to meet expectations set by the end of EYFS for behaviour. The data provided by the Foundation Stage Profile across six areas of learning and development suggests that boys are achieving less well than girls across all areas of learning and that more girls are working securely within the early learning goals than boys (DfES, 2007a: 2). A follow-up survey by Ofsted (DCSF, 2007) suggested that practitioners could address this imbalance if they took more responsibility for creating the right conditions for boys' learning. The survey recommended that, 'staff in settings should help boys to achieve more rapidly by providing opportunities for learning that engage them'. Effective practice for boys occurs when practitioners take account of the following:

- Find out how boys play at home and offer similar play opportunities in the setting as the starting point.
- Invite fathers in, enabling them to join in and act as positive role models to the boys, involving them in a wide range of activities, especially those that boys tend to avoid.
- Ensure that outdoor learning reflects indoor provision, because boys show greater enthusiasm outside and appreciate the space to spread out.
- Create situations in role-play provision that reflect boy's interests (Superheroes), work stations.

Currently, all settings are part of an inspection programme by Ofsted. The following is a list of what inspectors are advised to look for in children's personal, social and emotional development. Do staff:

- model positive behaviour towards each other, towards parents and towards children by establishing constructive relationships?
- support the development of independence skills, particularly for adults who are highly dependent upon adult support for personal care?
- understand attachment and its importance to children, who need warm, caring relationships with a small number of people, and so make sure that each child has a key person in the setting?
- plan opportunities for children to work alone and in small and large groups and activities that promote emotional, moral, spiritual and social development alongside intellectual development?
- ensure that there is time and space for children to focus on activities and experiences and develop their own interests?
- provide opportunities for play and learning that acknowledge children's particular religious beliefs and cultural backgrounds and promote positive attitudes to diversity and difference within all children, so children learn to value different aspects of people's lives?

When observing children, look out for them developing skills that will allow them to:

- *make relationships* (e.g. work as part of a group, share playground apparatus);
- *gain self-confidence and self-esteem* (e.g. how they show feelings and are sensitive to others);
- *learn to manage their behaviour and self-control* (e.g. do they explain what is right and wrong?);
- *develop dispositions and attitudes* (e.g. engage in a wide range of activities, are motivated, involved, concentrate and learn effectively);
- *develop self-care* (i.e. show care for their own personal hygiene and care and develop independence, such as washing their hands, decide to put on a coat to go outside);
- *develop a sense of community* (i.e. understand and respect their own and others' needs, views, cultures and beliefs).

What Ofsted found

A recent Ofsted survey (Ofsted, 2011) on the impact of the Early Years Foundation Stage found that PSED was satisfactory or better in all the schools and childcare providers visited. It is interesting to note that their key positive findings were linked to the routines that practitioners established and the high expectations they had of children's behaviour. Outcomes for children were better where the providers visited were clear about the stages of learning and development and specifically planned activities to cover all aspects of this area of learning.

Another key finding that endorses the effective practice checklist mentioned earlier was the good quality of the intuitive care. Provision overall was generally of a higher quality when staff, including child minders, had attended training and made use of the practice guidance for EYFS. Ofsted described one school where there were three waves of support for children's personal, social and emotional development in a Reception class. The first was the universal whole class-provision, which included 'emotion boards' in each classroom for the children to show how they were feeling and lots of circle-time activities. Wave two was a focus group for those children who had been identified as needing extra small-group input to strengthen their PSED skills. The third wave was the group work targeted at children who, because of significant emotional and social needs, required more extended opportunities to develop their self-confidence.

An area that posed problems for some providers and local authorities was the 'sense of community' aspects of the area of learning, especially in settings with very few or no pupils from minority ethnic cultures. This issue was most successfully addressed by visiting other schools with a more representative cultural and racial mix. This tends to surprise me, living and working in an area that is largely mono-cultural. Practitioners generally raise awareness of other cultures through celebrations, and they are also very effectively promoted through stories, such as *Handa's Surprise* (Browne, 1994).

Planning for personal, social and emotional development

The revised early learning goals for PSED are included at the end of this section. Firstly, there is the framework to support the summary development at 24–36 months (Table 8.1, p. 104) and then the proposed early learning goals (Table 8.6). The planning examples illustrated throughout this section are based on the current EYFS. The ELGs for each aspect of current

PSED are to be found at the end of the chapter in Tables 8.7 to 8.12. They readily show how planning for PSED is rarely a separate plan because PSED skills are always acquired within many areas of learning. This is very well illustrated in each of the following three examples from nursery schools. Tables 8.3 to 8.5 and Box 8.1 show a variety of formats. By examining a range of planning formats for PSED it seems to be appropriate to come up with some key planning principles. The finding by Ofsted (2011) that much of the successful PSED is 'intuitive' is reassuring, especially for child minders. There are some clear commonalities in planning. Essentially, the following must be considered when planning for PSED:

- Make reference to framework to support the summary of development.
- In long-term planning the *Development Matters statements* are clustered together and standalone alongside other areas of learning as the learning goals for the period.
- Be absorbed in planning for other areas of learning always in the medium term, because literacy, numeracy etc., very often provide the context for PSED.
- In short-term planning for any area of learning there is likely to be a PSED outcome or expectation identified.
- Specific reference to PSED is given a high priority in assessment and evaluations of learning.
- A session plan for PSED alone is more typical in a Reception class where schools are implementing SEAL.

(DCSF, 2008f; see Tables 8.3 and 8.4)

There are several examples of the planning formats in Tables 8.3 and 8.4 There is not one linked to SEAL as such because experiences suggest that too often the activity linked to PSED is seen as a lesson and does not emerge from the needs of the children and may not fit in with ongoing assessments of independent learning. The examples of long-term planning show how much PSED learning is expected in continuous provision planning. Each key person may have copies of long-term plans and will take from that the areas to develop and provide experiences with their children. This is one way. An alternative is for weekly planning meetings to use the long-term planning as a basis for discussion about assessment, and particularly the next steps for particular children, thus feeding into weekly or daily plans. For example, the short extract from a weekly plan covering all areas of learning in Table 8.5 is very specific in addressing areas of PSED that children may not meet in their everyday play.

The third planning example is for a class lesson showing how aspects of PSED are included in an 'All about me' lesson with a focus on knowledge and understanding of the world. This plan is very much the kind of plan that may be completed to inform a visitor to your setting, prepared by an inexperienced practitioner or for a different person working with the class (see Table 8.3).

Behaviour

Singling out one aspect of PSED may seem strange, but this links to the revised aspect of PSED, that is, managing feelings and behaviour. There is some rather disturbing recent research (Marmot, 2010) suggesting that 60 per cent of 5-year-olds in some of Britain's poorest areas do not reach a good level of behaviour and understanding. This is double that found in wealthier suburban parts of England. An earlier edition said that in effective settings there

TABLE 8.3 Daily session plan 'all about me'

WHOLE CLASS 20 MINS	GROUP ACTIVITIES	PLENARY 10 MINS	OBJECTIVES
Introduction What have we been thinking about over the past few weeks? Show IWB flipcharts Our first day at school Life Education Caravan Planting our first seeds in the garden Our first picture, painting of ourselves Trim Trail	Share activities available on the IWB. Children choose their names and choose an area to play in (free flow) to support learning from the whole class session.	What did you find out this lesson? Who used the mirrors? What did you find out? Who printed a picture of themselves/Would you like to share it?	***Knowledge and Understanding of the World*** *4. Investigates places, objects, materials and living things by using all the senses as appropriate.* *5. Asks questions about why things happen and how things work, looks closely at similarities, differences, patterns and change.*
Main part 15 mins Sitting in talking partners. Give out photos from home. Discuss questions from teacher and then feed back to the whole class when teacher chooses name out of a pot. Who are the people who live in your house? What is your favourite activity in school? *(watch use of this word!)* Who are your friends in class? What do you look like? What do you like doing when you are at home? What do you want to do when you grow up? Ask the children to 'network' with their talking partner – meet up with another pair and look at their photographs – what can you find out about them?	**Assessments** *Teacher/TA to observe and record using post-its/observation slips and take photographs of learning.*	Where would we like to go next with our learning? Make a list of things we might like to find out.	*6. Finds out about past and present events in own life, and in those of family members and other people.* ***Physical Development*** *8. Recognises the importance of keeping healthy and those things that contribute to this.* ***PSED*** *Displays high level of involvement in activities (40–60 mths)* *Continues to be interested, excited and motivated to learn (ELG)*
Circle Pick a photograph from the middle of the circle and see if we know anything about that child from the speaking and listening we have done so far.			*Talks freely about their home and community (30–50 mths)*

TABLE 8.4 Example of a weekly plan for PSED in a Reception class

AREA OF LEARNING	LEARNING INTENTION	ACTIVITY/ ACTIVITIES INCLUDING CONTEXT	LANGUAGE TO BE INTRODUCED	EVALUATION
PSED	Have an awareness of and an interest in cultural and religious differences. Have a positive self-image, and show they are comfortable with themselves.	Introduction to Chinese New Year – resources for this in box. Encourage children to talk about celebrations they are familiar with – birthdays, Christmas or Eid.	Vocabulary associated with Chinese New Year.	

TABLE 8.5 Planning for continuous provision in PSED

EYFS LONG-TERM PLANNING EXAMPLE – CONTINUOUS PROVISION BOOKS INDOOR/OUTDOOR

LONG-TERM KEY LEARNING OPPORTUNITIES

PSED	CLL
■ Continue to be interested, excited and motivated to learn. ■ Be confident to try new activities, initiate new ideas and speak in a familiar group. ■ Maintain attention, concentrate, sit quietly when appropriate. ■ Respond to significant experiences, showing a range of experiences when appropriate. ■ Have a developing awareness of their own needs, views and feelings, and be sensitive to the needs, views and feelings of others. ■ Have a developing respect for their own cultures and beliefs and those of other people. ■ Form good relationships with adults and peers. ■ Work as part of a group or class, taking turns and sharing fairly, understanding that there needs to be agreed values and codes of behaviour for groups of people, including adults and children, to work together harmoniously. ■ Understand what is right, what is wrong and why. ■ Consider the consequences of their words and actions for themselves and others. ■ Dress and undress independently and manage their own personal hygiene. ■ Select and use resources independently. ■ Understand that people have different needs, views, cultures and beliefs that need to be treated with respect. ■ Understand that they can expect others to treat their needs, views, cultures and beliefs with respect.	■ Enjoy listening to and enjoying using spoken and written language and readily turn to it in their play and learning. ■ Sustain attentive listening, responding to what they have heard with relevant comments, questions or actions. ■ Listen with enjoyment and respond to stories, songs and other music, rhymes and poems and make up their own music, songs stories and poems. ■ Extend their vocabulary, exploring the meanings and sounds of new words. ■ Speak clearly and audibly with confidence and control and show awareness of the listener. ■ Use language to recreate roles and experiences. ■ Explore and experiment with sounds, words and texts.

BOX 8.1 Example of long-term planning for PSED as part of a long-term plan for continuous provision covering role play indoors

- Continue to be interested, excited and motivated to learn.
- Be confident to try new activities, initiate ideas and speak in a familiar group.
- Maintain attention, concentrate and sit quietly when appropriate.
- Respond to significant experiences, showing a range of feelings when appropriate.
- Have a developing sense of awareness of their own needs, views and feelings, and be sensitive to the needs, views and feelings of others.
- Have a developing respect for their own cultures and beliefs and those of other people.
- Form good relationships with adults and peers.
- Work as part of a group or class, taking turns and sharing fairly, understanding that their needs to be agreed values and codes of behaviour for groups of people, including adults and children, to work together harmoniously.
- Understand what is right, what is wrong and why.
- Consider the consequences of their words and actions for themselves and others.
- Dress and undress independently and manage their own personal hygiene.
- Select and use activities and resources independently.
- Understand that people have different needs, views, cultures and beliefs that need to be treated with respect.
- Understand that they can expect others to treat their needs, views, cultures and beliefs with respect.

---

is planned promotion of positive behaviour which takes account of the needs of the parents as well as children. While this is still true, there is a further imperative today to work with parents to demonstrate the effective ways in which to develop in children an understanding of what is right, what is wrong, and why. Are we involving children well enough in identifying issues and finding solutions?

The EPPE research (Sylva *et al.*, 2004) found that the most effective settings adopted discipline/behaviour policies in which staff supported children in rationalising and talking through their conflicts. Where settings were less effective there was often no follow-up on children's misbehaviour and, on many occasions, children were distracted or simply told to stop. *Practice Guidance for the Early Years Foundation Stage* (DCSF, 2008f: 35) provides some good examples of effective practice in 'Appendix 2: Areas of Learning and Development'. Starting at birth and going through to 5 years, these are:

- Find out as much as you can from parents about young babies before they join the setting, so that routines you follow are familiar and comforting.
- Demonstrate clear and consistent boundaries and reasonable yet challenging expectations.
- Reduce incidents of frustration and conflict by keeping routines flexible so that young children can pursue their interests.
- Help children to understand their rights to be kept safe by others, and encourage them to talk about ways to avoid harming or hurting others.

- Share with parents the rationale of boundaries and expectations to maintain a joint approach.
- Demonstrate concern and respect for others, living things and the environment.
- Be alert to injustices and let children see that they are addressed and resolved.
- Ensure that children have opportunities to identify and discuss boundaries, so that they understand why they are there and what they are intended to achieve.
- Help children's understanding of what is right and wrong by explaining why it is wrong to hurt somebody, or why it is acceptable to take a second piece of fruit only after everybody else has had some.
- Involve children in identifying issues and finding solutions.

Research into to how to manage behaviours in pre-school provision has reported that the typical strategies used were exclusion, explanation or distraction. Staff prepared to raise with parents their concerns about problematic behaviours that endangered a child's safety or were out of character. A similar example read on the Mumsnet blog suggests that there are settings that still revert to the somewhat old-fashioned methods of control, such as time out for a 3-year-old, which are applauded by the large majority of other parent members! Do you agree with this? How should a refusal to do something be reprimanded in a 3-year-old? Surely, you do not agree that time out away from the other children is a satisfactory remedy? Adults need to have a discussion with the child concerned and identify and discuss the boundaries of what is acceptable behaviour and what is not. Importantly, this must be shared with a parent to ensure there can be reinforcement at home and further discussion.

Temper tantrums in 2-year-olds

It may seem unnecessary to cover the management of the behaviours of very young children. However, given the large number of web pages on the 'terrible twos' tantrum scenario, it is worth looking at strategies to deal with such a situation. Tantrums are a typical stage of child development. Toddlers are keen to do things as their mental and motor skills tend to develop more quickly than their ability to communicate. This can lead to frustration, and because they do not have the verbal skills to express their frustration they do so by throwing tantrums. In the case of a frustration tantrum the practitioner needs to send a clear message by walking away from a child using a tantrum to get his/her own way. By walking away, the child is taught that tantrums are not acceptable, which is part of toddler discipline. Sometimes frustration tantrums require empathy. Use the opportunity to bond with a child by helping out if they are struggling with a task, such as putting on a sock, for example. Tantrums may be triggered by being over-tired, hungry, unwell, or other reasons. Keeping a record of their frequency and what may be triggering the tantrum is a useful step in discovering what is causing the tantrum.

TABLE 8.6 Proposed early learning goals for PSED

PERSONAL, SOCIAL AND EMOTIONAL DEVELOPMENT			
ASPECT	EMERGING	EXPECTED (ELGS)	EXCEEDING
Self-confidence and self-awareness	Children join in a range of activities that interest them. They are confident to talk to other children when playing together. They can talk about what they need and what they enjoy doing, and make choices about the activities they prefer. They select and use resources with support.	Children are confident to try out new activities and can say why they prefer some. They talk about their ideas, choose the resources they need to plan and carry out activities they have decided to do and can say when they do or don't need help.	Children are confident to speak to a class group. They can talk about the things they enjoy, and are good at, and about the things they don't find easy. They are resourceful in finding support when they need help or information. They can talk about the plans they have made to carry out activities and what they might change if they were to repeat them.
Managing feelings and behaviour	Children are aware of their own feelings and know that some actions and words can hurt others' feelings. They can take turns and share, sometimes with support from others. They can usually adapt their behaviour to different events, social situations and changes in the routine.	Children can talk about how they and others show feelings and manage their feelings. They can talk about their own and others' behaviour and its consequences. They can work as part of a group or class and understand and follow the rules. They can adjust their behaviour to different situations and to changes in the routine.	Children know some ways to manage their feelings and are beginning to use these to maintain control. They can listen to each other's suggestions and plan how to achieve an outcome without adult help. They know when and how to stand up for appropriately. They can stop and think before acting and they can wait for things they want.
Making relationships	Children play as part of a group, and know how to make friends with others. They show some awareness of other children's needs.	Children can play cooperatively, taking turns when playing. They can take account of one another's ideas about how to organise their activity. They can show sensitivity to the needs and feelings of others and form positive relationships with adults and other children.	Children play group games with rules. They understand someone else's point of view can be different from theirs. They resolve minor disagreements through listening to each other to come up with a fair solution. They under stand what bullying is and that this is unacceptable behaviour.

TABLE 8.7 *Development Matters* statements for disposition and attitudes (DCSF, 2008f: 26)

AGE BAND	*DEVELOPMENT MATTERS* STATEMENTS (DISPOSITION AND ATTITUDES)
Birth–11 months	■ Develop an awareness and understanding of themselves. ■ Learn that they have influence on and are influenced by others. ■ Learn that experience can be shared
8–20 months	■ Become aware of themselves as separate from others. ■ Discover more about what they like and dislike. ■ Have a strong exploratory impulse. ■ Explore the environment with interest.
16–26 months	■ Learn that they are special through the responses of adults to individual differences and similarities. ■ Develop a curiosity about things and processes. ■ Take pleasure in learning new skills.
22–36 months	■ Show their particular characteristics, preferences and interests. ■ Begin to develop self-confidence and belief in themselves.
30–50 months	■ Seek and delight in new experiences. ■ Have a positive approach to activities and events. ■ Show confidence in linking up with others for support and guidance. ■ Show increasing independence in selecting and carrying out activities.
40–60 months	■ Display high levels of involvement in activities. ■ Persist for extended periods of time at an activity of their choosing.
Early Learning Goals	■ **Continue to be interested, excited and motivated to learn.** ■ **Be confident to try new activities, initiate ideas and speak in a familiar group.** ■ **Maintain attention, concentrate, and sit quietly when appropriate.**

TABLE 8.8 *Development Matters* statements for self-confidence and self-esteem

AGE BAND	*DEVELOPMENT MATTERS* STATEMENTS (SELF-CONFIDENCE AND SELF-ESTEEM)
Birth–11 months	■ Seek to be looked at and approved of. ■ Find comfort in touch and the human face. ■ Thrive when their emotional needs are met. ■ Gain physical, psychological and emotional comfort from 'snuggling in'.
8–20 months	■ Feel safe and secure within healthy relationships with key people. ■ Sustain healthy emotional attachments through familiar, trusting, safe and secure relationships. ■ Express their feelings within warm, mutual, affirmative relationships.
16–26 months	■ Make choices that involve challenge, when adults ensure their safety. ■ Explore from the security of a close relationship with a caring and responsive adult. ■ Develop confidence in own abilities.
22–36 months	■ Begin to be assertive and self-assured when others have realistic expectations of their competence. ■ Begin to recognise danger and know who to turn to for help. ■ Feel pride in their own achievements.

TABLE 8.8 (continued)

AGE BAND	DEVELOPMENT MATTERS STATEMENTS (SELF-CONFIDENCE AND SELF-ESTEEM)
30–50 months	■ Show increasing confidence in new situations. ■ Talk freely about their home and community. ■ Take pleasure in gaining more complex skills. ■ Have a sense of personal identity.
40–60+ months	■ Express needs and feelings in appropriate ways. ■ Have an awareness and pride in self as having own identity and abilities.
Early Learning Goals	■ **Respond to significant experiences, showing a range of feelings when appropriate.** ■ **Have a developing awareness of their own needs, views and feelings, and be sensitive to the needs, views and feelings of others.** ■ **Have a developing respect for their own cultures and beliefs and those of other people.**

TABLE 8.9 *Development Matters* statements for behaviour and self-control

AGE BAND	DEVELOPMENT MATTERS STATEMENTS (BEHAVIOUR AND SELF-CONTROL)
Birth–11 months	■ Are usually soothed by warm and consistent responses from familiar adults. ■ Begin to adapt to care-giving routines.
8–20 months	■ Respond to a small number of boundaries, with encouragement and support.
16–26 months	■ Begin to learn that some things are theirs, some things are shared, and some things belong to other people.
22–36 months	■ Are aware that some actions can hurt or harm others.
30–50 months	■ Begin to accept the needs of others, with support. ■ Show care and concern for others, for living things and the environment.
40–60 months	■ Show confidence and the ability to stand up for their rights. ■ Have an awareness of the boundaries set and of behavioural expectations in the setting.
Early Learning Goals	■ **Understand what is right, what is wrong and why.** ■ **Consider the consequences of their words and actions for themselves and others.**

TABLE 8.10 *Development Matters* statements for self-care

AGE BAND	DEVELOPMENT MATTERS STATEMENTS (SELF-CARE)
Birth–11 months	■ Anticipate food routines with interest. ■ Express discomfort, hunger or thirst.
8–20 months	■ Begin to indicate own needs by pointing, for example. ■ May like to use a comfort object.

TABLE 8.10 (continued)

16–26 months	■ Show a desire to help with dress and hygiene routines. ■ Communicate preferences.
22–36 months	■ Seek to do things by themselves knowing that an adult is close by, ready to support and help if needed. ■ Become more aware that choices have consequences. ■ Take pleasure in personal hygiene, including toileting.
30–50 months	■ Show willingness to tackle problems and enjoy self-chosen challenges. ■ Demonstrate as sense of pride in own achievement. ■ Take initiative and manage developmentally appropriate tasks.
40–60 months	■ Operate independently within the environment and show confidence in linking up with others for support and guidance. ■ Appreciate the need for hygiene.
Early Learning Goals	■ **Dress and undress independently and manage their own personal hygiene.** ■ **Select and use activities and resources independently.**

TABLE 8.11 *Development Matters* statements for sense of community

AGE BAND	*DEVELOPMENT MATTERS* STATEMENTS (SENSE OF COMMUNITY)
Birth–11 months	■ Respond to differences in their environment. For example, showing excitement or interest. ■ Learn that special people are a source of sustenance, comfort and support.
8–20 months	■ Learn that their voice and actions have effects on others.
16–26 months	■ Learn that they have similarities and differences that connect them to and distinguish them from others.
22–36 months	■ Show a strong sense of self as a member of different communities, such as their family or setting. ■ Show affection and concern for special people.
30–50 months	■ Make connections between different parts of their life experience.
40–60 months	■ Have an awareness of and an interest in cultural and religious differences. ■ Have a positive self-image and show they are comfortable with themselves. ■ Enjoy joining in with family customs and routines.
Early Learning Goals	■ **Understand that people have different needs, views, cultures and beliefs that need to be treated with respect.** ■ **Understand that they can expect others to treat their needs, views, cultures and beliefs with respect.**

TABLE 8.12 *Development Matters* statements for making relationships

AGE BAND	*DEVELOPMENT MATTERS* STATEMENTS (MAKING RELATIONSHIPS)
Birth–11 months	■ Enjoy the company of others and are sociable form birth. ■ Depend on close attachments with a special person within their setting. ■ Learn by interacting with others.
8–20 months	■ Seek to gain attention in a variety of ways, drawing others into social interaction. ■ Use their developing physical skills to make social contact. ■ Build relationships with special people.
16–26 months	■ Look to others for responses which confirm, contribute to, or challenge their understanding of themselves. ■ Can be caring towards each other.
22–36 months	■ Learn social skills and enjoy being with and talking to adults and other children. ■ Seek out others to share experiences. ■ Respond to the feelings and wishes of others.
30–50 months	■ Feel safe and secure and show a sense of trust. ■ Form friendships with other children. ■ Demonstrate flexibility and adapt their behaviour to different events, social situations and changes in routine.
40–60+ months	■ Value and contribute to their own well-being and self-control.
Early Learning Goals	■ **Form good relationships with adults and peers.** ■ **Work as part of a group or class, taking turns and sharing fairly, understanding that there needs to be agreed values and codes of behaviour for groups of people, including adults and children, to work together harmoniously.**

Discussion points

1. Discuss the behaviour management strategies used in your setting and compare these with the effective practice statements in *Practice Guidance for the Early Years Foundation Stage* (2008f).

2. How does your key person system work and what responsibilities do you each have?

9

Communication, language and literacy

Introduction

The EYFS review identifies 'communication and language' as a 'prime' area of learning with 'literacy' as one of the four specific areas of learning in which communication and language skills are applied. Tickell reports that 'communication and language are essential foundations for children's life, learning and success'. Concern was rightly raised in the consultation period that very young children were pressured to read and write at inappropriately young ages.

Notwithstanding the EYFS review, this chapter remains largely unchanged because there are separate sections on each of the three parts of the original area of learning. The existing *Development Matters* statements are still included alongside the recommended areas of learning to assist practitioners new to early years in their assessment and planning, although planning examples are slightly modified to reflect the new terminology.

The aim is to interpret the 'communication, language and literacy' area of learning (DCSF, 2008f) to provide guidance to support practitioners. Associated publications, *Mark Making Matters* (DCSF, 2008d), *Confident, Capable and Creative: Supporting Boy's Achievements* (DCSF, 2007a), *Supporting Children Learning English as an Additional Language* (DCSF, 2007d) and the *Inclusion Development Programme: Supporting Children with Speech, Language and Communication Needs* (DCSF, 2008a), are referred to in order to provide further illustrations of relevant practices for children with additional learning needs and English as an additional language.

The debates about the value of 'synthetic' phonics in the early reading process are informed by a critique from Scotland following the widespread adoption of 'synthetic' phonics in Scottish schools.

The chapter has three sections: language for communication and thinking (communication and language); literacy, including reading and writing; and providing for children with English as an additional language. The impact of ECAR (Every Child a Reader), which is highly praised in Tickell's review, is also outlined. The early learning goals and *Development Matters* statements from *Practice Guidance for the Early Years Foundation Stage* (DCSF, 2008f) to assist practitioners link their practice to the EYFS requirements and develop familiarity with development from birth to 5 are included in each section.

The revised framework for communication and language to support the summary of development at 24 to 36 (Table 9.13, p. 151) months and the proposed early learning goals are included at the end of the chapter (Table 9.14, p. 153). Other key features include: the role of the adult, planning and assessment examples; provision for children with additional learning needs; and the needs of boys. Chapter 7 also includes examples of the key role of parents and carers in their child's literacy, learning and development.

This chapter includes references to the key findings from Sure Start evaluations (Melhuish, 2010) and research into the ways in which young children learn to communicate, to read and to write from specialist developmental psychologists and other key players whose work informs what we know and understand about young children (DES, 1975; Johnston and Watson, 2005; Brierley, 1987; Bruner, 1960; Meadows and Cashden, 1997; Goswami and Bryant, 1997).

Communication and language

> Language is the most powerful tool in the development of any human being, it is undeniably the greatest asset we possess. A good grasp of language is synonymous with a sound ability to think. In other words, language and thought are inseparable.
>
> (Vygotsky, 1978)

Language development for 0 to 3s

The use of communication and language is at the heart of all learning. Learning to speak initially emerges out of non-verbal communication. It is important that practitioners value children's talk and appreciate the importance of making time for conversation with young children, both on a one-to-one basis and within small groups. One of the central objectives of Sure Start is to improve children's ability to learn. One of the means of achieving this is to reduce the number of children with speech and language problems requiring specialist intervention by the age of 4. Table 9.1 shows the aspects of speech and language development needing consideration. Law and Harris (2001) identified five key themes to set the context for helping children's communication skills:

TABLE 9.1 Terms used in speech and language development (Law and Harris, 2001: 7)

TERMS USED IN SPEECH AND LANGUAGE DEVELOPMENT	
Comprehension	The ability to understand words and sentences. A comprehension difficulty means that a child cannot understand what is said to him. Typically he cannot do as asked, or does only part of what is asked. (This may need to be distinguished from the case where the child can understand but will not cooperate!)
Expressive language	Using words and sentences. An expressive language difficulty means that a child might point or make noises instead of words; or that an older child uses only one word at a time instead of sentences.
Speech sounds	The accuracy of pronunciation. A speech sound difficulty means, for example, that a child says *tar* instead of *car*.

1. The importance of adult-child interactions, especially parent-child interactions.
2. The relationship between communication skills and other aspects of a child's general development.
3. The potential for a local community environment to impact on a child's development.
4. The importance of collaboration between the many people involved with a child's development.
5. The potential for a child's (or parent's) resilience to reduce the impact of potentially stressful circumstances and the importance of enhancing that resilience.

Listening to babies and children

In order to talk with a child, it is necessary to listen and watch. A child needs time and an opportunity to talk. When an adult listens, they give the child space to speak. When an adult watches, they can see what a child might want to talk about, even if words are not easy to understand. This means that the child's attempts to communicate can make sense to an interested adult. Then, at last, the adult can talk with the child. A child engaged in this way will learn new words and want to talk, because they know that their attempts to talk are heard and understood. A view promoted by EYFS is that of a listening approach because it gives a child much more scope for learning to talk than does an adult reliant on naming objects, or asking a child to name objects.

Babies and young children learn to focus on adult speech very early in their lives. It helps if adults make the communication easy for the child to listen to and understand. Parents often do this. They adapt their own language levels to those of the child to help them to listen effectively. The focus is on giving the child a listening and speaking part in the conversation. This contrasts with an adult using a high proportion of directive commands, which do not allow the child a turn to speak. It is true that the more parents talk to their children the more the children speak themselves. Practitioners can encourage conversation and extend the use of language through everyday situations, such as changing routines, mealtimes, shopping and cooking. An effective open partnership with parents is vital, as they most easily understand their child's communications and can help overcome any barriers that may occur. See examples of good practice in Table 9.2.

As a practitioner, what is a typical expectation of a 12-month-old child? According to EYFS practice guidance children should be starting to form words by the time they are a year old (*Development Matters*, Table 9.3). To communicate effectively children must understand what is being said to them and learn how to speak by forming the correct sounds within words, putting words together in short phrases and sentences and then learning to tell stories (Law and Harris, 2001: 7). Possibly, children with special needs will develop alternative systems for communicating, such as sign language, gestures or picture symbols. The following is list of strategies to use when talking to very young children:

- Speak about the here and now.
- Use simple words.
- Use key words only.
- Use few word endings.
- Use sentences which are one or two words longer than child's words are.
- Speak slowly and carefully.
- Repeat ideas.

TABLE 9.2 Good practice when talking to babies and children (Law and Harris, 2001)

Listening to children

WHY?	HOW?
See what child wants to say	Watch what your child is doing
Give your child a need to talk	Match what they do with what they try to say
Give your child time to talk	Repeat what your child says or tries to say

Effective practices

Sometimes practitioners gather together 'treasure baskets' which are collections of safe, natural materials for babies and young children to explore using all their senses. They make it possible to assess development across several areas, including cognitive, physical, emotional and communication skills. Importantly for child minders, they are a relatively cheap and effective resource if you have access to a range of market stalls in your area. Look for: measuring spoons, small colanders, whisks, bells, balls, ribbon, cones, pegs, brushes, napkin rings, and sponges, to name but a few items easily found.

Talking to 2- to 4-year-olds

Use a picture or actions to show what a new word means. Use a new word several times in one conversation. Repeat back correctly a sentence which your child has said in a childish way. Add in ideas to your child's sentence when you reply. Use sentences a little longer than your child uses. Give instructions clearly, in short parts. Speak clearly and not too fast. Repeat back correctly a word your child has said wrongly.

Enjoy rhymes and rhyming words. Storytelling provides a myriad of opportunities to promote 'possibility thinking.' At any point a child can be encouraged to think of alternative directions that a story might take. Figure 9.1 gives a flavour of how Keeley's communication and thinking skills are developed. Keeley attends a child minder on a full-time basis.

Children with English as an additional language (EAL)

There are increasing numbers of children entering EYFS settings for whom English is not their first language. Most of these children will already have well-developed communication and language skills in their home language, and will need support in schools and settings to develop their skills in English. The early years national strategy publications, provide practitioners and students with a wealth of guidance on supporting the learning of children with EAL and to develop their skills in English. This section of the chapter refers to this guidance.

A key first step for EAL children is the removal of the potential barriers that may have excluded them from accessing provision. It is the responsibility of local authorities (LAs) to ensure accessible information reaches those in most need of support. This responsibility is a direct result of the Early Years Outcomes duty, placed on LAs as part of the

PHOTO

Context for learning: visit to the park with a key worker

What did Keeley do?

Keeley and Sarah often visit the local park. On the way they pass the duck pond. Keeley says, 'Look, look, ducks! I *loke* ducks! Lots and lots and lots! I feed the babies first!' They fed the ducks. Sarah repeated Keeley's sentence, 'I <u>like</u> the ducks', thus modelling the correct pronunciation of the word without discouraging Keeley, who then pronounced the word correctly.

Keeley held out the bread as Sarah listened and watched her, at first hesitantly throwing some to the ducks with great glee as they all dived on the crumbs.

Keeley continued to chat about this experience as she walked back to the nursery, interspersed with comments about the wet grass, and what the ducks did.

What did Keeley learn?

- She understood and was able to speak in simple sentences.
- She learned some new words ('pond' and 'ducks', although she knew 'ducks' already) (16–26 mths LCT).
- She talked confidently about an enjoyable event just experienced and made links with visits there with her mum (22–36 mths LCT).
- Understands meaning from context (LFT 16–24 mths)
- Uses language to share experiences (LFT 22–36 mths).

Next steps
- Provide story books with similar theme and plenty of repetition for the key worker to read aloud.
- Encourage Keeley to talk about her visit to the park, show photos, ideally of the park to encourage a shared conversation about events and activities of interest to her.
- If Keeley is ready play games that require distinguishing the difference in sounds (DM 22–36 mths LCT).
- Provide books and resources to engage in symbolic play.

FIGURE 9.1 Developing communication, language and literacy skills in a 2-year-old

Children Act (DCSF, 2006b). This requires them to address the gaps in achievement between different groups of children at the end of the Foundation Stage measured by the Foundation Stage Profile outcomes. In many LAs these children form an increasing percentage of the lowest achievers at the end of the Foundation Stage. A key principle is the importance of the home language.

> Bilingualism is an asset, and the first language has a continuing and significant role in the identity, learning and the acquisition of additional languages.
>
> (DCSF, 2007d: 4)

TABLE 9.3 *Development Matters* statements for language for communication (DCSF, 2008)

AGE BAND	*DEVELOPMENT MATTERS* STATEMENTS (LANGUAGE FOR COMMUNICATION)
Birth–11 months	■ Communicate in a variety of ways including crying, gurgling, babbling and squealing. ■ Make sounds with their voices in social interaction.
8–20 months	■ Take pleasure in making and listening to a wide variety of sounds. ■ Create personal words as they begin to develop language.
16–26 months	■ Use single-word and two-word utterances to convey simple and more complex messages. ■ Understand simple sentences.
22–36 months	■ Learn new words very rapidly and are able to use them in communicating about matters which interest them.
30–50 months	■ Use simple statements often linked to gestures. ■ Use intonation, rhythm and phrasing to make their meaning clear to others. ■ Join in with repeated refrains and anticipate key events and phrases in rhymes and stories. ■ Listen to stories with increasing attention and recall. ■ Describe main story settings, events and principal characters. ■ Listen to others one-to-one or in small groups when conversation interests them. ■ Respond to simple instructions. ■ Question why things happen and give explanations. ■ Use vocabulary focused on objects and people that are of particular importance to them. ■ Begin to experiment with language describing possession. ■ Build up vocabulary that reflects the breadth of their experiences. ■ Begin to use more complex sentences. ■ Use a widening range of words to express or elaborate on ideas.
40–60 months	■ Have confidence to speak to others about their own wants and interests. ■ Use talk to gain attention and sometimes use action rather than talk to demonstrate or explain to others. ■ Initiate conversation, attend to and take account of what others say. ■ Extend vocabulary especially by grouping or naming. ■ Use vocabulary and forms of speech that are increasingly influenced by their experiences of books. ■ Link statements and stick to a main theme or intention. ■ Consistently develop a simple story, explanation or line of questioning. ■ Use language for an increasing range of purposes. ■ Use simple grammatical structures.
Early Learning Goals	■ **Interact with others, negotiating plans and activities and taking turns in conversation.** ■ **Enjoy listening to and using spoken and written language, and readily turn to it in their play and learning.**

What does your environment for EAL children look like?

Everything you provide for children whose first language is English is relevant for children learning English as an additional language. However, there are key principles and provision that makes for more effective learning and development for EAL children. It is vital that your

TABLE 9.4 *Development Matters* statements for language for thinking

AGE BAND	DEVELOPMENT MATTERS STATEMENTS (LANGUAGE FOR THINKING)
Birth–11 months	■ Are intrigued by novelty and events and actions around them.
8–20 months	■ Understand simple meaning conveyed in speech. ■ Respond to the different things said to them when in a familiar context with a special person.
16–26 months	■ Are able to respond to simple requests and grasp meaning from the context.
22–36 months	■ Use action, sometimes with limited talk that is largely concerned with the 'here and now'. ■ Use language as a powerful means of widening contacts, sharing feelings, experiences and thoughts.
30–50 months	■ Talk activities through, reflecting on and modifying what they are doing. ■ Use talk to give new meaning to objects and actions, treating them as symbols for other things. ■ Use talk to connect ideas, explain what is happening and anticipate what happens next. ■ Use talk, actions and objects to recall and relive past experiences.
40–60 months	■ Begin to use talk instead of action to rehearse, reorder and reflect on past experience, linking significant events from own experience and from stories, paying attention to how events lead into one another. ■ Begin to make patterns in their experience through linking cause and effect, sequencing, ordering and grouping. ■ Begin to use talk to pretend imaginary situations.
Early Learning Goals	■ **Use language to imagine and recreate roles and experiences.** ■ **Use talk to organise, sequence and clarify thinking, ideas, feelings and events.**

environment has additional visual support for children learning English. You need to continue to speak to children even when they do not respond because many children go through a 'silent phase' when learning a new language. Children will usually understand far more than they can say. Try to respond to children's non-verbal communication. They will then start to echo single words and phrases, joining in with repetitive songs and stories.

Whether the environment is a home or a childcare setting or school, the principle for all children is that it will play a key role in supporting and extending children's development and learning. Plan an environment that is rich in signs, symbols, notices, numbers, words, rhymes, books, pictures, music and songs that take into account children's different interests, understandings, home backgrounds and cultures. Make sure there is plenty of time for children to share these resources with adults and other children. Are children confident to explore inside or outside? Have you considered where children will gather for stories, songs and rhymes? Consider how you are going to plan for learning and development, whether it is for children to explore independently or working with an adult indoors or outdoors.

The role of the practitioner

The practitioner can have a powerful impact and influence on the lives of children:

- Ensure that they provide a learning environment in which black children and their families feel welcomed, respected and valued.
- Enter into genuine partnership with parents of black children by creating space for dialogue by listening to the voices of black children and their parents.
- Provide a rich learning environment with relevant, appropriate, creative and challenging learning opportunities.
- Recognise that good teaching is a vital ingredient in achievement and ensure that black children experience good role models in all areas of learning and development.
- Keep careful records to track children's progress from entry to the setting, ensuring that expectations and progress of black children is in line with other groups and investigating possible causes where variance rises.
- Consider assessment procedures – are observational assessments of black children fair, honest and free from incidences of stereotyping?
- Reflect honestly on personal attitudes, feelings, preconceptions and tendencies to stereotype.
- Examine their own attitudes and awareness and reflect on those of their colleagues, co-workers and community.
- Challenge negative attitudes and practice within the setting.
- Make race equality training a priority for whole setting professional development.
- Review and implement, monitor and evaluate their race equality policy.

Planning for language and communication

There are various ways of looking at planning for communication and language for very young children particularly. Indeed, the most effective way may not be to plan at all because the likelihood is that practitioners may find themselves imposing an experience on the children that is not within their understanding or interest. This can lead to too many of those 'silent periods' mentioned earlier. I remember a video used many years ago to demonstrate how to help children with EAL converse. A birthday cake was presented and candles were lit to help Mohammed understand 'birthday cake'. However, to no avail as he courageously offered the word 'blow' because he was told to 'blow the candles out'. Our understanding has moved on as a result of extensive guidance, including the *Practice Guidance for the Early Years Foundation Stage* (DCSF, 2008f). But has our practice moved on? Do we all really know how to trigger the interest, engagement and cooperation of a 3-year-old intent on building a sand castle? In August 2009, Megan Pacey, the Chief Executive of Early Education, stressed that there was still a need to provide additional guidance and support in three areas, one of which was planning, listed alongside supporting child-initiated activities and demonstrating progress.

★ ★ ★

The key to planning is that it is there to provide a scaffold for teaching, a sense of what the next steps might be as you are supporting or extending child-initiated activities or an adult-led activity, although with the under-3s there should be less of this. Planning will always need to be linked to assessment and is likely to be a result of an assessment (see 'next steps' or sections on what children enjoyed last week in sample plans in other chapters).

Familiarity with the *Development Matters* statements are crucial because they provide the scaffold for you to use to extend children's learning, knowledge and understanding as they go about their activities in a setting. This may sound too simplistic because it is important to capture what children are interested in and that may necessitate adult intervention by introducing a topic or theme. The practitioner's familiarity with what it is reasonable to expect children to do is crucial because without that knowledge, how can they know what comes next? There are several examples of planning provided (see Figures 9.2 and 9.3) for key worker assessment of

We are starting to talk

Ethan 14 months

Points and makes his views known by squealing. Sits and plays with his voice by blowing and babbling. Sometimes calls for Dadda.

Begins to understand what he cannot do.

Enjoys listening to stories and a favourite programme *In the Night Garden*.

Can turn pages in a favourite book.

Possible practices

- Be physically close and make eye contact, use touch and voice to converse with babies.
- Learn and use key words in home language.
- Share stories and rhymes.
- Tune in to messages children try to convey.
- Wait and watch before responding.
- Use non-verbal communication.
- Talk to babies about what you are doing to link words with actions.
- Watch for their understanding.
- Use talk to describe what children are doing.

Ella 16 months

Listens to others and enjoys musical sounds.

Understands simple requests, wash your hands and hold the spoon.

Begins to talk to dolls in role play and mimics what she may have heard.

Begins to share and talk to others.

Mat 17 months

Chatters to others and makes his views clear.

Curious and keen to talk about interests in the nursery — train set and small-world play.

Knows several nursery rhymes.

Bethany 12 months

Slightly reserved, watches but is not communicating verbally.

Begins to listen to others.

Lacks curiosity in things around her and is very tearful at times.

Development Matters

- Make sounds with their voices in social interaction.
- Take pleasure in making and listening to a wide variety of sounds.
- Use single-word and two-word utterances.
- Understand simple sentences.
- Create personal words as they begin to develop language.
- Are intrigued by novelty and events and actions around them.
- Understand simple meanings conveyed in speech.
- Respond to the different things said to them when in a familiar context with a special person.
- Are able to respond to simple requests and grasp meaning.

Assam 19 months (EAL)

We are not making headway with Assam. He does not appear to respond to verbal commands. Chat with colleague raises a possible hearing issue as he shows elation when signs are made — wave, gestures, etc., but otherwise is not engaging in play.

FIGURE 9.2 Language development planning and assessment for under-3s key worker group

Observing and assessing sheet

Child's name	
Adult observer	
Area of provision	
Date	**Time/duration**

What happens/happened

PSED	CLL	PSRN	KUW	PD	CD

What was learned about the child's interest, abilities or needs?

Possible lines of development

FIGURE 9.3 Observing and assessing an aspect of communication, language and literacy

the under-3s. It will be useful for practitioners to evaluate these to come to a consensus in the setting as to the method they prefer.

Reflecting on practice

The key principle in the EYFS framework of the *Unique Child* encourages practitioners to reflect on their practice. In terms of developing speech, language and communication skills, practitioners need to ask themselves if they:

- Have a thorough knowledge of child development and the development of speech, language and communication.
- Understand how children progress at different rates in communication and language.
- Get a good picture of children's communication and language outside the setting.
- Make time in their staff team to discuss children's level of development.
- Take account of the fact that some children will understand considerably more language than they use.
- Recognise that some children who have a lot to say don't always understand everything that is said to them.
- Know the difference between children who are shy or reserved and those who have speech, language and communication needs.
- Recognise and support the different methods of communication that children use.
- Think about the language skills that are involved in the activities they are providing and ensure that all children can access them.

(DCSF, 2008f: 21)

Literacy

Reading (including linking sounds and letters)

In the revised EYFS framework (DfE, 2011a), literacy is now a 'specific' area of learning with two aspects being 'reading' and 'writing'. There are two assessment stages. When children are 2 they will be assessed in the communication and language areas. Then, at the end of the Foundation Stage, assessment of reading and writing will take place. I make no apologies for linking reading with linking sounds and letters in this chapter. I will draw on the findings of recent research to explain why the move from the 'searchlight' model of reading to the 'simple view of reading' has taken place.

The issue that needs to be debated is whether the statutory requirement to teach young children to read, making prime use of *Letters and Sounds* (DCSF, 2007c), is the most effective method. I readily endorse the early warnings coming from TACTYC in a recent Times Educational Supplement letter that acknowledges the key role that phonics plays in learning to read, although there are other factors such as vocabulary that have a greater impact when children reach 11.

This section of the chapter takes the *Practice Guidance* sections for reading and linking sounds and letters as the baseline because the *Development Matters* statements are compatible with the development stages of the typical child from birth to the end of the Foundation Stage. Table 9.5 shows the combined *Development Matters* statements for linking sounds and letters and reading.

Perhaps, as hinted earlier, the most powerful influence on reading development in recent years is *The Rose Review: The Independent Review of the Teaching of Early Reading* (DfES, 2006a). This review, while acknowledging the contribution of the National Literacy Strategy found that the 'searchlight' model for reading promoted by the Strategy and a previous seminal review of literacy known as the *Bullock Report* (DES, 1975) was overtaken by more recent understanding of the reading process (Goswami and Bryant, 1990; McGuinness, 1998) and concludes that it is time to move on from previous models in order to support practitioners to further improve their teaching of early reading. It recommends a 'simple view' of reading. This conceptual framework identifies two components of reading: 'word recognition' and 'language comprehension', both of which, it claims, are essential to developing fluent and effective reading. It is worth reinforcing that this is just one view of the way in which children learn to read and it is crucial that you are open-minded when teaching reading to the reality that there are children who do not learn to read in this way.

There is the worry that phonological awareness or 'synthetic phonics' may be seen in isolation to the reading process and not as part of it. In a previous edition (Rodger, 1999: 73) identified this as an area fraught with controversy at that time following on from the 'real' books approach to teaching reading. Essentially, this is because of the different beliefs which are held by educationalists and psychologists about how children learn to read and write. An increasingly widespread view, which is beginning to influence the way in which children are introduced to the printed word, relates to the way in which children are taught to sound out words. In early speech children are concerned to understand the meanings of words and pay very little attention to the sounds that words make. But as children begin to learn to read and write words the component sounds of the words begin to take on a new meaning. Children are fascinated by rhymes and enjoy using them, in both real and invented words. Rhyme has a direct link with some aspects of learning to read. In my own teaching experience with 3- and 4-year-olds, poems such as the one in Figure 9.4 leave the children in paroxysms of laughter.

To help children to understand the different sounds made by the symbols in our alphabetic system, children need to be able to distinguish separate sounds within the stream of language they hear when people talk and read aloud. This is 'phonological awareness'. Children's sensitiv-

I Have a Cat

I have a cat who walks with grace
I have a cat with a blue face
I have a cat with purple eyes
I have a cat who makes sand pies

I have a cat who likes to eat snails
I have a cat with a spiky tail
I have a cat who drinks lemonade
I have a cat who plays with a spade

I have a cat who goes out to tea
I have a cat who plays in the sea
I have a cat whose name is Fred
I have a cat who sleeps on my bed

FIGURE 9.4 Playing with language

TABLE 9.5 *Development Matters* statements for reading and linking sounds and letters

AGE BAND	*DEVELOPMENT MATTERS* STATEMENTS (READING)	*DEVELOPMENT MATTERS* STATEMENTS (LINKING SOUNDS AND LETTERS)
Birth–11 months	■ Listen to familiar sounds, words or finger plays.	■ Listen to, distinguish and respond to intonations and the sounds of voices.
8–20 months	■ Respond to words and interactive rhymes, such as 'clap hands'.	■ Enjoy babbling and increasingly experiment with using sounds and words to represent objects around them.
16–26 months	■ Show interest in stories, sings and rhymes.	■ Listen to and enjoy rhythmic patterns in rhymes and stories.
22–36 months	■ Have some favourite stories, rhymes, songs, poems or jingles.	■ Distinguish one sound from another. ■ Show interest in play with sounds, songs and rhymes. ■ Repeat words and phrases from familiar stories.
30–50 months	■ Listen to and join in with stories and poems one to one and also in small groups. ■ Begin to be aware of the way stories are structured. ■ Suggest how the story might end. ■ Show interest in illustrations and print in books and print in the environment. ■ Handle books carefully. ■ Hold books the correct way up and turn the pages. ■ Understand the concept of a word.	■ Enjoy rhyming and rhythmic activities. ■ Show awareness of rhyme and alliteration. ■ Recognise rhythm in spoken words.
40–60 months	■ Enjoy an increasing range of books. ■ Know that information can be retrieved from books and computers.	■ Continue a rhyming string. ■ Hear and say initial sounds in words and know which letters represent some of the sounds.
Early Learning Goals	■ **Explore and experiment with sounds, words and texts.** ■ **Retell narratives in the correct sequence, drawing in language patterns of stories.** ■ **Read a range of familiar and common words and simple sentences independently.** ■ **Know that print carries meaning and, in English, is read from left to right and top to bottom.** ■ **Show an understanding of the elements of stories, such as main character, sequence of events and openings, and how information can be found in non-fiction texts to answer questions about where, who, why and how.**	■ **Hear and say sounds in the order in which they occur.** ■ **Link sounds to letters, naming and sounding the letters of the alphabet.** ■ **Use their phonic knowledge to write simple regular words and make phonetically plausible attempts at more complex words.**

ity to rhyme is directly linked to the ease with which they begin to decipher print (Bradley and Bryant, 1985). The work of Goswami and Bryant (1990) supports the research findings stated earlier that some aspects of rhyming are strong predictors of later reading ability. Alphabetic letters represent sounds, and strings of letters, by representing a sequence of sounds, can signify spoken words. According to Goswami and Bryant (1990) children may recognise the word as a visual pattern without paying much attention to the individual letters or to the sounds that they represent. The assumption being, therefore, that children's awareness of sounds – or phonological awareness – plays an important part when they learn to read and write.

Children demonstrate different kinds of 'phonological awareness' because there are different ways in which words can be divided up into smaller units of sound (see Table 9.6).

McGuinness (1998), with her cognitive and educational psychology background, states that 'children must be trained to hear the individual sounds (phonemes) of their language. They must be able to disconnect, or "unglue", sounds in words in order to use an alphabetic writing system' (p. xiii). Her research has discovered that where the sequence of reading and spelling instruction is compatible with the logic of the alphabetic code *and* with the child's linguistic and logical development, learning to read and spell proceeds rapidly and smoothly *for all children*, and is equally effective for poor readers of all ages. While her work focuses on the children who have difficulty learning to read there are messages for those of you working with young children.

In her publication *Why Children Can't Read* (1998), McGuinness provides guidance to parents. The issue, she believes, is not *when* children are taught to read, but that they are taught correctly. The successful conditions in which children learn to read she sums up simply as:

- talking to your child;
- reading to your child;
- encouraging pre-writing skills.

These are very much part of the early literacy repertoire of most early years practitioners, and generally accepted by practitioners as central to their practices. However, the area where McGuinness's views challenge some of the current practices is more interesting. For instance, teaching letter names in isolation is claimed to be harmful and should be replaced by providing the sound of the letter within a familiar word. The only function reciting the alphabet serves is to help children to find their way around a dictionary or an index where this skill is required.

The term 'emergent literacy' was coined by Marie Clay in 1966. This term still encapsulates that very early stage of exploration and play as children come to terms with their different

TABLE 9.6 Three ways to divide words into component sounds (Goswami and Bryant, 1990: 2)

	SYLLABLE	ONSET AND RHYME	PHONEME
'cat'	cat	c-at	c-a-t
'string'	string	str-ing	s-t-r-i-n-g

environments, and thankfully is also embraced by the *Development Matters* statements for the under-3s in EYFS guidance.

The findings of a seven-year, school-based study in Clackmannanshire, which began in 1997, led the way in recognising the merit of a phonic-based approach to early reading. The outcomes of the study found that children involved in the phonic-based synthetic phonic programme were seven months ahead of their peers in reading and nine months in spelling. The gains in children's reading were impressive, and it was found to help children from quite deprived backgrounds particularly well. Its strengths were reported to be in the intensive teaching of the sounds of all letters and blends of letters, so that children quickly learn all the building blocks needed to read. A consequence of this is that those children arriving in school not knowing their letters are not disadvantaged for long. This creates a more level playing field with those children with greater literacy-based pre-school experience. Boys did not lag behind girls either.

Theory into practice: providing for early reading in a range of settings

Letters and Sounds (DfES, 2007c) is now used extensively in settings and EYFS classes in primary schools. This section of the chapter outlines implications for practitioners and provides examples of planning from nursery and Reception class settings. A checklist of priorities within day-to-day provision to encourage children to become interested in books from a young age is also included.

Typically, settings will have discrete plans for phonic sessions, such as the ones shown in Tables 9.7, 9.8 and 9.9. A word of caution needs to be exercised here and it is imperative that practitioners recognise that not all children will benefit from this approach to early reading. An article in *The Guardian* (Scott, 2007) questions the merit of this by asking the question: are some children missing out? Scott comments on the statistics for reading standards at the end of Key Stage 1. 'Two years on, however, reading attainment appears to have remained static'. In discussion with others – the president of the UK Literacy Association, for example – Scott states that, 'More attention needs to be paid to the other elements of what it means to become a reader as well as the phonic element. Phonics is necessary but it is not sufficient to become a reader in the rounded sense'. This view is supported by the Scottish academic Sue Ellis, saying that: in England you have a very centralised curriculum where the government, the policy-makers, have to be seen to be doing something, but are often quite distant from the people who have to make their decision work. In Scotland there is a much more devolved system where decisions are made much closer to those who will have to implement them. Most current research shows that children need literacy teaching that is tailored to the individual. The article cites the West Bartonshire phonics experiment, which was launched in 1997 with aim of eradicating pupil illiteracy within a decade. At the time, the area had one of the poorest literacy rates in the UK with 28 per cent of children leaving primary school at 12 as functionally illiterate. In 2007, the council reached its target of full literacy, the first education authority in the world to do so. Synthetic phonics were at the core of the scheme, but only one strand in a ten-step programme that included extra time in the curriculum for reading, home support for parents and the fostering of a literacy environment in the community.

Generally, practitioners are planning separately for *Letters and Sounds*, which tends to be taught in small groups according to the children's understanding and age, especially in an EYFS unit comprising 3- and 4-year-olds. A successful approach to sharing books in

TABLE 9.7 Weekly plan for letters and sounds

Learning objectives

Letters and Sounds Phase 2 – week 1. Observations Metal Mike: 40–60 months – *hear and say initial sounds in words and know which letters represent some of the sounds. Say sounds in words in the order in which they occur. Outside: general observations CLL 2.3 – links some sounds to the letters.* Teacher group observation: *blends sounds with words*

■ To develop the oral blending and segmenting of sounds in words
■ To know the phonemes 's', 'a', 't' and 'p'

	MONDAY	TUESDAY	WEDNESDAY	THURSDAY
Revisit/Review	Play Inky's gym p. 55 (practising oral blending)	Toy Talk p. 43 (practising oral segmenting) Recall 's' using IW, uncover grapheme with action. Check with picture	Play Inky's gym (practising oral blending) Recall 's' and 't' using IW, uncover grapheme with action. Check with picture	Toy Talk (practising oral segmenting) Recall 's', 't' and 'a' using IW, uncover grapheme, all to make phoneme with action. Check with picture
Teach	Teach 's' using Jolly Phonics	Teach 't' using Jolly Phonics. Inky's 't' pot, can we sort the objects (CLL 2.2)	Teach 'a' using jolly phonics. Inky's board, 'a' and 's', can we sort the objects ? (CLL 2.2)	Teach 'p' using jolly phonics. Inky has left a message, something has broken in the classroom – 'tap' Introduce Sound buttons p. 58 – blending for reading
Practise	– I Spy p. 43 (practising oral blending). Inside Bear's cave – I spy a b-e-d, s-oa-p. Children can then lead the game, trying to segment word. Include 's' magnetic letters, encourage children to articulate phoneme – Metal Mike p. 38 (practising oral segmenting). CVC food for Mike to eat. Mike only understands robot talk	– I Spy p. 43 (practising oral blending). Inside Bear's cave – I spy a b-e-d, s-oa-p. Children can then lead the game, trying to segment word. Include 's' and 't' magnetic letters, encourage children to articulate phonemes – Metal Mike p. 38 (practising oral segmenting). CVC food for Mike to eat. Mike only understands robot talk	– I Spy p. 43 (practising oral blending). Inside Bear's cave – I spy a b-e-d, s-oa-p. Children can then lead the game, trying to segment word. Include 's', 't' and 'a' magnetic letters, encourage children to articulate phonemes – Metal Mike p. 38 (practising oral segmenting). CVC food for Mike to eat. Mike only understands robot talk	– I Spy p. 43 (practising oral blending). Inside Bear's cave – I spy a b-e-d, s-oa-p. Children can then lead the game, trying to segment word. Include 's', 't', 'a' and 'p' magnetic letters, encourage children to articulate phonemes – Metal Mike p. 38 (practising oral segmenting). CVC food for Mike to eat. Mike only understands robot talk

TABLE 9.7 (continued)

	– Outside activity – mini-beast remote-controlled toy, children can direct toy over matting with 's' letters and pictures – snake, sausage	– Outside activity – mini-beast remote-controlled toy, children can direct toy over matting with 's' and 't' letters and pictures – snake, sausage, tennis, table	– Outside activity – mini-beast remote-controlled toy, children can direct toy over matting with 's', 't' and 'a' letters and pictures – snake, tennis and ant	– Outside activity – mini-beast remote-controlled toy, children can direct toy over matting with 's', 't', 'a' and 'p' letters and pictures – snake, ant, tennis, pig
Opportunities to apply	Outside – paint letters outside and alphabet cards included clipboards for writing Storytelling 's' props, Clipboards and alphabet cards. Alphabet jigsaws. Painting easel	Outside – paint letters outside and alphabet cards included, clipboards for writing Storytelling 't' props, Introduce puzzle boards – 's' and 't', pictures to be sorted	Outside – paint letters outside and alphabet cards included, clipboards for writing Storytelling 'a' props. Clipboards and alphabet cards. Alphabet jigsaws, painting easel, puzzle board – 's', 't' and 'a', pictures to be sorted. Letter hunt – magnets and magnetic letters 's', 't' and 'a'	Outside – paint letters outside and alphabet cards included, clipboards for writing Storytelling 'p' props. Clipboards and alphabet cards. Alphabet jigsaws, painting easel, puzzle board – 's', 't', 'a' and 'p', pictures to be sorted. Letter hunt – magnets and magnetic letters 's', 't', 'a' and 'p'

small groups too tends to work more effectively when children are grouped by similar readiness to listen to stories and contribute. Very young children may find it very hard to join a large group and find this a stressful experience. This may manifest in what appears to be disruptive behaviour, and indeed it often is. The answer may lie in a gradual approach to large-group work. It is rarely ideal for 3-year-olds to be grouped in a large group for a story. Preferably, continuous provision should give a high priority to promoting literacy skills by ensuring there is always an adult to encourage children to share books, role play in the puppet theatres and making use of listening devices to hear favourite stories. Table 9.8 is an example of planning for literacy.

Planning takes many formats covering long, medium and short term (see Chapter 2). In this section there are samples of long-, medium- and short-term plans. Practitioners in different parts of the country use these to ensure they are meeting the statutory EYFS framework. The formats presented here vary and are presented completed.

As a start, practitioners may wish to audit their provision to ensure there is a high priority to literacy development and learning. The checklist in Figure 9.5 provides a starting point.

Providing for children with English as an additional language

The intention is that all the examples and guidance outlined in each chapter will be equally applicable to children whose first language is not English, but it is important that, as well as celebrating the similarities between children, their differences are also accepted in the spirit of us all being different, whatever our ethnic and/or cultural background. Nonetheless, it is widely acknowledged that EAL children who have limited access to the Foundation Stage are more likely to have poor outcomes at the end of it. How often does one hear the comment, 'Oh! He doesn't talk/can't talk because …'? It is unacceptable to accept the status quo for such children because their early development and learning of the English language is imperative if they are to cope with the later, more linguistic demands of primary education. The opening paragraph of *Supporting Children Learning English as an Additional Language* (DCSF, 2007d: 2) states:

> For growing numbers of settings, providing care and learning opportunities for children and families new to English, or at various stages of proficiency, is a new experience.

So what needs to be in place to ensure all our children have equal opportunities? Of course there are LA responsibilities that were acknowledged in the *Primary National Strategy* (DCSF, 2007e: 3) but day by day some readers will have bilingual children in their care. The recognition that some children may have competence in several languages with English just one of many is important and may suggest that those children have an aptitude to acquire English readily. The National Strategy referred to above identifies the principles and theories that underpin approaches to supporting children learning EAL. These are:

- the importance of building on their existing knowledge about language;
- the impact of attitudes towards them personally and their culture, language, religion and ethnicity on learning their identity;

Resource areas and resources

- ➤ Domestic role-play area.
- ➤ Imaginative role play-area.
- ➤ Cosy story telling area – undercover?
- ➤ Library corners in several areas with books displayed with front cover visible.
- ➤ Comfortable seating, such as throws, rugs, cushions.
- ➤ Mark-making materials in the domestic play area.
- ➤ Magazines and newspapers.
- ➤ Materials for writing stories – well-resourced with paper, crayons and pencils, etc.
- ➤ Headsets and tapes of stories.
- ➤ Magnetic boards with alphabet letters.
- ➤ Puppets linked to stories.
- ➤ Use of children's labels and captions.
- ➤ Alphabet at child eye height.
- ➤ Interactive whiteboard at child height if possible, but create a platform if not (boys love this).
- ➤ Pencils attached to painting easel to encourage children to write their name.
- ➤ Self-registration board with forename first, before adding surname too.
- ➤ Checklist displayed for children to record snack taken.
- ➤ Computers, desk and laptops in technology area.
- ➤ Signs on everything to recreate the richness of the visual literacy environment outdoors.
- ➤ An area for parents to read with their children.

Try to replicate as much of the above as possible outside.

FIGURE 9.5 Preparing the early years environment to promote communication, language and literacy development

Some important issues are as follows:

- ■ English should not replace the home language; it will be learned in addition to the language skills already learned and being developed within the language community at home.
- ■ Children may become conversationally fluent in a new language in two or three years but may take five or more years to catch up with monolingual peers in cognitive and academic language.

- Children learning EAL are as able as any other children, and the learning experiences planned for them should be no less challenging.

- Additional visual support is vital for children learning English and using illustrations and artefacts will support and enhance the learning experiences of their monolingual peers.

- It is essential that adults continue to talk to children with the expectation that they will respond.

- Adults and children should respond positively and encouragingly to children's non-verbal communication. As they observe, listen and explore the setting, children will be applying the knowledge they already have in their new context. As they start to echo single words and phrases and join in with repetitive songs and stories, their attempts should be sensitively praised and encouraged.

(DCSF, 2007d: 5)

The DCFS publication from the National Strategy is comprehensive in identifying effective practice and guidance on how to reflect on practice. References are made in the next section.

Reflecting on practice when working with EAL children

Earlier the 'silent' period of an EAL child was mentioned. Clarke (1992: 17–18) cites ten ways to encourage the participation of children during their 'silent' period. She recommends:

1. Continued talking even when children do not respond.
2. Persistent inclusion in small groups with other children.
3. Use of varied questions.
4. Inclusion of other children as the focus of the conversation.
5. Use of the first language.
6. Acceptance of non-verbal responses.
7. Praising of minimal effort.
8. Expectations to respond with repeated words and/or counting.
9. Structuring of programme to encourage child-to-child interaction.
10. Providing activities which reinforce language practice through role play.

A case study (9.1) of the way in which a group of Reception-aged children in a primary school responded to a structured play environment in an inner city school in Manchester highlights points 9 and 10 in Clarke's list of ways to encourage children in their 'silent' period. When reflecting on your own practice you may wish to ask yourself the following questions, which relate to two of the key EYFS principles in this chapter – *Enabling Environments* and *Learning and Development*:

- Does your environment celebrate linguistic and cultural diversity?
- How well informed are you of the languages, culture and circumstances of the families you work with?
- Have you considered the additional support EAL learners may need in order to access routines?

CASE STUDY 9.1 Using structured play to promote language development for children with EAL

In the Reception classroom, the structured play area was developed to provide opportunities to extend the topic 'Light and Dark' by setting up as a bear's cave. The space to do this in the classroom was very restricted, but as it turned out this was a bonus because of the security and intimacy provided for children in the cave. Ingeniously designed walls and flaps over the entrance ensured there was a high degree of privacy and authenticity for the two children able to play together. The stimulus for the story was *Do Little Bears Sleep?*, copies of which were displayed inside the cave along with other stories familiar to the children. Creatures suspended from the ceiling and cushions on the floor provided a comfortable, concealed environment away from the hustle and bustle of the classroom. Torches of various sizes and colours were available to see the pictures in the book. A clipboard with outlines of 'Mr Blobbie' was available for the children's use. The class teacher routinely targeted pairs of children with EAL to explore and work in the cave. Her intentions went beyond allowing the children to construct their own literacy and play experiences. Her curriculum plans identified the ways in which this environment was planned to support children's learning. She encouraged the children to share a story, always pairing a linguistically capable child with a less confident one. Children who spoke the same home language were encouraged to work together, thus providing support and encouragement for the less fluent speaker of English and also to enable the children to share the story in their home language.

(Rodger, in Halsall, R., *Teacher Research and School Improvement*, 1997: 127)

TABLE 9.8 Key worker literacy group plan for nursery

Key worker groups – morning nursery

	OBJECTIVE	ACTIVITY	EVALUATION
Tuesday	■ To listen to and join in with stories (30–50 mths) ■ Listen to stories with increasing attention and recall ■ Begin to talk in pretend imaginary situations 40–60 mths) ■ To use a wide vocabulary to talk about sounds daddy/baby bear's voice/ footsteps (Phase 1 Letters and Sounds) patterned language within the text and questioning regarding sound descriptions T/TA to record observations The intention of this session is to extend the children's learning building upon child-initiated play from the previous week	Revisit and share text 'Goldilocks and the Three Bears'. Carry out role play with props, modelling and encouraging the children to speak in role. Invite children to make their own suggestions for different characters e.g. How would daddy/baby bear's voice/footsteps sound? (Link to Letters and Sounds. Phase 1 – Story sounds p. 17) T/TA To challenge Katie, Stephanie and Jodie by: asking them to identify and repeat	

TABLE 9.9 Short-term planning for CLL: overview of expectations for one week for older Foundation Stage children

FOUNDATION STAGE SHORT-TERM PLANNING EXAMPLE		
Communication, language and literacy week		
NUMBER OF WEEKS: 1	**CORE TEXT: THE ICE HAND – MODELS FOR WRITING**	
Learning intentions		
Speaking and listening Listen with enjoyment and respond to stories, songs, and other music, rhymes and poems and make up their own stories, songs, rhymes and poems. Sustain attentive listening, responding to what they have heard by relevant comments, questions or actions. Extend their vocabulary, exploring meaning and sounds of new words. Interact with others, negotiating plans and activities, and taking turns in conversation. Use talk to organise, sequence and clarify thinking, ideas, feelings and events.	**Reading** Show an understanding of the elements of stories, such as main character, sequence of events, openings and how information can be found in non-fiction texts to answer questions about where, who, why and how. Know that print carries meaning and, in English, is read left to right and top to bottom. Extend their vocabulary, exploring the meaning and sounds of new words. Retell narratives in the correct sequence, drawing on the language patterns of stories.	**Writing** Attempt writing for various purposes, using features of different forms, such as lists, stories and instructions.
Sentence level Write their own names and other things such as labels and captions and begin to form simple sentences and sometimes use punctuation.	**Word level** Use phonetic knowledge to write simple regular words and make phonetically plausible attempts at more complex words.	**Presentation** Use a pencil and hold it effectively to form recognisable letters, most of which are correctly formed.
Key outcome – to create a non-fiction book about the ice hand, constructing our own sentences		

- Do you model language enough in relation to the contexts in which you are working? Ask open questions, talk alongside the children naming the equipment you are playing with, then ask them to pass so and so, thus providing a context. Self-talk through the activities to give the children a commentary.
- Are you giving the children time to think?

Writing and handwriting

In this section the focus of mark making is linked to literacy rather than numeracy (see the next chapter), although there are clear links between each in young children's development and learning.

Young children will make literary and numeracy marks simultaneously where they are provided with the conditions in which to do so. Many years of experience and initiative after initiative to improve young children's ability and skill in independently writing leave me somewhat bewildered as to what to suggest to young practitioners entering the profession. The examples of writing in Figures 9.6a, b and c were written by a girl in a Reception class.

Young children will scribble and make patterns and marks as they develop. They will 'emerge into literacy', to borrow a phrase from Marie Clay (1996). The skill of the early years practitioner is to ensure that children are able to demonstrate a readiness to form letters, begin to write words and copy letters and words. Readiness is important because without the early stages of fine motor skill acquisition, children, especially boys, are being set up to fail in their first attempts at writing.

So how do practitioners motivate children to develop their handwriting and writing skills? An important starting point before children come into an early years environment are the writing/mark-making experiences in their home. Do they see writers – writing shopping lists, messages, birthday cards, calendar entries, etc. – in action? Have they access to mark-making materials? Home visits prior to the children starting the nursery will give practitioners useful background knowledge about this.

What does the EYFS practice guidance suggest?

The guidance for early mark making is clear and rightly starts with what children do and how adults can extend initial explorations of materials (see the *Development Matters* statements in Table 9.12). Familiarise yourself with this, as it provides excellent guidance, although, quite rightly, a higher priority is given to language and reading development. Useful additional guidance is available in *Mark Making Matters* (DCSF, 2008d). A recommendation as to the experiences and resources to support mark making describes the indoor and outdoor activities to provide.

A crucial practice must be to ensure that children develop those very early emergent writing skills in 'an active, play-based learning environment' so that children have many different ways of representing their thoughts and feelings. Children will realise that marks can be used symbolically to carry meaning. The observations of such actions by practitioners are vital.

What are the letters and words that children are familiar with? Children will see their name prominently displayed on their coat peg when they start nursery. They may see it elsewhere too. Build on this knowledge, encourage children to 'write' their name on completed drawings and observe for their application of letters into their drawings. Figure 9.7 is an example of independent writing by an able 5-year-old girl in a Reception class where a topic on celebrations provided the stimulus for her party list.

From marks to writing

Younger children continue to make marks that may appear to be random, but it is interesting to note how readily children turn to mark making. Do girls do this more often than boys? Children model what others are doing and possibly children's home experiences differ, with girls copying writing a shopping list, or if children are very reluctant to mark it is because they do not see

TABLE 9.10 What are children learning to do? Part 2

Weekly CLL Planning Example Monday–Thursday

	DAY 1	DAY 2	DAY 3	DAY 4
What we want children to learn (*Development Matters*)	To be able to talk about what they see and retell a sequence of events.	To write captions to go with the pictures of the melting ice hand. To use a word bank to support our spelling.		To think of ideas for speech bubbles and attempt to write them.
Adult-led activities (whole class)	As a whole class we spend the morning watching the ice hand as it melts. Begin discussion with lots of child-initiated thoughts about how it was made, etc. Take children to ICT suite to introduce publishing package, model own ideas about the ice hand.	Using big book, read captions to go with each picture together. Children match the caption to the picture. Model reading strategies and ask particular children to help. Show children the new set of pictures we are going to use – model writing one or two captions using the children's ideas. Use this as the start to introduce the idea of a word bank to help them make their writing even better. Continue to encourage phonic strats.		Show the children the plastic animals frozen in the ice – discuss how they are feeling. What do you think they are saying? Introduce the idea of a speech bubble. Have one pre-written, can we read it? Can we write our own? Teacher to scribe ideas.
Adult-led activities (independent or group work)	Children create a drawing on 2publish to show their interpretation of the ice hand – more able to attempt independent sentence. Children with adult support also sequence a set of pictures taken during various stages of the melting.	In small, well-supported groups (1 adult – 4 children). Each child will create their own caption to go with 3 or 4 sentences depending on their ability. Captions will then be cut into strips and made into books – see sample in file. Children use the word bank, alphabet strips and phonic strats for spelling. More able to use full stops and think about capital letters to start.		Children in pairs to attempt to make own speech bubble for trapped animal. They help each other with writing and spelling, checking each other's letter formation on a letter chart.

TABLE 9.10 (continued)

Opportunities for children to explore and apply	Winter activities on the writing table – Icy 1 on sound table, pouring water into different plastic gloves. Ice cold animals.	Ice hands of the side to observe with magnifying lens. Ice cubes in water tray. Books about snow and ice in reading area.	Speech bubbles in writing area attached to different animals from the zoo. Books which show examples of speech bubbles.
Look, listen and note	Make notes as children talk about the ice hand, also note ICT skills.	Make specific notes about phonic strats and use of word bank.	Make specific notes about PSED, paired work and handwriting standard.
Assessment opportunities	Print out a copy of each ice hand picture to talk about. Stick into KUW books.	Please complete writing assessment prompt sheet.	Annotated work.

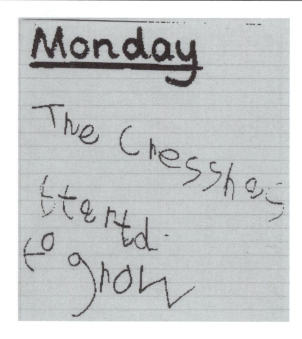

FIGURE 9.6a Contexts for writing (i)

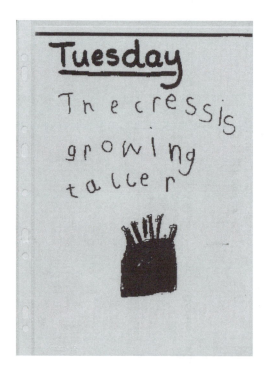

FIGURE 9.6b Contexts for writing (ii)

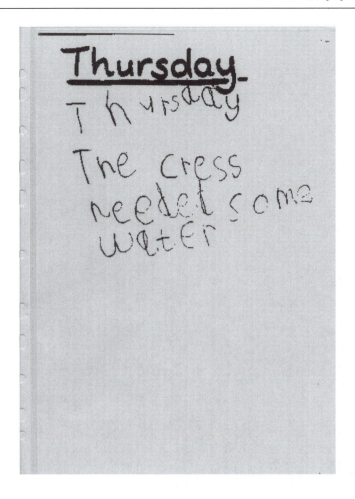

FIGURE 9.6c Contexts for writing (iii)

examples of this (Athey, 1990: 181). As practitioners, do you model writing regularly? A print-rich environment does not model the writing process. Observation of very young children's mark making is crucial because it helps to make their thinking visible and helps to understand the intellectual development of the child. Young children, from birth, demonstrate some repeatable patterns of behaviour and thought (schemas). The mark making begins to help the identification of a child's interests. For example, a child intent on drawing circles and playing with balls is showing an interest in 'dynamic circular' schemas. To nourish this, continuous provision can add further opportunities for provision to maintain interest. The whole area of schematic development (Athey, 1990) is covered in Chapters 2, 9 and 11. How, then, do practitioners plan for writing and provide opportunities for child-initiated learning? The lists below make suggestions for experiences and resources for indoors and outdoors.

TABLE 9.11 Long-term planning for CLL (adapted from Burnside EYFS Unit, Durham LA 2008)

LONG-TERM KEY LEARNING OPPORTUNITIES – CONTINUOUS PROVISION

CLL

- Enjoy listening to and using spoken and written language and readily turn to it in their play and learning.
- Sustain attentive listening and respond to what they have heard with relevant comments, questions or actions.
- Listen with enjoyment and respond to stories, songs and other music, rhymes and poems and make up their own stories, songs, rhymes and poems.
- Extend their vocabulary, exploring the meanings and sounds of new words.
- Speak clearly and audibly with confidence and control and show awareness of the listener.
- Use language to imagine and recreate roles and experiences.
- Explore and experiment with sounds, words and texts.
- Retell narratives in the correct sequence, drawing on language patterns of stories.
- Read a range of familiar and common words and simple sentences independently.
- Know that print carries meaning, and, in English, is read from left to right and top to bottom.
- Show an understanding of the elements of stories, such as main character, sequence of events and openings, and how information can be found in non-fiction texts to answer questions about where, who, why and how.

POSSIBLE EXPERIENCES

- Discover how to handle books carefully
- Hold the book the right way up and turns the pages one at a time
- Enjoy looking at pictures
- Opportunities for different voices to tell stories
- Talk about how characters from different stories feel
- Have some favourite stories, rhymes and poems
- Developing listening skills
- Begin to be aware of the way stories are structured
- Suggest how the story might begin/end
- Show an interest in illustrations and print in books and their environment
- Understand that print carries meaning and is a means of communication
- Enjoy an increasing range of books
- Understand that information can be retrieved from books

RESOURCES ACROSS THE PROVISION

- Children's favourite books
- Big books
- Picture, rhyme, poetry books
- Interest books
- Books linked to themes or topics of interest
- Home-made books, children's own books
- CDs of and tapes of rhymes, stories, songs and spoken words
- Posters, pictures and postcards
- Puppets and props
- Story or rhyme sacks or boxes
- Comics and newspapers
- Instruction leaflets, recipe cards/books
- Atlas, road, street maps
- Objects and games to support phonological awareness
- Environmental print

TABLE 9.11 (continued)

ADULT'S ROLE AND LINK TO EYFS	
UNIQUE CHILD	POSITIVE RELATIONSHIPS
Reading stories about everyday events help children to keep themselves safe Encourage, listen and respond to children's communications Value each child's contribution Follow individual interests, be aware of print, signs and symbols from different cultures Give children time to think about stories and reflect on them, making choices	Play and enjoy looking at books alongside and with peers Promote the value of every child's contribution in story telling Use photographs and homemade books to share with parents Motivate children to concentrate and persevere Sharing books with key person, support children, model active listening Encourage children to respect books and keep them tidy
ENABLING ENVIRONMENTS	LEARNING AND DEVELOPMENT
Observe ■ Fine motor co-ordination and skill development ■ Imaginative talk while story telling ■ How child relates story to their play ■ How they express feelings when discussing and retelling stories ■ Empathise with children and support their emotions	**Support and encourage** Creativity in story telling Show genuine interest, clarify ideas, offer encouragement and ask open questions Help children make connections in their learning and extend their thinking Keep children's interest by allowing them to develop some independence and make choices Opportunities to learn through experience Model handling books, re-enacting and story telling

TABLE 9.12 *Development Matters* statements for writing and handwriting

AGE BAND	DEVELOPMENT MATTERS STATEMENTS (WRITING)	DEVELOPMENT MATTERS STATEMENTS (HANDWRITING)
Birth–11 months	■ Use arms and legs and increasingly use them to reach for, grasp and manipulate things.	■ Play with own fingers and toes and objects around them.
8–20 months	■ Begin to make marks.	■ Begin to bring together hand and eye movements to fix on and make contact with objects.
16–26 months	■ Examine the marks they and others make.	■ Make random marks with their fingers and some tools.
22–36 months	■ Distinguish between different marks they make.	■ Begin to show some control in their use of tools and equipment.
30–50 months	■ Sometimes give meaning to marks as they draw and paint. ■ Ascribe meanings to marks that they see in different places.	■ Use one-handed tools and equipment. ■ Draw lines and circles using gross motor movements. ■ Manipulate objects with increasing control.
40–60 months	■ Begin to break the flow of speech into words. ■ Use writing as a means of recording and communicating.	■ Begin to use anti-clockwise movement and retrace vertical lines. ■ Begin to form recognisable letters.
Early Learning Goals	■ **Use their phonic knowledge to write simple regular words and make phonetically plausible attempts at more complex words.** ■ **Attempt writing for different purposes, using features of different forms such as lists, stories and instructions.** ■ **Write their own name and other things such as labels and captions, and begin to form simple sentences using punctuation.**	■ **Use a pencil and hold it effectively to form recognisable letters, most of which are correctly formed.** (Model holding a pencil between the thumb and forefinger and encourage this in children, but observe to see whether they are ready for this.)

Inside experiences

- self-registration board or register;
- name writing – on pictures, attach pencil to easels;
- diaries and calendars to record events, days of the week, weather;
- cooking recipes displayed, charts to add times and ingredients – modelling writing by an adult;
- home/setting diaries;
- pads, notebooks, paper, clipboards and writing implements all around the setting – book corners, construction area, whiteboards;
- finger painting;
- pattern painting.

TABLE 9.13 Framework to support summary of communication and language development at 24–36 months (revised ELGs)

COMMUNICATION AND LANGUAGE			
ASPECT	24–36 MONTHS	36–48 MONTHS	EARLY LEARNING GOALS
Listening and attention	Children listen with interest when adults read stories to them. They recognise and respond to many familiar sounds. They can shift their attention to a different task if their attention is fully obtained.	Children listen to others one-to-one or in small groups when the conversation interests them. They join in with repeated refrains and anticipate key events and phrases in rhymes and stories. They can focus attention by shifting between an activity and listening.	Children listen attentively in a range of situations. They listen to stories, accurately anticipating key events and respond to what they hear with relevant comments, questions or actions. They can give their attention to what is being said to them and respond appropriately, whilst still being involved in an activity.
Understanding	Children can identify action words by pointing to the right picture. They understand 'who', 'what', and 'where' in simple questions. They are developing an understanding of basic concepts.	Children respond to instructions containing positional language. They can identify objects by their use. They attempt to answer 'why' and 'how' questions using words like 'because'.	Children can follow instructions involving several ideas or actions. They answer 'how' and 'why' questions about their experiences and in response to stories and events.
Speaking	Children learn new words very rapidly and are able to use them in communicating. They use action, sometimes with limited talk, that is largely concerned with the 'here and now'. They talk in basic sentences and use a variety of questions.	Children use talk, actions and objects to connect ideas and recall past experiences. They can retell a simple past event in correct order and talk about things that will happen. They question why things happen and can give explanations.	Children express themselves effectively showing awareness of listeners' needs. They use past, present and future forms accurately when talking about events that have happened or are to happen in the future. They develop their own narratives and explanations by connecting ideas or events.

Outside experiences

- rolls of paper on the ground;
- paper, pads in the tent, gazebo, shed;
- mark-making trolley;
- large chalks for the ground;
- sticks and natural materials for mark making.

Case Study 9.2 shows how a skilled practitioner combines effective literacy learning with enjoyment for her 3-, 4- and 5-years-olds.

FIGURE 9.7 Early writing at the end of Reception

CASE STUDY 9.2 Exemplary literacy learning (Laurel Avenue Primary School, Durham LA)

Based on their very low skills and ability when they start in the nursery, children make excellent progress by the time they leave the Foundation Stage unit in all areas of learning. They quickly settle into the routines. Home visits help to allay any parental concerns and begin to give children confidence. It is the view of parents that their 'children come on in leaps and bounds'. 2007 was an exceptional year and children exceeded the level expected for their age by the time they started in Year 1. However, there is fluctuation year-by-year and not all children attending the nursery transfer to the school. Overall, most

(continued on p. 154)

TABLE 9.14 Revised early learning goals for communication, language and literacy (2011)

ASPECT	EMERGING	EXPECTED (ELGS)	EXCEEDING
COMMUNICATION AND LANGUAGE			
Listening and attention	Children listen to others one to one or in a small group when the conversation interest them. When listening to familiar stories and rhymes children can join in at relevant points with repeated refrains and phrases and can anticipate events. They can focus their attention by shifting between an activity and listening.	Children listen attentively in a range of situations. They listen to stories, accurately anticipating key events and respond to what they hear with relevant comments, questions or actions. They can give their attention to what is being said to them and respond appropriately, whilst still being involved in an activity.	Children listen to instructions and follow them accurately, asking for clarification if necessary. They listen attentively with sustained concentration to follow a story without pictures or props and can listen in a larger group, for example, at assembly.
Understanding	Children respond to instructions when, for example, they are asked to get or put away an item, and understand the meaning of words such as 'on' and 'under'. They can identify familiar objects by the way in which they are used.	Children can follow instructions involving several ideas or actions. They can answer 'how' and 'why' questions about their experiences and in response to stories and events.	After listening to stories children can express views about the events or characters in the story and answer questions about why things happened. They can carry out instructions which contain several parts in a sequence.
Speaking	Children can connect ideas using talk, actions or objects and can retell a simple past event in the correct order. They question why things happen and give simple explanations.	Children express themselves effectively showing awareness of listeners' needs. They use past, present and future forms accurately when talking about events that have happened or are about to happen in the future. They develop their own narratives and explanations by connecting ideas or events.	Children show some awareness of the listener by making changes to language and non-verbal features. They recount experiences and imagine possibilities, often connecting ideas. They use a range of vocabulary in imaginative ways to add information, express ideas or to explain or justify actions or events.
LITERACY			
Reading	Children know that print carries meaning. They show interest in books and can suggest how a story might end. They can segment the sounds in simple words and blend them together, and join in with rhyming and rhythmic activities.	Children read and understand simple sentences in stories and information books, using phonic knowledge to decode regular words and read them aloud accurately. They demonstrate understanding when talking with others about what they have read, or what has been read to them.	Children can read phonetically regular words of more than one syllable as well as many irregular but high frequency words. They use phonic, semantic and syntactic knowledge to understand unfamiliar vocabulary. They can describe the main events in simple stories they have read.
Writing	Children give meaning to the marked they make as they draw, paint and write. They can segment words orally, and use some clearly identifiable letters to communicate meaning, representing some sounds correctly and in sequence.	Children write their own labels, captions, messages and simple stories which can be read bythemselves and others. They use their phonic knowledge to spell words in ways which match their spoken sounds, and make use of high frequency spelling.	Children can spell phonetically regular words or more than one syllable as well as many irregular but high frequency words. They use features of narrative in their own writing.

children reach the expected level and an increasing number reach beyond it. Achievement is outstanding bacause teaching is exemplary and fully engages children in everything they do. Not an opportunity is missed to encourage children to develop their literacy skills, whether it is reading their name when choosing a fruity snack, self registering when they come into school or reading the instructions to make a cup of tea during outdoor play. Children enjoy learning because it is fun. An investigation into the range of everyday utensils and crockery very successfully helped to improve children's early language skills. Teapots, jugs, kettles and different kinds of tea generated a wealth of learning that helped to improve the speech and understanding of many children. Personal, social and emotional development is very well promoted too. Children grow in confidence and play calmly and productively at all times. Children delight in brushing their teeth as soon as they arrive into the unit. Assessment is exemplary and fulfils two main purposes excellently, to guide future learning for the children and to inform parents of their child's progress. Leadership of the unit is outstanding bacause of the excellent model of exemplary teaching and the impact of this talent on other staff.

TABLE 9.15 Observing and assessing mark making

OBSERVING AND ASSESSING MARK MAKING			
Child's name	X		
Adult observer	Xx		
Area of provision	Mark making		
Date:	17/11/08	**Time/ duration**	30 minutes

What happens/ happened

X was playing in the mark making area. She as using the scissors to cut some paper to the specific size she required.

X then began to write small marks on the pieces of paper. I asked X what she was writing, and she replied, 'I'm write Daddy.' X said she would like to know how to write daddy 'for my letter'. I repeated back to her the word daddy, stretching put the sounds for her to hear, and asked her to listen carefully. I then demonstrated how to write 'daddy', saying the sounds in the word slowly as I modelled the writing. X then proceeded to imitate my writing.

X then began to write on one of the other pieces of paper. 'That letter for grandma and grandad'. X asked for envelopes to put her letters in, thse were provided and x put her letters inside. X put lines on the back of the envelope. 'Those are my words' she said.

X then got the hole punch. 'I just got to do clicks,' she said. X put her envelope in to the hole punch and made one hole in each. 'Look, I made one hole'.

X then returned to making small lines on the backs of the envelopes. 'These are writes and this says to daddy'. X picked up both her envelopes. 'Now I'm need to post them'. X went to post the letters in the box.

TABLE 9.15 (continued)

PSED	CLL	PSRN	KUW	PD	CD
	Writing and handwriting			Using equipment and materials	

What was learned about the child's interest, abilities or needs?
Child: X understands that words can be written down, and that words have meaning when written down. X is interested in making marks
Parent: X's parents tell us, that when letters arrive, she asks for the envelopes to do her writing on.
Practitioner: X showed great interest in the party invitations and envelopes given out by another child
Possible lines of development
Provide post office resources to develop x's interest in creating and sending letters. Encourage X to write other letters so we can take her to a real post box and post the letter to her house.

TABLE 9.16 The development of writing (Gorman and Brooks, 1996)

The development of writing

STAGE	INDICATORS
1 **Drawing and sign writing**	• Makes shapes and lines on the page • Shapes often have a clear meaning to the child • Shapes do not look like letters • Understands there is a difference between pictures and words
2 **Letter-like forms**	• Knows there is a difference between drawing and words • Cannot write letter shapes • Draws symbols which simulate letter shapes • Letters in own name are close approximate to letter shapes • Attempts at writing over letters shows some pencil control
3 **Copied letters**	• Over-writing shows good control of letter shapes • Copies letter shapes quite accurately/accurately • Copies letter shapes from a separate piece of writing
4 **Name and letter strings**	• Writes letters quite voluntary without copying • Writes own name • Writes lines of letters which convey meaning • Controls letter shapes quite well • May/may not group letters into words
5 **Words**	• Uses strings of letters to write words • Some words can be read • Words not written as separate units in a sentence • Words written as separate units in copying sentences
6 **Sentences**	• Writes in sentences • Some words within sentences can be read
7 **Text**	

3-year-old children in the nursery may exhibit aspects of stage 1 and 2. The opportunities to write are likely to be met in a playful context – imaginative play in a post office, surgery or shop for example.

Discussion points

1. Review the planning examples provided to identify those that provide the most useful guidance on activities and teaching that most effectively contribute to children's learning. You may wish to look at examples for under-3s and over-3s in communication, reading and writing and handwriting.

2. Has synthetic phonics become an end in itself, rather than a key building block in a more comprehensive reading strategy?

3. Brainstorm your provision for mark making and early writing and the opportunities your children have to observe writing and get parents involved.

10

Physical development

Learning begins when life begins … the period of early childhood has special significance, for not only is physical growth faster at this time than at any other time later in life but it is during these years that the foundations of personality are laid.

(Her Majesty's Stationery Office, 1969: 5)

Introduction

The above statement is taken from a booklet prepared by the Department of Health and Social Security, the Home Office, the Department of Education and Science, the Scottish Home and Health Department and the Scottish Education Department in 1969, which was written to guide those parents who felt that their children were ready for experiences outside their home and to those that found it necessary to place their children with other people. What a journey the development of childcare has made in the past 40-plus years!

Clare Tickell (2011), author of the revised recommendations for the EYFS curriculum, has recommended that physical development becomes a 'prime' area of learning. I can almost feel the pleasure this news will bring to many practitioners. This priority is closely linked to the renewed emphasis on healthy development for all children and the need for children to have increasingly more control over their bodies as they get older in order to succeed in applying the basic skills of writing.

The 'prime' areas of learning are connected to each other. Research says that physical development supports personal, social and emotional development as increasing physical control provides experiences of self as an active agent in the environment, promoting growth in confidence and awareness of control; it supports communication and language because a child who can effectively use large movements, gestures and the fine movements involved in speech is able to convey messages to others.

There are two aspects to physical development in the revised EYFS: 'moving and handling' and 'health and self-care' (see Table 10.1 for a breakdown of the expectations for development in this area of learning for 2-year-olds and Table 10.2 for the end of the Foundation Stage).

As in previous editions, this chapter will provide a rationale for the importance of physical development based on the most recent research and focus on the crucial contribution of outdoor learning to children's health and well-being and to their overall development.

TABLE 10.1 Framework to support summary of physical development at 24–36 months (DfE, 2011a)

PHYSICAL DEVELOPMENT			
ASPECT	24–36 MONTHS	36–48 MONTHS	EARLY LEARNING GOALS
Moving and handling	Children gain increasing control of their whole bodies and are becoming aware of how to negotiate the space and objects around them.	Children maintain balance when they concentrate. They negotiate space successfully when playing racing and chasing games, adjusting speed or changing direction to avoid obstacles. They handle tools effectively for the purpose, including mark making.	Children show good control and coordination in small and large movements. They move confidently in a range of ways, safely negotiating space. They handle equipment and tools effectively, including pencils for writing.
Health and self-care	Children can communicate their physical needs for things such as food and drink and can let adults know when they are uncomfortable. They are beginning to be independent in self-care, e.g. pulling off their socks or shoes or getting a tissue when necessary but still often need adult support for putting socks and shoes back on or blowing their nose.	Children can recognise and express their own need for food, exercise and the toilet, rest and sleep. They can put on a jumper or coat with little assistance and can fasten big buttons. They usually have bladder and bowel control and can attend to most toileting needs most of the time themselves.	Children know the importance of good health of physical exercise and a healthy diet and talk about ways to keep healthy and safe. They can manage their own basic hygiene and personal needs successfully, including dressing and going to the toilet independently.

The EYFS review recommendations for physical development

The current EYFS guidance (DCSF, 2008f) makes a key statement as to the requirements of physical development for babies and children, which is fully supported by the Tickell review. The guidance states that:

> provision must be provided for children to be active and interactive and improve their skills of coordination, control, manipulation and movement. They must be supported in using all their senses to learn about the world around them and to make connections between new information and what they already know. They must be supported in developing an understanding of the importance of physical activity and making healthy choices in relation to food.

> (DCSF, 2008f)

Tickell takes these statements further by stating that, 'physical development is an essential foundation for healthy development, for the early development of physical movement and dexterity as well as healthy eating and exercise, the key starting point for their understanding of how to remain healthy in later life' (DfE, 2011a: 20).

In the event that the two-year health and development programme becomes universal, children will have an integrated health and early years review when they are 2 years old. Physical development meets the recommendation of two of the characteristics of effective teaching and learning which are *playing and exploring* and *active learning*.It can be argued that the third characteristic of *creating and thinking critically* encompasses all aspects of physical development, particularly in the outdoor environment. Table 10.1 is an example of the framework for assessing physical development between 24–36 months. This assessment will provide a secure baseline for children's learning as they enter whatever form their pre-school experience takes.

The research basis for including physical development as a prime area of learning

The research review (Evangelou *et al.*, 2009: 92) describe children's fundamental development in interconnected domains with children primed to encounter their environment through relating to and communicating with others, and engaging physically in their experiences. The evidence gathered for the review found that physical development was cited by 40 per cent of respondents as the third most important assessment area. Many thought that physical development was underemphasised, particularly for children from birth to 22 months, and was important because of the health aspect.

As young children begin to develop concepts they define these in terms of touch, movement and senses. Observe young children as they begin to develop concepts which they define in terms of movement and space, developing schemas to repeat and test ideas. Chapter 6 has a case study describing the physical play of an 18-month-old child. The ability to practice his skills and develop control as he moved around the garden learning how to manipulate a bucket and stirrer is a typical example of using schemas to repeat and test ideas (Athey, 1990).

TABLE 10.2 Early learning goals for physical development at the end of the Foundation Stage (DfE, 2011a)

PHYSICAL DEVELOPMENT			
ASPECT	EMERGING	EXPECTED (ELGS)	EXCEEDING
Moving and handling	Children can maintain balance when they concentrate. They run skillfully and negotiate space successfully, adjusting speed or direction to avoid obstacles. They are beginning to hold a pencil and crayon with thumb and two fingers.	Children show good control and coordination in large and small movements. They move confidently in a range of ways, safely negotiating space. They handle equipment and tools effectively, including pencils for writing.	Children can hop confidently and skip in time to music. They hold paper in position and use their preferred hand for writing, using a correct pencil grip. They are beginning to be able to write on lines and control letter size.
Health and self-care	Children can tell adults when they are hungry or tired or when they want to rest or play. They can dress with some assistance and can usually manage personal needs such as washing their hands and toileting.	Children know the importance of good health, physical exercise and a healthy diet and can talk about ways to keep healthy and safe. They can manage their own basic hygiene and personal needs successfully, including dressing and going to the toilet independently.	Children know about and can make healthy choices in relation to healthy eating and exercise. They can dress and undress independently, successfully managing fastening buttons or laces.

As the observer of this activity it was very apparent that it would have been impossible to replicate this experience indoors. Many aspects of *moving and handling* were evident. It was a classic example of the way in which the physical environment enabled exploration, control and confidence in a child who was an active agent in the environment.

The work of Maude (2006) is cited in the evidence review as it links children's physical development to daily practices in early years environments. Suggestions made by Maude are that children's physical development curriculum needs to include:

- physical development to stimulate growth, enhance physical development and to provide healthy exercise;
- movement development to build on existing movement vocabulary, to develop coordination and body tension and to extend movement vocabulary;
- movement skill acquisition to develop fundamental motor skills to the mature stage, to introduce the dynamics of movement, to develop coordination and teach accuracy in movement;
- movement confidence development to teach movement observational skills, to develop movement experimentation and expression, to enhance self-expression and to enhance self-confidence, self-image and self-esteem;
- general education to teach movement observation, to teach appropriate vocabulary for discussing and explaining movement, to stimulate thought processes, to encourage independence and ownership of learning, to sustain periods of enjoyment.

(Maude, 1996: 194)

The importance of play in developing a movement curriculum for young children should be a high priority according to Maude, and indeed is fully reinforced in the current EYFS and in the review. The value of outdoor learning is firmly acknowledged in the EYFS framework and its profile further developed by creating physical development as a 'prime' area of learning.

Outdoor learning and physical development

The EYFS review's evidence base corroborates very strongly the vital role of play in fostering learning and development across all domains of learning – social, cognitive, and emotional. Bruner (1960) describes the welcome, non-threatening context in which children learn about their world and develop the skills necessary for adult life. Observations of children outside often show them concentrating, persevering and investigating at a level not always evident indoors. So how does this come about? There are some key principles to observe when looking to develop your outdoor provision. The EYFS principle *Enabling Environments* describes the outdoor environment in the following ways:

- Being outdoors has a positive impact on children's sense of well-being and helps all aspects of children's development.
- Being outdoors offers opportunities for doing things in different ways and on different scales than when indoors.
- It gives the child first-hand contact with weather, seasons and the natural world.
- Outdoor environments offer children freedom to explore, use their senses, and be physically active and exuberant.

(DCSF, 2008f)

Perhaps the most authoritative voice on outdoor learning is Helen Bilton (2002, 2004). A starting point, she says, must be the quality of the outdoor environment, resources and what your children want from this aspect of their early learning experiences. The notion that the outdoors reflects what is provided indoors is a common one. However, there must be priority given to outdoor physical activity that is unavailable inside. Maude (1996) sees this as: provision of an adventure playground; a secret garden; a playground with suitable markings to encourage challenge in movement; a tarmac area with wheeled toys, including trucks, tricycles, bicycles and other ride-on and push-along toys; an indoor space with soft-play or gymnastic apparatus; and grass and hard areas with balls, bats, etc.

Planning for outdoor learning

This section will take two approaches to planning for outdoor learning. The first one is likely to have a greater impact on those practitioners who work in a nursery, Children's Centres or private or voluntary settings. This reflects what I am seeing in visits to settings. It is important to have planning that reflects your planning methodology overall. For example, Table 10.3 is a blank table of the provision indoors and outdoors in a sample from three settings in the north east of England, all of which are in different authorities but have essentially the same approach. The second set of examples (Table 10.4) is from settings in the same authorities but has clearly-stated activities on the plans. Evaluate these to come to a decision as to the planning methodology that fits with your philosophy.

The next step in the planning example in Table 10.3 is to begin to compile the learning journey for the targeted children that week. This will effectively act as evidence of what learning has taken place and can provide the impetus for next steps in their learning. For those children in Reception classes or those entering Reception classes from nursery, the learning journey is a record of learning and development so far. Case Study 10.1 describes an innovative approach taken by an early years teacher in Newcastle-upon-Tyne.

CASE STUDY 10.1 Example of a learning journey

This case study describes a well-contextualised record of one boy's *Learning Journey*. Nadine, an early years practitioner, has produced sheets of self-adhesive labels colour coded for age bands covering the *Development Matters* statements in each area of learning. They are colour coded to indicate the age bands the statements refer to in order to protect parents from concern that their child may not be achieving in line with their chronological age, although the colours provide evidence needed for practitioners. The activity example describes the progress of Sam as he told his 'tea party story'. When playing in the water, Sam decided that he wanted to make 'cups of tea' for everyone. He sorted all of the cups onto the table and then went into the sand to get the teapot. He then filled the cups with water and handed them to different people. 'Here you are Anne, its tea', he said confidently. He stayed playing and repeating what he was doing for some time, staying fully engrossed. A series of photographs and written descriptions chart Sam's development and learning as he sustains interest in developing this schema. Small stickers indicate his achievement in an unobtrusive manner. The record of his learning is transferred to the on-line assessment tracker completed for all children to enable a setting-based profile for the LA.

TABLE 10.3 Outdoor planning: building on children's learning weekly plan

OUTDOOR AREA	NEXT STEPS EXTENDING LEARNING ACTIVITY AND DATE ADDED
Construction area	
Writing area/writing boards	
Number area/climbing fame	
Role play	
Music area	
Creative area	
Garden	
Yard/bike area	
Digging area	
Grass area	
Small construction	
Water	
Gazebo	
Weekly evaluation (names of children please) Additions to Learning Journeys	

TABLE 10.4 Continuous curriculum weekly spaces for play plan (indoors/outdoors) EY Unit

GOLDILOCKS AND THREE BEARS	LEARNING INTENTION/EMPHASIS	INDOORS	OUTDOORS	OBSERVE CHILDREN'S INTERESTS	POSSIBLE NEXT STEPS
Book/listening	To extend topic/know that print carries meaning and understand the story To listen to the story To retell the story	Books about bears, listening centre	Books about bears		
Construction	To build using different materials		Blocks, crates and cardboard boxes		
Creative	To use creative materials to represent features		Represent bears using plates and materials		
Physical/movement	To handle equipment and tools To use pencils for writing (HA)		Write names/mark for name on bear models Use paste spreaders		
Investigation	Children interested in why things happen and how things work To listen to instructions		Making meal in Goldilocks cottage		
Malleable	Children create simple representations Use what they have learned about media (HA)		Paintings of bears, models of bears using found materials		
Mark making	Children give meaning to marks they make		Letters to Goldilocks, self-initiated activities		
Music	Children explore sounds Children listen and talk about the story of Goldilocks		Listen and begin to sing 'when Goldilocks went to the house of . . .'		
Role play	Children engage in imaginative role play based on their experiences To retell story of Goldilocks				
Small world	Children talk about the characters and what they do				

Practitioners work with a range of trainees. To support training, one practitioner produced a check list of questions to ask based on 'Look, Listen and Note' opportunities for outdoor activities. The guidance suggests that these notes are used to inform formative assessment. Research mentioned earlier has shown that many practitioners need prompts to help with open questioning (see Chapter 6) as this was found to be a weak area in the EPPE projects (Siraj-Blatchford, 2007). Consider this kind of brainstorm in weekly review meetings to ensure that all colleagues are confident in understanding how to extend children's learning. The example below is from a Reception class.

BOX 10.1 Look, listen and note opportunities

- Do children play alongside peers, initiate conversation, show purpose in their play?
- Can children use the outdoor area independently?
- Can children recognise any numerals? If so, do they have a personal significance (age, own door number, etc.)?
- Can children use number names correctly?
- Do children notice anything about the shape of the numbers?
- Do children know which number comes before or after a given number?
- Can children count using one-to-one strategies?
- Can children negotiate the space in the outdoor area safely?
- Can the children use the bikes, etc., with some control and confidence?
- Can children climb, swing safely and with control?
- Do children play imaginatively? Can they imitate real life in their role play?
- Do children turn what they have heard from books and stories into their play?
- Do children use appropriate language in their role play?
- Do children recognise the coins and use them in their play to pay and to give change?
- Can children use the measuring sticks, tapes, feet, etc., to measure their feet properly?
- Can children select and buy items in the shop using the correct money?
- Do children match number and quantity correctly?
- Can children talk about patterns, shape, colour, etc., in their feet creations?
- Do children explain their shoe designs with clarity and using descriptive language? Can they explain what they have done and why?

The questions in Box 10.1 are an example of how the specific areas of learning, that is, mathematical development, are embedded within the outdoor environment and the physical development 'prime' area of learning. The specific areas are providing a context for building on early learning and development beyond the prime areas. It is likely that the specific areas of learning are dependent on the prime areas and cannot be encountered in isolation from not only physical development but also from CLL and PSED. A further example (see Table 10.5) shows very clearly the 'symbiotic relationship between prime and specific areas of learning' (DfE, 2011a: 96). The completed planning demonstrates very effectively the extent of the 'instructional yet playful teaching' and the 'planned purposeful play' with a balance of adult-led and child-initiated learning as recommended in the *Early Years Review*. Differentiation could include the three possible outcomes for the revised ELGs. Table 10.7 illustrates a different example of a Reception class outdoor area planning grid. Table 10.6 is a blank copy of this grid.

TABLE 10.5 Outdoor continuous curriculum

OUTDOOR CONTINUOUS CURRICULUM – ADULT/CHILD-INITIATED PLAN (SAMPLE OF SOME OUTDOOR AREAS)

OUTDOOR AREA: JANUARY 2009

AREA	AREA OF L&D	WHAT DO WE WANT CHILDREN TO LEARN? KEY QUESTIONS	WHAT MAY CHILDREN DO?	RESOURCES	ADULT INTERACTION/ DIFFERENTIATION	WHAT DID THE CHILDREN LEARN?
Large construction	MD PD	Construction materials can be used as props in play as well as for building purposes *Talk about what they are doing. Ask children to estimate how many more crates they will need to finish the construction*	Use the crates and hollow blocks for a purpose in their play Estimate how many more crates they will need	Crates and hollow blocks	Supervision for safety. LA – may need support to understand 'estimating' AA – encourage and praise efforts HA – should be able to guess amounts	
Small construction	MD PD	Different construction material *Talk about what they are doing, listen and extend with open questions*	Use small construction to create something in their play	Lego, Duplo, wooden blocks	By outcome	
Shoe tying station	PD UW	How to tie shoe laces *What do we do next?*	Use laces to tie bows	Shoes, feet boards, laces,	Show how to tie a knot praise and support	
Mark-making area	W PD	Develop motor skills and early writing, handle pencil correctly Use mark making for a purpose in their play *Talk about what they are doing, ask questions*	Plan the design of the shoe they are creating. Use resources to support their play, create props	Marker pens, paper, chalks, water, brushes, whiteboards, magazines, chalk board and chalks	Encourage children to participate. Be on hand to ensure they fully understand the task	
Magnetic board	MD R & W	Attempt to spell out words, investigate letters and numbers *Ask what they are*	Use magnetic letters and numbers	Magnetic letters and numbers	LA – Adult support needed AA – Some adult support	

TABLE 10.6 Blank adult-directed learning plan for outdoor continuous provision

AREA (ADD OUTDOOR AREAS)	AREA OF L&D	WHAT DO WE WANT CHILDREN TO LEARN? KEY QUESTIONS	WHAT MAY CHILDREN DO?	RESOURCES	ADULT INTERACTION/ DIFFERENTIATION	WHAT DID THE CHILDREN LEARN?

Discussion points

1. As a staff team or group of trainee practitioners, brainstorm your concerns about outdoor provision and how you can manage this with limited staffing, especially in a Reception class.

2. Identify the table toys and games that encourage the development of physical dexterity.

TABLE 10.7 Reception outdoor planning grid

RECEPTION OUTDOOR AREA PLANNING

OUTDOOR AREA	AREA OF LEARNING	LEARNING INTENTION	WEEK: KEY QUESTION	FOCUS: ACTIVITY	RESOURCES	ASSESSMENT CRITERIA
Sand	CLL	Find and read letters and link to sounds	Can you find the s/a/t/p/i/n/m/d letters and match to letters on the clipboard?	During CI play, ask the children to match letters in the sand to corresponding letters on clipboard	Laminated letters and clip boards with matching letters on A4 laminated sheets.	I can link sounds to letters I can recognise s/a/t/p/i/n/m/d
Water	MD/PD/PSE	To use maths vocabulary tall/short bottles to pour water into bottles, to share equipment, handle bottles	Can you pour water from the tall bottle to the short bottle? Can you share the bottle with your friends?	During CI play children may pour water into the short bottle or vice versa and share with peers	Variety of sized bottles	I can use vocabulary related to size in my play I can share with my friends
Bridge and tower	CLL/MD	To use experiences from home in play: to use imagination in play	Which story do you know that has three chairs/ bowls in it?	During CI play, use the props in their play to extend play Develop the Three Bears story from play	Three bowls, three chairs	I can use experiences from home in my imaginative play
Bike and cars	CLL/PD/PSE	To use pedal-powered toys with care, to share with my friends, to link letter sounds and initial letter sounds	Can you find the objects beginning with i/n/m/d and put them in the matching lettered hoop?	During literacy and AI play, ride to the hidden objects and place them in the corresponding lettered hoop	Objects beginning with i/n/m/d Hoops lettered with i/n/m/d Cars and bikes	I can pedal a bike/car I can match initial letter sounds with a grapheme
Seating	CLL/PSE	To handle books carefully; to understand	Can you read the story of the three	Using the Three Bears	Three Bears book	I can handle books carefully and retell a story

TABLE 10.7 (continued)

		the main characters and re-tell a storyline in a known book	bears to your friend?	story, read the story to their friends		
Grass	UW/CLL	To talk about change and explore the environment	Can you draw and write about the signs of autumn?	Use clipboard and paper to draw and write about autumn	Four clipboards with paper and pencils and crayons	I can make marks and talk about my drawing/writing I can explore the environment around me
Garden	UW	To explore the environment around them	Can you name the vegetables that are growing in the garden? What do they need?	Talk about the vegetables that are growing in the garden		I can talk and name the vegetables
Cottage	PSE	To play alongside my friends	Can you make up a story to play with your friends?			I can play with my friends
Balance beams	PD	To show increasing control using equipment for balancing	Can you balance along the beams?	During CI, can they walk along the beam?	Beam and stepping stones	I can walk along the balance beam
Chalk boards	CLL/PD	To ascribe meaning to my marks, to begin to form letters correctly	Can you write on the chalk board?	Begin to form letters on the chalkboard	Chalk, clipboards	I can begin to write I can link sounds and letters

11

Mathematical development

Introduction

This chapter aims to share with practitioners the requirements of the EYFS guidance for mathematical development and the recommendations of the *Independent Review of Mathematics Teaching in Early Years Settings and Primary Schools* (DCSF, 2008b), known as the Williams review. The revised ELGs are provided later in the chapter.

It is relevant to remind readers here that this area of learning is not now perceived to be a 'prime' area as it was in EYFS (DCSF, 2008f). Mathematical development is a 'specific' area of learning in which the prime areas are to be applied. The revised early learning goals are reduced and as this is not a prime area, learning and progress are not assessed until children are 3 years old. Table 11.1 indicates the revised ELGs for mathematical development.

Three key publications from the National Strategies provide advice on learning, teaching and resourcing. These are: *Mark Making Matters* (DCSF, 2008d); *Children Thinking Mathematically: PSRN Essential Knowledge for Early Years Practitioners* (DCSF, 2009b); and *Numbers and Patterns: Laying Foundations in Mathematics* (DCSF, 2009g). A relatively recent concept, that of mathematical graphics (Carruthers and Worthington, 2006), as highlighted in the Williams Review (DCSF, 2008b), is covered in some detail. As well as looking at research findings relating to mark making, more recent studies (McCrink and Wynn, 2004; Sarnecka and Carey, 2002; Thompson, 2008) linked to calculation and numerosity are outlined with implications for teaching and learning.

Examples of planning from a range of settings including nursery classes attached to primary schools, some with Reception-aged children working alongside the younger children, Children's Centres caring for children from 6 months to 5 and by child minders. There are excellent examples of cross-curricular mathematical learning adventures and experiences across a wide range of settings. The importance of the role of the home environment in developing early mathematical understanding is reinforced by research with babies.

Recent research

The findings of a longitudinal research study (Sylva *et al.*, 2004) emphasised the long-term benefits of pre-school mathematical learning. They found that children who received a rich

TABLE 11.1 Revised early learning goals for mathematical learning (DfE, 2011)

MATHEMATICS			
ASPECT	EMERGING	EXPECTED (ELGS)	EXCEEDING
Numbers	Children match and compare the numbers of objects in two groups of up to 5 objects, recognising when the sets contain the same number of objects. They show curiosity about numbers by offering comments or asking questions. They find one more or one less from a group of up to 5 objects.	Children use numbers up to 10 in order to do simple addition and subtraction to solve practical problems. They can find a total by counting on, and can calculate how many are left from a larger number by counting back.	Children estimate a number of objects and check quantities by counting up to 10. They solve practical problems that involve combining groups of 2, 5 or 10, or sharing into equal groups.
Shape, space and measures	Children identify and describe shapes in simple models, pictures and patterns. They can compare properties of objects which are 'big' or 'small', or their position in relation to one another such as whether one is 'behind' or 'next to' another.	Children use everyday language to describe and compare size, weight, capacity, time, position and distance. They know and talk about patterns and the properties of flat and solid shapes.	Children estimate, measure, weigh and compare and order objects and talk about properties, position and time.

variety of home learning before they started school achieved measurably better results in mathematical tests at age 10. There are similar findings too for children with special educational needs.

Sure Start evaluation reports (Melhuish *et al.*, 2008 and 2010) highlight the difficulties centres have in getting to those hard-to-reach families and help parents and their young children to access support.

There are key pointers from the Williams review which have influenced the guidance provided to practitioners. The review places a priority on providing practitioners with guidance on mathematical mark making, as well as the recommendation to include time and capacity in the early learning goals. Crucially, the review comments on mathematical pedagogy in the early years and especially mathematical learning through play activities. The review cites the findings of the *Effective Provision of Pre-School Education Project* Sylva, 2004) and fully endorses the findings that effective pedagogy includes interaction traditionally associated with the term 'teaching', the provision of instructive learning environments and 'sustained shared thinking' to extend children's learning (DCSF, 2008f: 33). Chapter 6 goes into more detail about 'sustained shared thinking', 'joint involvement episodes' and 'schemas', and the importance of the inter-relationship between the home environment and the early years setting, with the parent (or carer) seen as the most important educational influence in a young child's early development.

The key features of effective mathematical pedagogy are:

- skilled practitioners interacting with children in a rich, stimulating and interesting environment;
- practitioners' use of mathematical language in open-ended discussions (see Box 11.1)
- building on play;
- making the most of everyday routines and spontaneous learning to develop mathematical skills and concepts;
- practitioners supporting, challenging and extending children's thinking and learning through sustained shared thinking and the use of accurate mathematical language;
- giving children opportunities to record their understanding and thoughts in early mathematical mark making.

The final point is the key and an area in which, historically, practitioners have not encouraged children to mark make in a mathematical context. The ground-breaking practitioner research by Elizabeth Carruthers has led to new approaches in early years settings and the inclusion of mathematical learning in the DCSF publication on mark making mentioned earlier.

Mathematical mark making

Carruthers and Worthington (2003) coined the term 'mathematical mark making' or 'graphics' to describe children's own marks and representations that they use to explore and communicate their mathematical thinking. This is evident in the scribbles, drawings, writing and tally-type marks which lay the foundations for understanding mathematical symbols and later use of standard forms of written mathematics (Carruthers and Worthington, 2006). It is through mark making that a child is truly creative. A single drawing, for example, may help a child to develop concepts relating to problem-solving, reasoning and numeracy or knowledge and understanding of the world, as well as improving their physical coordination (DCFS, 2008e: 3). Mark making is thinking on paper (Carruthers and Worthington, 2006). It is useful for practitioners to recognise this in planning and assessing early mathematical skills. Table 11.6 shows the DM statements for *Numbers as Labels for Counting* including additional statements to remind you of the need to encourage mathematical graphics.

Counting and recognising numbers ('numerosity') and calculation

Historically, much research into mathematical learning is in the area of numeracy, with a marked change in the findings of researchers in recent years. There are aspects of counting that need consideration in early years settings. The traditional 1:1 matching activities of objects as a first step towards counting is less effective in helping children learn object to word. The 1:1 principle is more likely to be learned through 1:1 number word to object matching when modelling counting. So instead of matching sets of objects by 1:1 correspondence, more should be made of recognising equivalence, greater than and less than when comparing sets (Thompson, 2008).

It is further postulated by other researchers that there can be confusion for children in the cardinal principle, in that the count word assigned to the final object indicates the cardinality (how many) of the whole set. This can confuse children and it is suggested that there could be more attention in early years to the idea that number words and written symbols represent quantity rather than being a function of counting and the relationship between consecutive counting numbers as representing one more or one fewer (Sarnecka and Carey, 2008). When items were added to or removed from a set of hidden objects babies recognised this, thus indicating an innate understanding of calculation (McCrink and Wynn, 2004). Other researchers have noted that 3-year-olds understand such tasks with larger numbers, recognising which sets would have more when there are additions or removals of objects. Children demonstrate an innate understanding of addition and subtraction at the age of 3 which is not evident in children's emergent counting abilities.

What this research is showing is the value of informal mathematical learning in the early years which can embed understanding in a practical context that lays the foundation for later understanding in more formal school mathematics. Are there enough opportunities created for this informal understanding of calculation? Later problems can arise when children are lacking in confidence in counting forwards or backwards. This has implications for practices such as counting words forwards, backwards and from a given number rather than one, in order to aid subsequent calculation strategies. Once children start to count fluently they recognise small quantities without counting, this is known as subitising. Children continue to subitise when looking at dice and patterns. Box 11.1 lists some key vocabulary for this area of learning.

BOX 11.1 Key mathematical language in the early years

More/less
Bigger/smaller
Longer/taller/shorter
Higher/lower
Full/empty
Heavier/lighter
Wider/narrower
Faster/slower
Too much/too little
Same/different
Before/after
Balance
Both
Altogether
Add/take away
Share
In/out/on/under/beside
Above/between/behind/in front
Names of numbers, shapes, days, months, year, coins
Round/flat, straight/curvy/corner/line

Source: Dorsetforyou.com

Research basis for the review of the revised EYFS framework

There is an evidence base that states that achievement in mathematical activity on entry to school is a clear indicator of subsequent achievement in later years (Aubrey *et al.*, 2006) according to researchers in England, the United States and Finland. Young children are much more likely to develop an understanding in socially contextual activities than non-contextual mathematical contexts (Mix, 2002). Early years, it is suggested, could have a greater emphasis on number words as representing a quantity rather than a function of counting (Sarnecka and Carey, 2008). There needs to be lots of informal learning in the early years. For example, being able to count on and back is a first step to being able to solve addition or subtraction problems later. However, there is research reported by Aubrey (2003) of a European study which shows that beginning formal instruction at an early age does not improve subsequent mathematical achievement.

Planning for mathematical development

The *Enabling Environment* principle captures the essence of mathematical activities required for young children. Children should be encouraged to investigate things about shape, distances and measures in their outdoor environment, count along with their peers as they sing number rhymes and talk about what day it is, how many days there are in a week etc. Block play is an ideal environment to learn about shapes and sizes as long as there is a more knowledgeable persona able to provide the new words for emerging understandings. The tree house in an outdoor area of a nursery class attached to a primary school in the north east illustrated well how children develop their ability to count as they climbed the eight steps to the entrance and walked back down.

Children like to count from a fairly young age. They count their age in candles with enthusiasm, they count the objects on a page to match the number in counting books. They march, skip and step out as they count on the way. Table 10.4 (p. 163) has the potential for mathematical learning linked to the Goldilocks tale.

★ ★ ★

I understand the argument for the designation to 'specific' areas of learning, but to have a curriculum framework that only expects assessment of mathematical learning at the end of the Foundation Stage will certainly reduce the attention given to children's learning in this area. The research used to support this change is referred to earlier in the chapter. Practitioners will decide how this area will stand in the future.

This section shares examples of planning provided by practitioners in nursery schools, Reception classes and Children's Centres. The characteristic feature of these is the close references to the *Development Matters* statements on the plans to ensure the needs of all children are considered and information about learning contributes to assessment records. Case Study 11.1 describes how a Reception class teacher implements her planning. To assist practitioners there is a breakdown of the *Development Matters* statements for each strand of mathematical development – numbers and shape, space and measures. See Tables 11.2 and 11.3. In addition, the revised, differentiated ELGs for mathematical development are included in Table 11.1.

CASE STUDY 11.1 Montpelier Primary School Foundation Unit

A class of Reception children in their first term in school are all involved in activities covering all areas of learning, with a balance between child-initiated and adult-led activities with the balance towards child-initiated learning. Some children work with adults and others are engaged in a range of activities planned in response to the children's interests. These activities are all identified on the daily plan with all the ongoing (continuous) provision planned, with possible learning outcomes identified covering the 'knowledge and understanding of the world', 'creative development', 'physical development' and 'personal, social and emotional development' areas of learning. The planning for 'mathematical development' and 'communication and language' is in greater detail. An excellent feature of the planning is the section called 'What has happened before?' and 'Next steps planned' in response to children's interests (see Table 11.2).

TABLE 11.2 Lesson: mathematical development – input and activities

WHAT HAS HAPPENED BEFORE?	NEXT STEPS PLANNED
– Learning journeys – X and Y completed linking elephant puzzle, unsure in identifying some numerals and during observation did not know a strategy to use to find out. – Counting baseline observations indicate many children are finding it difficult to count given a small number of objects.	– Teach strategy so able to identify numerals independently. I can use a number line. – Teacher activity – counting a given number of objects found in the caves, encouraging 1:1 counting. Use the number line to find the correct number. Independent Bear Hunt in the classroom.

All children gather on the carpet for the short introductory session to listen to an explanation of how to use a number line given by a more able child, followed by an impressive program linked to the theme of bears around the classroom. Children are encouraged to move bears in and out of the virtual cave and count to three using the number line to support getting the three bears into the cave. The number of bears entering the cave increases to six based on the children's readiness to understand this. Following this the children go about their tasks, with the girls requesting ice cream play dough very happy to go off and make ice cream. A clay challenge is provided to make a construction to help the bear family cross the bridge. Small groups of children engage in the play-based numeracy activities to count the spiders in the cave and match the number correctly to the group. Another group are packing baskets for the picnic and use the number line to check counting numbers of strawberries, etc. The planning for this is featured in Box 11.2.

BOX 11.2 What we want children to learn: adult-directed teaching

MD
Says some number names in familiar contexts, Says number names in order.

Register, counting lunches, number of children in the class.
Red room

■ The bears have all left their caves and R has been asked to put them back. R does not know his numbers and he has the cave numbers to find out how many bears live there. Can we help? Model how to use a number line. Match number and count along the line to find out number. Count teddies 1:1.
I can use a number line.

Blue room Teacher group observations *MD 1.2/3 Counts up to 3/6 objects correctly. 40–60 mths. Select the correct numeral to represent 1 to 5 objects. Extend MD 1.6 Counts up to 10 objects correctly. Recognises numbers 1–9.*

- Children to count numbers of spiders found in the cave.
- We need to help the bear match the number to the spiders.
- Model using the number line to find the correct number. Find the correct number, then food for the bear. Can you pack a basket? Children to use number line to identify numeral and then count that number of strawberries for the bear.

Purple room *MD 1.2/3/6 Counts up to 10 objects correctly. Selects the correct number to represent objects.*

- Outside activity – Cave Street, caves labelled 0–9 and groups of bears, children to count the bears and place in the correct cave.

The planning illustrated is only for mathematical development and is based on PSRN in the previous EYFS framework, so there is the use of DM statements. Nonetheless, this is an excellent example of how differentiation to provide for the range of ability in the class is provided. Table 11.3 is an indication of the planning for all the other areas of learning.

TABLE 11.3 Opportunities for children to explore and apply

PSED	KUW	CD	PD
30–50 mths: form friendships with other children. Encouraged to help others with aprons and special helper role 30–50 mths: show increasing independence in selecting and carrying out activities. Children to select own trays.	30–50 mths: know how to operate simple equipment. Listening corner – the wheels on the bus. KUW 1.3 Construct in a purposeful way, using simple tools and techniques. Exploring collage and reclaimed materials. Children may choose to make a construction to help the family cross the mud or may choose to use materials for other purposes.	CD 1.1 Explore different media. CD 1.2 Create simple representations of events. Easel – paint and chalk.	40–60 mths: explore malleable materials. Handle tools and malleable materials basic control. Clay table, playdough – vanilla ice cream cones. Scoops, tubs. PD 1.3 Use a range of small and large equipment. Bikes, building box with bear hunt props.

Ongoing: KUW Sand tray – socks, scoops and spades. Water tray – playdough with stars, astronauts and play paper. Construction 1 – jungle duplo. Construction 2 – snowflakes. Construction 3 – 3D shapes.
CD: sing simple songs from memory – singing songs as a class, singing songs from memory. Nursery rhymes and number actions. Use a range of small and large equipment. Travel around, under, over and through balancing and climbing equipment – outside play equipment, bikes, mini assault course. Move with control and coordination: jigsaws, table top games, tracing, threading beads, morning cutting and handwriting activities. Work as part of a large group taking turns and sharing fairly: circle games, table top games, snack time.
Are developing an interest in books. Know that print conveys meaning. Book corners.

The features of excellence in this example are the ways in which prior learning is considered and the differentiation indicated in the planning by referring to the age bands. Learning mathematically is embedded into creative and imaginative experiences for the children. The rigour in planning provided a prop and guide for the practitioners. Table 11.4 is an example of a very familiar format for planning and usefully includes the key mathematical language targeted. The key vocabulary introduced is useful, but possibly the allocation of activities to particular staff would be a helpful addition.

TABLE 11.4 An example of short-term planning for numeracy

AREA OF LEARNING	LEARNING INTENTION	ACTIVITIES, INCLUDING CONTEXTS	LANGUAGE TO BE INTRODUCED	EVALUATION
MD	Say and use number names in order and in familiar contexts. Use language such as more or less than to compare basic quantities. Use everyday words to describe position.	Basic counting – songs, rhymes, stories with apparatus, etc. Using pegs, beads, etc., to introduce the vocabulary of addition and subtraction. Outdoor activity. Children to follow instructions to extend their positional vocabulary.	Number names, count and check. More, less, count, check, add, take away. In front, behind, next to, in between.	

The practitioner in a mixed Reception and Year 1 class adjusted her planned activities to accommodate the wide age range in her class by applying assessment for learning (AFL) principles – all, most and some outcomes (see Table 11.5, showing two days of a weekly plan). This example fits well with the revised EYFS framework ELGs which are phrased in the same fashion of all (emerging), most (expected) and some (exceeding [ELGs])

TABLE 11.5 Assessment for learning planning

	LEARNING INTENTION	DIFFERENTIATED ACTIVITIES
Mon	Counting in 1s, 2s and 10s. Number names, more, add, plus, count, check. Know by heart all the pairs of numbers with a total of 10/ find one more/one less than a number from 1–10.	Unifix making steps to show number bonds to 10. **All:** Count the bricks/pegs for each number 1–10. **Most:** Say a number one more than a given number from 1–10. **Some:** Find pairs of numbers which total 10.
Wed	Number rhymes and songs. Number names, next, after, next, steps, jumps. Know by heart all the pairs of numbers with a total of 10/find one more/one less than a number from 1–10.	Using a number line – start at a given number, how many jumps needed to make 10. **All:** Enjoy joining in with number rhymes and songs. **Most:** Recite the number names in order continue the count forward from a given number. **Some:** Describe and extend number sequences in ones.

The website dorsetforyou.com provides some straightforward, practical guidance for early years practitioners. There are some examples of blank planning sheets in Chapter 4 which provide guidance on what to add into the 'What happened before' and 'Next steps planned' boxes.

Implications of the revised EYFS framework

Mathematical development is now a 'specific' area of learning with only two aspects. These are:

1. numbers (formerly two aspects – numbers for labels and for counting and calculating);
2. shape, space and measures (see Table 11.1 for revised ELGs).

As said in other chapters, but worth reinforcing here, the 'specific' areas of learning provide a context for building on early development and learning beyond the prime areas. The specific areas are dependent on the 'prime' areas and are unlikely to be encountered in isolation from communication and language, personal, social and emotional development, and physical development, since the child is always experiencing the world through emotions, communication and physical and sensory involvement. Tickell states that the 'specific' areas of learning are influenced by the times we live in and societal beliefs about what it is important for children to learn. In terms of learning mathematically, it is crucial that there is the support of adults to help children to encounter and use the cultural 'tools for thinking' which include systems of symbolically representing concepts such as numbers. This is an interesting idea and one that is easily tested in almost any early years setting.

I feel I can claim with confidence that the incidents of mathematical learning were fairly scarce in many early years settings in the past precisely because practitioners shied away from presenting mathematical activities. The EYFS framework did rectify this in many respects. One can just be hopeful that this is not a 'baby thrown out with the bathwater' situation. Research mentioned earlier tends to support the notion of very young children engaging with mathematical thinking as they seek patterns and make connections. They recognise relationships through finding out about and working with numbers and counting according to the EYFS Framework (DCSF, 2008f).

Resourcing mathematical learning

Mathematical displays are crucial to provide children with clues and a reference point for their own conversations, but make sure the displays are either at child level or sufficiently bold to be visible from afar. Consider having number lines of different lengths to show children that numbers go beyond ten. A string or a pegged line of numbers to encourage children to discuss numbers is another useful resource. Number tracks made by children with chalk outside are also useful. Devise games that encourage children to record their score numerically in their play. Large floor jigsaws of interlocking numbers are a familiar sight, but remember to have an adult playing with children engaged in this activity to help provide children with the number names. Now that mathematical development is regarded as a 'specific' area of learning, do not regard this as a demotion of its status in the early years curriculum. What this does is to ensure that mathematical learning is embedded in practical activities that provide a much greater chance of ensuring the practical application of mathematical activities.

TABLE 11.6 *Development Matters* statements for numbers as labels and for counting

AGE BAND	DEVELOPMENT MATTERS (NUMBERS AS LABELS AND FOR COUNTING)
Birth–11 months	■ Respond to people and objects in their environment. ■ Notice changes in groupings of objects, images or sounds.
8–20 months	■ Develop and awareness of number rhymes through their enjoyment of action rhymes and songs that relate to their experience of numbers. ■ Enjoy finding their nose, eyes or tummy as part of naming games.
16–26 months	■ Say some counting words randomly. ■ Distinguish between quantities, recognising that a group of objects is more than one. ■ Gain an awareness of one-to-one correspondence through categorising belongings, starting with 'mine' or 'mummy's'.
22–36 months	■ Have some understanding of 1 and 2, especially when the number is important for them. ■ Create and experiment with symbols and marks. ■ Use some number language such as 'more' and 'lot'. ■ Recite some number names in sequence.
30–50 months	■ Use some number names and number language spontaneously. ■ Show curiosity about numbers by offering comments or asking questions. ■ Use some number names accurately in play. ■ Sometimes match number and quantity correctly. ■ Recognise groups with one, two or three objects. ■ *Continue to create and experiment with written numbers*.*
40–60 months	■ Recognise some numerals of personal significance. ■ Count up to three or four objects by saying one number name for each item. ■ Count up to six objects from a larger group. ■ Count actions or objects that cannot be moved. ■ Begin to count beyond 10. ■ Begin to represent numbers using fingers, marks on paper or pictures. ■ Select the correct numeral to represent 1 to 5, then one to 9 objects. ■ Recognise numerals 1 to 9. ■ Count an irregular arrangement of up to ten objects. ■ Estimate how many objects they can see and check by counting them. ■ Count aloud in ones, twos or tens. ■ Know that numbers identify how many objects there are in a set. ■ Use ordinal numbers in different contexts. ■ Match then compare the number of objects in two sets.
Early Learning Goals	■ **Say and use number names in order in familiar contexts.** ■ **Count reliably up to ten everyday objects.** ■ **Recognise numbers 1 to 9.** ■ **Use developing mathematical ideas and methods to solve practical problems.** ■ **Attempt to record using numbers*.**

* Added by author

Discussion points

1. Share the ways you introduce mathematical learning in your setting.

2. Discuss the implications of the research that suggests a number card should be used to represent a quantity or total of numbers and not as a means of counting. Carry out an activity with children to show how they show confusion about this.

12

Providing a context for learning

Understanding the world

Finding out and exploring is concerned with children's open- ended, hands-on experiences which result from innate curiosity and provide the raw sensory material from which children build concepts, test ideas and find out.

(DfE, 2011a: 89)

Introduction

The focus of this chapter is to show how an understanding of the world provides the context for learning about the environment, the people in it and the activities that children engage with in their explorations and investigations of what is intrinsically and extrinsically interesting about the world around them. Understanding of the world also provides a secure basis for learning concepts, attitudes and skills in all areas of learning. Explorations, investigations and enjoyment experienced by children in the outdoor environment are central to the chapter. Therefore, there are no apologies for having a strong focus on outdoor learning. Examples of case studies from practices observed in a variety of settings are included.

Ideas and the plans of practitioners provide a valuable context for children's learning. They are not to straightjacket children into doing things they do not wish to do. This is such an easy claim to make with regard to this area of learning which, along with physical and creative development, is at the heart of children's learning and enjoyment.

The EYFS review has created two tiers of learning goals with *Understanding the World* as one of the four 'specific' areas of learning. This is means that this is 'experience dependent' and is one of those areas where the social and cultural context of children's development is influential. Adults are likely to be the spur for triggering an understanding of the world, whether it is an understanding of peoples' work, places and experiences children undergo or a developing understanding of places and technology. Specific areas of learning are culturally determined whereas prime areas are universal to all societies.

Understanding the world

The revised area of learning has an increased emphasis on the 'concentric approach to learning' (DfE, 2011a: 104). This is a recognition that children learn first about themselves and the people and the things that are important to them. It then focuses on the inter-relationship of people and communities and of living and non-living things. There is an increase on the focus on children using a computer. This is a reflection on the growth of children's understanding of the application of many types of technological devices. I am sure practitioners will agree with this explanation and welcome the child-centred approach.

A child's first encounter with early years provision is often in the form of a record 'All about Me.' In a previous edition I wrote:

> The opportunity to apply communication, numeracy, literacy, observational and investigational skills to practical situations is at the heart of knowledge and understanding of the world ... this area of learning is fundamental to young children's learning.
>
> (Rodger, 2003: 152)

The activities and experiences in which children take part ensure they deepen their understanding about themselves, their friends and families. For example, watching the traffic passing and counting the lorries rumbling past provides a context for the application of basic skills in a meaningful way. The activity is about recording how many vehicles they see. It is also about observing similarities and differences between different types of vehicles. That such activities like counting the bulbs as they are planted is described as geography or mathematics, or personal and social development is largely irrelevant. The subject or area of learning label is for the adults to know about for their assessment and record keeping and to inform their planning. Children benefit from the richness and first-hand nature of a range of experiences. They use all their senses to hear the traffic, to see the different vehicles, to record the number seen or simply to tell someone about it. The experience is everyday within the child's understanding and importantly will have some meaning for that child, who will begin to identify with the world around him/her.

CASE STUDY 12.1 How many areas of learning?

A group of Reception class boys are playing with some miniature animals in the 'rainforest area' of the classroom. They are in the second term of their time in this class and have attended part-time in the school nursery.

DAMIEN: Look at mine hanging off (about the monkey).
PAUL: Mine's hanging.
PAUL: Right! Crocodiles can't fly.
JOHN: Crocodiles can't fly. They can't jump.
DAMIEN: Jaguars can't climb.
JOHN: Snakes can slither. You don't know where my monkey is?
DAMIEN: Sss, Sss, Sss.
PAUL: Two jaguars come out of the forest.
DAMIEN: We haven't got five.

All the boys count the animals together: One, two, three, four, five, six, seven, eight.

JOHN: There are seven (There are seven).
PAUL: I've got three (He has).
JOHN: Where does the monkey live?
DAMIEN: On top of the trees.
JOHN: Which live on the bottom?
PAUL: I know, the spiders.

The boys continue with their play, describing to other children who come to the table the movements of each of the animals. The activity lasts about 15 minutes.

Case Study 12.1 exemplifies the range of learning taking place in an activity that was planned to help the children learn what animals can do and how they live, and did not include any reference to mathematics. Nonetheless, the boys accurately applied their numeracy knowledge, demonstrating the case for this as a 'specific' area of learning.

The case study highlights the key importance of observational assessments of self-initiated activities to be able to accurately assess embedded learning.

A key principle of EYFS, that 'the environment plays a key role in supporting and extending children's development and learning', is fundamental to this area of learning. The importance of the outdoor environment is reiterated in the description of the learning environment necessary for children:

- Being outdoors has a positive impact on children's sense of well-being and helps all aspects of children's development.
- Being outdoors offers opportunities for doing things in different ways and on different scales than when indoors.
- It gives children first-hand contact with weather, seasons and the natural world, and the opportunity to be active and exuberant.

(DCSF, 2008f)

Therefore, it is well worth thinking of this area of learning holistically. This is demonstrated admirably in Case Study 12.2 about Ben, a 3-year-old with special educational needs in a north east nursery school. It is clear from all the examples of planning seen that this is indeed how practitioners are planning for *Understanding of the World*. By providing a context to enable children to find out about themselves, where they live, what people around them do and how they make sense of the environment, you are helping children to make sense of the world. You are recognising that children learn most effectively when they are actively involved and interested.

The three key learning characteristics that are assessed by practitioners provide an excellent prompt as to what kinds of activities and experiences should be available to young children. To remind you these are *playing and exploring, active learning* and *creating and thinking critically*. However, what is critical as children attend nursery is the enrichment that needs to be provided to extend learning and maintain children's interest. I recently observed children in a nursery unit learning about living outdoors – in tents, a tree house and gazebo. It was the tents that generated all the interest because, once inside, they provided privacy and security for the children.

There are revised early learning goals. See Table 12.1 for the differentiated goals expected to be achieved by the end of the Foundation Stage.

CASE STUDY 12.2 Outdoor learning

I am reminded as I begin to write this chapter of Ben (6 years old) at the end of his nursery experience. Fortunately for him his parents want him to go to school in the area. There is no suitable school catering for his special needs and so he stays in the nursery full-time until a suitable school can be found. He has his own teacher for two hours every day. His parents want him to go to the school his brothers attend, across the road from the nursery. The head of the school is not so sure. Ben remains in the nursery.

Ben is a paraplegic. He has profound hearing loss and is partially sighted. His communication skills are minimal. He communicates via signing (a little) and expresses delight by hugging anyone around. He has just spent half an hour of his daily two hours allocation of a special educational needs support teacher in the quiet room, where they work through a programme of literacy and numeracy activities recommended by the support service. He can count to five now. The support teacher is a very experienced former nursery teacher. She is making little headway with Ben as she struggles to sustain his attention on the picture book they are sharing.

Ben and she go outside and head for the climbing platform in the middle of the field near the railings which separate the nursery field from the main road. She cajoles him to climb to the centre where they can easily see both main roads coming to a junction. Once again she gets out the picture book and encourages Ben to point to the lorry and say 'l-o-r-r-y'. Squirming and wriggling, Ben's attention wanders. Suddenly, rumbling round the corner comes a builder's lorry. Pointing excitedly Ben cries out, 'LORRY!' and hugs his teacher, who smiles and glows at this tremendous achievement.

TABLE 12.1 Revised early learning goals for understanding the world

UNDERSTANDING THE WORLD			
ASPECT	EMERGING	EXPECTED (ELGS)	EXCEEDING
People and communities	Children can recognise some special times in their lives and the lives of others. They know some of the things that make them unique, and can talk about some of the ways they are similar to, or different from their friends or family.	Children talk about past and present events in their own lives and in those of family members. They know that other children don't always enjoy the same things and are sensitive to this. They know about similarities and differences between themselves and others and amongst families, communities and traditions.	Children know the difference between past and present events in their own lives and some reasons why people's lives were different in the past. They know that other children have different likes and dislikes and that they may be good at different things. They understand that different people have different beliefs, attitudes, customs and traditions and why it is important to treat them with respect.
The world	Children show an interest in aspects of their familiar world such as the place where they live or the environment. They	Children know about similarities and differences in relation to places, objects, materials and living things. They	Children know that the environment and living things are influenced by human activity. They can describe some actions

TABLE 12.1 (continued)

ASPECT	EMERGING	EXPECTED (ELGS)	EXCEEDING
	are curious and interested in why things happen and how things work. They can talk about some of the things they have observed such as plants, animals, natural and found objects.	can talk about features of their own immediate environment and how environments might vary from one another. They can make observations of animals and plants and explain why some things occur, and talk about changes, including simple experiments.	which people in their own community do that help to maintain the area they live in. They know the properties of some materials and can suggest some of the purposes they are used for. They are familiar with basic scientific concepts such as floating, sinking experimentation.
Technology	Children show an interest in technological toys with knobs or pulleys, or real objects such as cameras or mobile phones. They show skill in making toys work by pressing parts or lifting flaps to achieve effects such as sound, movement or new images.	Children recognise that a range of technology is used in places such as homes and schools. They select and use technology for particular purposes.	Children find out about and use a range of everyday technology. They select appropriate applications that support an identified need – for example in deciding how best to make a record of a special event in their lives, such as a journey on a train or steam train.

The Reggio Emilia approach

To those of you who are unfamiliar with the Reggio system (Edwards and Redfern, 1998) I am including a very short review of the basic tenets of the approach to early childhood education implemented in a unique collection of schools for young children in northern Italy. It is appropriate to include it in this chapter because of the importance attached to the outdoor environment. Essentially, the Reggio approach's principal educational aim involves children in long-term projects to develop their intellect through a systematic focus on symbolic representation.

> Young children are encouraged to explore their environment and express themselves through all of their available 'expressive, communicative, and cognitive languages', whether they be words, movement, drawing, painting, building, sculpture, shadow play, collage, dramatic play, or music, to name a few.
>
> (Edwards *et al.*, 1998: 7)

Several examples of such projects are included in the book and are relevant to this chapter in that they take the topic-based approach to early learning to be the centre of all learning. For instance, one example describes 4- and 5-year-old children carrying out a study of a neighbourhood supermarket. The core of the programme, unlike the pre-planned experiences we offer in the UK, is one of problem-solving and problem-setting. Rules and routines are less important than the creation of the effective adult-child relationship. Recording of the activities and representations created by the children form the basis of the *documentation* unlike our curriculum planning, which generally includes information about the way in which we intend children to reach particular goals.

I have some reservations about the fervour with which the Reggio Emilia approach is capturing the hearts of early years educators the world over. Haven't we in the UK been tinkering with such an approach to the early years curriculum since the days of Plowden?

The children are seen as active participants in learning in the Reggio Emilia approach. They initiate and interact with their environment. The environment is the third educator after the teacher and the parent. Indoor areas have lots of paint, drawing materials and clay to encourage children to represent their concepts as they learn in a hands-on way. The involvement of parents is the key as they come to understand through visits, photographs and workshops how their children are learning. The role of the teacher as partner, nurturer and guide in Reggio Emilia has the following features:

- Promoting children's learning in cognitive, social, physical and affective domains.
- Managing the classroom.
- Preparing the environment.
- Providing nurturance and guidance.
- Communicating with important constituencies (parents and colleagues).
- Seeking professional growth.

(Edwards, 1998: 181)

In addition, there are two other components that are seen as essential: engaging in political activism to defend the cause of public activism, and conducting systematic research on daily classroom work for the purposes of curriculum planning, teacher development and professional dissemination.

It has been said that the teacher in Reggio Emilia should work to promote the intellectual life of children by listening, recording and documenting what is observed and then using it a as a basis of decision-making. Listening is defined as seeking to follow and enter into the active learning that is taking place. The application of Vygotskian theory is very evident in this situation. Indeed, the *spiralling,* that is the reciprocal connections between educators, children and parents, is crucial to learning. There are continual cycles of revisiting and re-representation. The Reggio teacher assesses what is happening with children within a cycle of days. Such a spiralling way of thinking is characteristic of Reggio educators. This approach is gaining ground in the England and is typified by the openness that characterises learning in some English settings where skilled staff engage with children and extend their learning.

Children learn to understand the world through their involvement with it. This may be through visiting different parts of it, learning about the environment outside and through their lives as members of a family. This then gives practitioners an idea of the agenda needed to ensure that children engage with planned activities covering this area of learning. However, the revised EYFS curriculum has removed this area of learning to be a 'specific' area in which the 'prime' skills are applied. I am aware that this chapter began with an assertion that this area of learning most usefully provides a context in which to apply higher order skills and concepts that in the current climate are personal social and emotional development, communication and language and physical development. So there is to be a change of emphasis or one could say priorities, but I am very optimistic that this area of learning will continue to provide an excellent context for the prime areas. The investigative and exploratory skills that characterise the *Development Matters* statements for knowledge and understanding of the world are firmly part of children's learning characteristics that are assessed along with progress towards the early learning goals.

Planning for understanding the world

Unusually in a book about planning in the early years, I am suggesting in this chapter that planning for understanding the world is not something that needs to be done as a discrete area of learning. The essence of the chapter is that this area of learning provides the context in which the 'prime areas' are developed. Therefore, included in this section are examples of plans that include other areas of learning alongside understanding the world.

As this will be a 'specific' area of learning, there is no requirement to assess progress towards the ELG for children in preschool provision. It is likely that in their play the under-3s will be demonstrating many of the understanding the world skills and certainly the learning characteristics, such as active learning, playing and exploring and creating and thinking critically. Examples of Tables provided for other areas of learning include elements of understanding of the world.

There are blank planning formats which can be used as a basis for your own plans (Table 12.3). The planning example used in the next chapter is a starting point for continuous provision planning.

CASE STUDY 12.3 Mini-beast hunt

Children have been finding out about mini-beasts (see Table 12.2 for the medium-term plan). They have read stories, such as *The Very Hungry Caterpillar* (Carle, 1995) and *The Bad-Tempered Ladybird* (Carle, 1985). They know that insects are found outside and they sometimes fly. A small group of children armed with information books, posters and magnifying lenses set off to gather small creatures and hopefully to find ladybirds and caterpillars. Very carefully their findings are collected in transparent containers and taken back to the classroom for further observation. Great care and concern is shown by the teacher and the children as they allow the ladybirds to rest on their hands while they count their spots and number of legs, talk about the colour of their bodies and their relative size compared to a butterfly which was found outside earlier in the day. The children are engrossed. They are using and acquiring a range of scientific and language skills initially. The teacher does not want to lose the momentum of their interest and enthusiasm so she quickly provides each child with a selection of coloured play dough to make their version of the ladybird.

TABLE 12.2 Medium-term planning for the mini-beast hunt

TOPIC: MINI-BEASTS	AREA OF LEARNING: CLL AND UW LEARNING CHARACTERISTICS: ALL	TERM: SUMMER 2/2
LEARNING INTENTIONS – LINK TO CLL, UW, MD, PSED, PD	AREAS/RESOURCES, INSIDE/OUT, SELF-INITIATED	ADULT-DIRECTED ACTIVITIES
Children know the similarities and differences between the creatures (legs, size, colour, wings) link to MD.	Collection of mini-beasts.	Children encouraged to sing 'We're all going on an insect hunt' with NN.
Children observe the mini-beasts, talk about what they see.	Children use the magnifiers and posters correctly and observe the insects.	CT asks children to describe the insects they see (assess).
Some children talk about the insects' habitat.	Children go the library to get information books.	Teacher encourages talk about insect similarities and differences (assess).
Some children use reference book to identify insects.	Children engage in role play outside to make an insect hide, home, as they decide.	Children make a ladybird from playdough with help.
Children use the magnifiers with skill.	Children draw and paint their insects from observation and with support.	Children draw and label with help.
Children listen to *The Hungry Caterpillar* and *The Bad-Tempered Ladybird* stories.		Stories in the book corner linked to activity.
Children draw an insect and some add a caption.		Movement linked to how the insects move on outside grassy area.
Children take turns and share the tools.		Talk about caring for creatures.

TABLE 12.3 Long-term planning spaces for play

LONG-TERM KEY LEARNING OPPORTUNITIES				
PSED	CL	PD	MD	UW
			Lit (reading and writing)	EA&D
PERMANENT RESOURCES	POSSIBLE EXPERIENCES	ADULT'S ROLE AND LINK TO EYFS		
		Unique child	Positive relationships	
		Enabling environments	Learning and development	

CHAPTER

13

Expressive arts
and design

Having their own ideas covers the critical area of creativity – of generating new ideas and approaches in all areas of endeavour. Being inventive allows children to find new problems as they seek challenges, and to explore ways of solving these.

(DfE, 2011a: 90)

Introduction

At the time of writing this chapter the recommendations of the EYFS review are in the consultation stage. Expressive arts and design is to be one of the 'specific' areas of learning in which the prime skills are applied. The new area of learning builds on the former creative development. Although it appears that the number of aspects has been reduced this is not the case. The focus is much more clearly on *children's experience* of exploring and learning about creative and artistic expression in parallel with their desire to express and represent their learning in diverse ways. The intention is to emphasise the children's aesthetic experiences, which are defined as, 'belonging to the appreciation of the beautiful'. Is this really how one would define 'aesthetic experiences' for young children? One can look to a seminal educational publication by HMI in 1989, which describes aesthetic and creative areas of learning as 'central to learning' (HMI, 1989: 29).

Table 13.1 identifies the proposed early learning goals for expressive arts and design. The issue for practitioners is to allow the children to respond as they see fit to the range of experiences provided for them. The didactic model of learning, in which children are told exactly what to do, is not appropriate for any area of learning, but particularly for this one. It is about eliciting children's thoughts and ideas. The weekly planning example in Table 13.2 suggests that children are to be given an adult-prepared outline of a leaf and asked to add sticky pieces of paper to it. What do children understand about autumn? Can they draw their own leaf based on observations of leaves? There is much scope to learn more than this.

Research findings

Interestingly, it is appearing that the research review in previous editions of this book are more in accord with the way in which the curriculum is developing as a result of the recent report

TABLE 13.1 Expressive arts and design area of learning

EXPRESSIVE ARTS AND DESIGN			
ASPECT	EMERGING	EXPECTED (ELGS)	EXCEEDING
Exploring and using media and materials	Children imitate and create movement in response to music, join in with dancing games and sing a few familiar songs. They explore and differentiate between colours, begin to describe the texture of things, and create 3D structures.	Children sing songs, make music and dance with ways of changing them. They use and explore a variety of materials, experimenting with colour, design, texture, shape and form.	Children develop their own ideas through selecting and using materials and working in processes that interest them. Through their explorations they find out and make decisions about how media and materials can be combined and changed.
Being imaginative	Create simple representations of events, people and objects. They sing to themselves, explore sounds, and tap out simple, repeated rhythms. They engage in imaginative play and role play based on their experiences.	Children use what they have learned about media and materials in purposeful and original ways. They represent their own ideas, thoughts and feelings through art and design, music, dance, role play and stories.	Children talk about the ideas and processes which have led them to make music, designs, images or products. They can talk about features of their own and others' work, recognising the differences between them and the strengths of each.

by Clare Tickell (DfE, 2011a). The influence of Vygotsky (1978) and Athey (1990) reinforce the idea that the basic skills of getting on with each other and learning to talk and listen can be very effectively provided within many contexts, in this case expressive arts and design. It is widely acknowledged that children who function well creatively are those who discuss what they are doing.

An area that is absent in this area of learning is any mention of the senses, although it is mentioned in other areas. It is important to recognise the importance of sensory development. This is a particularly crucial aspect of the development of very young children. Children use and develop their senses as they interact with the environment. They look and listen and learn to respond to familiar sounds and smells as they grow and develop. Brierley (1987: 76) said that 'building up knowledge of the world through our senses by trial and error is the basis of all later intellectual activity'.

Vygotsky (1978) reinforces the crucial role of imagination in the development of the human mind and in the case of very young children, that 'pretend play' is a leading factor in development. Role play is a key area to enable children to escape into fantasy, but importantly to allow children to understand the perspective of others (Harris, 2000: 36). It is from the age of 2 that children begin to construct events that are not in the real world. Other research into comparing children drawing at home and in a Children's Centre reveals how parents seem to be much more tuned into their children's needs than the setting practitioners. A link between a creative role-play activity such as 'Super Heroes' can lead to imaginative drawings of a higher quality

TABLE 13.2 Example of adult-directed planning for creative development from a weekly plan

AREA	AREA OF LEARNING	LEARNING INTENTION	ACTIVITY/KEY QUESTIONS	NO. OF CHILDREN AND RESOURCES	GROUPS	DIFFERENTIATION/SEND
Cut and stick	CD PD CLL	To make collages and to use scissors with increasing control and safety	Can you make a collage of an autumn leaf? (check meaning of collage with children and explain) Can you use the scissors to cut the paper?	2 Leaf outlines!! coloured paper, scissors and glue	Friendship AI/CI	Support children who need help with scissors and glue spreaders
Paint	CD PD MD	To make paintings: to choose and mix colours for a purpose, to use language tall and short as they paint	Can you paint a picture of a tall object? Can you paint a picture of a short object?	4 Powder paint, water, brushes, thin brushes, sponges of different lengths	Friendship CI	Encourage children to mix paint independently Discuss the tall and short objects Use the visual reminder in the art area
Role play	CD CLL	To engage in imaginative play; to introduce a storyline into their play; to begin to write for a purpose	Can you play in the baby hospital? Can you write in the appointment book? Can you use the telephone as you play?	4 Baby clothes, nurse, doctor outfits, appointment books, pencils and telephone	Friendship CI/AI	Model correct responses in the role play Encourage use of correct vocabulary AI Adult initiated CI Child initiated

compared to a direct instruction to draw an Easter egg, for example, or cut out a template of a leaf. The link between a child's imaginative processes and the task needs to be recognised and encouraged. This may have implications for provision. As practitioners, is enough time provided to allow children to share their drawings with each other and to discuss their 'stories'?

Music and dance are subsumed into being imaginative. Again, this is because this is all central to the child's aesthetic experiences. Infants love to play with sound. Listening to nursery rhymes develops children's musicality and their language and literacy skills. The opportunities for music for the under-3s should enable children to begin to interact with others (Evangelou *et al.*, 2008). The way provision is organised and the fluidity of what is expected is discussed with practitioners so that children's own ideas and experiences are fostered and developed. Does this have implications for planning and learning? What should the priorities be? The next section draws on the (DCSF, 2008f) for some answers.

Learning and development

The principles which guide the work of all early years practitioners are grouped into four themes. The four guiding themes work together to underpin effective practice. They put the legal requirements into context, and describe how practitioners should support the development, learning and care of young children. The review of EYFS recommends that the themes and principles should stay as they are. The *Learning and Development* and *Enabling Environments* principles are central to expressive art and design. The suggested contexts for learning provide a very clear steer for planning and provision in early years settings:

Contexts for learning

- Children need plenty of space and time to play, both indoors and outdoors.
- Children who are allowed to play with resources and equipment before using them to solve a problem are more likely to solve the problem successfully.
- Making dens and dressing-up are an integral part of children's play and don't require expensive resources.
- Role-play areas allow children to take on and rehearse new and familiar roles.

(DCSF, 2008f)

Learning through experience

- Children have to play physically and emotionally.
- Children play alone or with others.
- In their play children use the experiences they have and extend them to build up ideas, concepts and skills.
- While playing, children can express fears and re-live anxious experiences. They can try things out, solve problems and be creative and can take risks and use trial and error to find things out.

(DCSF, 2008f)

Case Study 13.1 shows how a 3-year-old responds to investigating outside on a frosty morning.

CASE STUDY 13.1 A frosty morning

Following a frosty day when puddles froze and children explored the ice and watched it melt in the sunshine, the practitioner set out some trays of ice in various stages of melting. Savita, aged 3, held an ice cube. The practitioner observing her said in Gujurati: 'Look! It is melting because your hands are warm.' She then repeated the word 'melting' in English and Savita too used this word to show her developing competence in learning English.

Effective planning and assessment

There is the expectation that all early years practitioners will need to understand the different ways in which children learn in order to provide effective support. Tickell recognises that this is implicit in the previous EYFS (DCSF, 2008f) (see earlier in this chapter); she feels that the EYFS would be a better product if the following were made explicit as the three characteristics of effective teaching. These characteristics that are now embodied in all learning are very central to the expressive arts and design:

1. playing and exploring;
2. active learning;
3. creating and thinking critically.

In order to show that the implications for practice in early years are changed very little, settings do not need to change their planning greatly in order to meet changes to the curriculum. The reality is that planning for expressive arts and design will show as part of cross-curricular planning on medium-term plans, with specific plans for adult-led learning activities where particular skills are developed. However, the skills are just as likely to be language and communication skills or indeed any of the 'prime' areas of learning. Matthews' (1994) view of the development of children's drawing from birth to 6 years is shown in Table 13.3. The question for practitioners is whether they go for the planning models included in Figure 13.1 and Table 13.2 or create the opportunities for children to reach the emerging, expected or exceeding steps towards the ELGs in their investigations and experiences gained from self-initiated activities. Tickell uses the term 'playful teaching' and stresses that 'skilled practitioners should spend most of their time interacting directly with children to guide their learning' (DfE, 2011a: 30).

The key to assessing development must be the critical observations of children's learning in whatever situation these activities occur. Assessment of learning could embrace many areas – linked to mark making, for example. The assessment provides a scaffold for the planning of the next steps for learning, bearing in mind the priority to the 'prime' areas. Practitioners could have the dilemma of knowing what this activity is from a planning point of view. The all-embracing area of learning 'exploring and using media and material' and 'being imaginative' becomes exactly what the new EYFS expects. Table 13.6 is an example of an assessment record that will contribute to children's learning journeys. One of these could very easily be completed for a separate area of learning if a practitioner was observing a small group of children engages in a creative or imaginative activity such as role play, baking or collage. The planning examples shown are worthy of discussion (see

TABLE 13.3 Magic planning based on children's ideas

	MONDAY	TUESDAY	WEDNESDAY	THURSDAY	FRIDAY
Tinkering table (problem solving)	Cauldron counting (adding 1 more to 5) E-interest in making spells	As Monday – continued interest/planned observation opportunity	Sorting jewels/buttons according to more than one criteria E-interest in Winnie's jewels	CP (consolidation time)	Cauldron counting (adding 1 more to 10) E-interest in making spells
Role play (Winnie's house)	Establish roles of characters from *Winnie the Witch* (focus text)	As Monday – adults to support play with S&L focus (turn taking/using magic vocabulary)	As Monday – adults to support play with S&L focus (turn taking/using magic vocabulary)	CP (consolidation time)	CP (consolidation time)
Cosy story area	Selection of books about magic E-interest in witches and magicians	Selection of books about magic E-interest in *Room on the Broom*	Retelling *Room on the Broom* using story sack and props (adult focus)	CP (consolidation time)	CP (consolidation time)
ICT/smart board	Cbeebies site E-interest in *Grandpa in My Pocket* so focus to be on this/navigation skills	Cbeebies site E-interest in *Grandpa in My Pocket* so focus to be on this/navigation skills	Magic paintings on smart notebook – selecting tools to use (stars, rainbows, etc.) E-interest in *Magic Finger*	Magic paintings on smart notebook – selecting tools to use (stars, rainbows, etc.)	CP (consolidation time)
Construction/ small world (carpet)	Black fabric, mini-beasts, cauldron to make spells E-interest in spell-making	Black fabric, mini-beasts, cauldron to make spells E-interest in spell-making	CP (consolidation time)	CP (consolidation time)	CP (consolidation time)
Creative area (messy table)	Glitter in the paint – thin brushes E-interest in sparkle	Glitter in the paint – thin brushes E-interest in sparkle	CP (consolidation time)	CP (consolidation time)	CP (consolidation time)
Workshop (consolidation time)	CP	CP (consolidation time)	Making witches hats E-interest *Winnie the Witch*	CP (consolidation time)	CP (consolidation time)

TABLE 13.3 (continued)

Sand	CP (consolidation time)	Wet sand E-interest in shape moulds	Wet sand E-interest in shape moulds	Wet sand E-interest in shape moulds	CP (consolidation time)
Role play (magic carpet)	Adult focus – model going on a magic carpet ride	Adult focus – model going on a magic carpet ride	CP (consolidation time)	CP (consolidation time)	CP (consolidation time)
Mark making area	CP (consolidation time)	Writing spells (rhyming focus)	Writing spells (rhyming focus)	CP (consolidation time)	CP (consolidation time)
Investigation station	Torches, magic set (rings, pots and balls, cards) E-interest in magic shows	Torches, magic set (rings, pots and balls, cards) E-interest in magic shows	Torches, magic set (rings, pots and balls, cards) E-interest in magic shows	CP (consolidation time)	CP (consolidation time)
Busy fingers	Black sparkly play dough CP	CP (consolidation time)	CP (consolidation time)	CP (consolidation time)	CP (consolidation time)
Water	Spell making – glitter, jewels, green colouring	Spell making – glitter, jewels, green colouring	Spell making – glitter, jewels, green colouring	CP (consolidation time)	CP (consolidation time)
Outdoor area	Fairy ring, campfire, tyre play, witch den making, making potions CP	Fairy ring, campfire, witch den making, making potions CP	Fairy ring, campfire, tyre play, witch den making, making potions CP	Fairy ring, campfire, tyre play, witch den making, making potions CP	Fairy ring, campfire, tyre play, witch den making, making potions CP

Creative	Autumn 2 Animals
1. Explores different media and responds to a variety of sensory experiences. Engages in representational play.	
2. Creates simple representation of events, people and objects and engages in music making. 3. Tries to capture experiences using a variety of different media. 4. Sings simple songs form memory. 5. Explores, colour, texture, shape and space in two and three dimensions.	
6. Recognises and explores how sound can be changed. Recognises repeated sounds and sound patterns and matches music to movement. 7. Uses imagination in art and design, music, dance, imaginative and role play and stories. 8. Responds in variety of ways to what s/he sees, hears, smells, touches and feels. 9. Expresses feelings and preferences in response to art work, drama and music and makes some comparisons/links between pieces.	

Nursery objectives

Nursery and reception objectives

FIGURE 13.1 Medium-term plan for creative development in a nursery unit

question below) because the activity column tends to list a series of closed questions that could inhibit creativity. It will be useful for practitioners to debate how to make sure that questioning gives a child a chance to explain their understanding before a 'yes' or 'no' answer is given.

The planning example in Table 13.4 shows how child-initiated and continuous provision were planned to build on the enthusiasm and interests of the children in a nursery class. In this example, children began to be excited and interested in magic incidents after hearing the story *Room on the Broom* (Donaldson, 2002). A range of story books continued to capture the children's enthusiasm and delight, typically *Winnie's Flying Carpet* (Thomas, 2009) and other Winnie stories captured the children's creativity and scope to develop imaginative activities

Any child's first steps into the education system has the potential to be a traumatic experience if handled incorrectly. Children today are fortunate in the sensitivity of practitioners to ensure the smooth transition between home and school. In many cases this is almost seamless because parents are so welcomed into settings, practitioners are known to children because of their home visits and the staggered entry period ensures a gradual settling in.

TABLE 13.4 The development of children's drawing (Matthews, 1994)

AGE BAND	FEATURES OF CHILDREN'S DRAWING
Birth–1 year	■ Imitate actions and movement using their whole body ■ Are aware of patterns which have strong contrasts and resemble the human face ■ Make intentional marks, for example, with food using finger and hand ■ Are aware that movements result in a mark
1–2 years	■ Make a variety of marks, sometimes described as scribbling ■ Are aware that that different movements make different marks ■ Grip pen or crayon using palm of hand ■ Make marks that record and represent the movement of their bodies and other objects ■ Draw overlapping and layered marks
2–3 years	■ Use pincer grip to hold graphic materials ■ Produce continuous line and closed shape to represent inside and outside ■ Combine lines and shapes ■ Produce separate but linked shapes
3–4 years	■ Name marks, and symbolic representation is emerging ■ Experiment with the variety of marks that can be made by different graphic materials, tools and surfaces ■ Unaided, use a circle plus lines to represent a person, often referred to as a 'tadpole person' ■ Start to produce visual narratives
4–5 years	■ Are able to produce a range of shapes and sometimes combine them, for example to produce a sun ■ Draw shapes and figures that appear to float in space on the page ■ Draw figures which include more details, such as arms, legs, hands, fingers, eyebrows ■ Subdivide space on page to show higher and lower
At 6 years	■ Draw figures that are grounded and use lines for ground and the sky ■ Display depth by making figures in the distance smaller to indicate further away ■ Include more details in their drawings, for example, windows, doors and chimneys on buildings ■ Drawings have more narrative features, for example, may feature a number of episodes of the same story

I am sure many of you can recall the trauma associated with those first steps into the alien environment of a Reception class, as can I. The following anonymous poem captures the frustration felt by a boy trying to explore his feelings through drawing because he did not have the words to express them any other way. There are other ways to interpret this, but what it illustrates so well is the power of creativity and, unfortunately in this poet's case, the way creativity was stifled. The transition from home to nursery was a memorable experience for the child in this poem that has lasted for many years. I am very optimistic that this is an example of what happened in the past and, hopefully, not a taste of the future.

About School – Anonymous

He always
He always wanted to explain things, but no one cared,
So he drew.

Sometimes he would just draw and it wasn't anything.
He wanted to carve it in stone or write it in the sky.
He would lie out on the grass and look up in the sky and it would
be only the sky and things inside him that needed saying.

And it was after that he drew the picture,
It was a beautiful picture. He kept it under his pillow and would
let no one see it.
And he would look at it every night and think about it.
And when it was dark and his eyes were closed, he could see it still.
And it was all of him and he loved it.

When he started school he brought it with him,
Not to show anyone, but just to have with him like a friend.

It was funny about school.
He sat in a square brown room, like all the other rooms,
And it was tight and close, and stiff.

He hated to hold the pencil and chalk, with his arm stiff and
his feet flat on the floor, stiff, with the teacher watching
and watching.

The teacher came and spoke to him.
She told him to wear a tie like all the other boys,
he said he didn't like them and she said it didn't matter.
After that he drew. And he drew all yellow and it was the way
he felt about the morning. And it was beautiful.

The teacher came and smiled at him. 'What's this?' she said.
'Why don't you draw something like Ken's drawing?
Isn't it beautiful?'

After that his mother bought him a tie and he always drew
airplanes and rocket-ships like everyone else.
And he threw the old picture away.
And when he lay all alone looking at the sky, it was big and blue,
and all of everything, but he wasn't anymore.

He was square and brown inside and his hands were stiff.
And he was like everyone else. All the things inside him that
needed saying didn't need it anymore.

It had stopped pushing. It was crushed.
Stiff.
Like everything else.

TABLE 13.5 Medium-term planning (Islington LA)

EYFS medium-term planning for fictional playgroup/nursery
Spring term – second half /related theme 'Transport'

MAIN FOCUS: TRANSPORT	ASSESSMENT:	ENVIRONMENT AND RESOURCES:
DISPLAYS:		
Photo display of different types of transport in local area Gather photos/artefacts of transport from different countries Table top displays for children – rotate weekly small-world train set/airport/mobilo to make vehicles	Narrative observation and discussion with parents and child to be completed for all children this half-term Set timetable for each child to be allocated as 'focus child' this half term and ensure their interests are linked to weekly planning	Walk in the local area – take photos of different types of transport seen Take children on visit to local train station Trip to local park
Personal, Social and Emotional Continue to develop profile books and encourage children to share these with their friends during small group time sessions Developing children's motivation to learn by ensuring that their interests are linked to planning Develop children's self-help skills – range of dressing-up clothes to support dressing and undressing/encourage independence at meal/snack times Resources to promote cooperative play – e.g. wheeled toys, bats and balls, balancing beams	**Physical** Add labels and signs to the outside area – e.g. add props to wheeled toys to make in to trains, buses, fire engines, ambulances, taxis Set up obstacle courses with climbing equipment Trip to local park to develop large physical movement Opportunities to develop sand, water and malleable play	**Communication, Language and Literacy** To adapt and develop further home corner provision To introduce additional role-play area outside – 'the train station' Build up familiarity with books – *Mr Gumpy's Outing*, *Mr Gumpy's Motor Car* and *The Train Ride* and rhymes that feature transport To play alongside children in the role-play areas to encourage emergent writing Opportunities for large-scale mark making outside – 'footprints', rolling tyres and wheels in paint on to wall paper, etc.

TABLE 13.5 (continued)

PSRN	Creative	Knowledge and Understanding
Introduce numbers as labels in the outside area – e.g. number plates on vehicles, chalked out number parking bays	Make props to act out number rhymes	Encourage children's curiosity – e.g. testing cars down ramps
Opportunities to explore shapes – using recyclable materials to make their favourite transport models	Use large strong boxes for creative imaginative play outside	Adults to model asking questions about why things happen
Numbers in the 'train station' role-play area – tickets, timetables, etc.	Resources to support role play with wheeled toys, e.g. AA boxes, fire hose	Provide problem-solving opportunities – making vehicles for favourite toys
	Well-resourced and organised workshop area to encourage open-ended creative opportunities with emphasis on 'process' not product	Opportunities for using ICT – computer, digital camera, cd player, programmable toys

Parents
Run 2 Workshop sessions – to invite parents to stick photos in their child's profile books and contribute their observations to the book
Invite parent 'X' in to talk to children about his job as a bus driver
Give parents dates of trips and ask if they can volunteer to help on local trips

TABLE 13.6 Example of a learning story format for assessment

LEARNING STORY		
ADULT OBSERVER:	DATE:	TIME/DURATION:

The scene:

What happens:

Selected dialogue:

Any surprises:	What I need to do next:

Discussion points

1. Review the planning example in Table 13.2 to identify the key questions you might ask to support children's learning.

2. Discuss the favourite stories you have used to develop enriching learning activities in your setting. Use Table 13.3 'Magic planning: building on children's interests' as a starting point for activities.

Bibliography

Abbott, L. and Rodger, R. (eds) (1994) *Quality Education in the Early Years*. Buckingham: Open University Press.

Alexander, R. (2009) *Children their World, their Education: Final Report and Recommendations of the Cambridge Primary Review*. London: Routledge.

Allen, G. (2011) *Early Intervention: The Next Steps*. An Independent Report to Her Majesty's Government. London: The Centre for Social Justice. Available online at: www.centreforsocialjustice.org.uk.

Allen, G. MP and Duncan Smith, I. MP (2008) *Early Intervention: Good Parents, Great Kids, Better Citizens*. The Centre for Social Justice. The Smith Institute: London.

Athey, C. (1990) *Extending Thought in Young Children*. London: Paul Chapman Publishing.

Aubrey, C. (2003) Count me in: taking in early mathematical experiences. *Primary Mathematics*, 7(3), 17–20.

Aubrey, C., Dahl, S. and Godfrey, R., (2006) Early mathematical development and later achievement: further evidence. *Mathematics Education Research Journal*, 18 (1), 27–46.

Auerbach-Major, S. and Queenan, P. (2003). Preschool emotional competence: pathway to social competence. *Child Development*, 74, 238–256.

Biemiller, A. (2003) Vocabulary: needed if more children are to read well. *Reading Psychology* 24, 323–335.

Bilton, H. (2002) *Outdoor Play in the Early Years: Management and Innovation* (2nd ed.). London: David Fulton.

Bilton, H. (2004) *Playing Outside*. London: David Fulton.

Blakemore, S. J. and Frith, U. (2005) *The Learning Brain: Lessons for Education*. Oxford: Oxford Blackwell Publishing.

Bradley. L. and Bryant, P. (1985) *Rhyme and Reason in Reading and Spelling*. Ann Arbor: University of Michigan Press.

Brierley, J. (1987) *Give Me a Child until He Is Seven. Brain Studies and Early Childhood Education*. London: The Falmer Press.

Bronfenbrenner, U. (1979) *The Ecology of Human Development*. Cambridge, MA: Harvard University Press.

Browne, E. (1994) *Handa's Surprise*. London: Walker Books Limited.

Bruner, J. (1960) *The Process of Education*. New York: Vintage Books.

Carle, E. (1995) *The Very Hungry Caterpillar*. London: Puffin.

Carle, E. (1985) *The Bad-Tempered Ladybird*. London: Puffin.

Carruthers, E. and Worthington, M. (2003) 'Making sense of mathematical graphics: the development of understanding abstract symbolism'. Presentation at the *European Early Childhood Education Research Association* (EECERA) Conference, September 2003 at University of Strathclyde.

Carruthers, E. and Worthington, M. (2006) *Children's Mathematical Making Marks, Making Meaning*. London: Sage Publications.

Chandiramani, R. (2011) *Children and Young People Now*. Available online at: cypnow-bulletins@haymarket.com.

Clay, M. (1985) *The Early Detection of Reading Difficulties*. Auckland, New Zealand: Heinneman.

Clarke, P. (1992) *English as a Second Language in Early Childhood*. Victoria, Australia: Resources Centre, Richmond.

Convention of Scottish Local Authorities (COSLA) (2008) *The Scottish Curriculum for Excellence*. The Scottish Office.

DCSF (2006a) *The Rose Report: Independent Review of the Teaching of Early Reading*. Nottingham: DCSF.

DCSF (2006b) *The Childcare Act*. London: DCSF.

DCSF (2007a) *Confident, Capable and Creative: Supporting Boys' Achievement*. London: DCSF. Available online at: www.standards.dcsf.gov.uk.

DCSF (2007b) *Childcare and Early Years Providers Surveys Primary Schools with Reception and Nursery Classes*. London: DCSF.

DCSF (2007c) *Letters and Sounds*. Nottingham: DCSF. Available online at: www.standards.dfes.gov.uk.

DCSF (2007d) *Supporting Children Learning English as an Additional Language*. London: DCSF.

DCSF (2007e) *Primary National Strategy*. Nottingham: DCSF.

DCSF (2008a) *Inclusion Development Programme, Supporting Children with Speech, Language and Communication Needs: Guidance for Practitioners in the Early Years Foundation Stage*. Nottingham: DCSF.

DCSF (2008b) *Independent Review of Mathematics Teaching in Early Years Settings and Primary Schools*. Nottingham: DCSF.

DCSF (2008c) *EYFS Profile Handbook*. London: DCSF.

DCSF (2008d) *Mark Making Matters*. Nottingham: DCSF.

DCSF (2008e) *Social and Emotional Aspects of Development: Guidance for Practitioners Working in the Early Years Foundation Stage*. Nottingham: DCSF Publications.

DCSF (2008f) *Practice Guidance for the Early Years Foundation Stage*. Nottingham: DCSF.

DCSF (2009a) *Progress Matters: Reviewing and Enhancing Young Children's Development*. Nottingham: DCSF.

DCSF (2009b) *Children Thinking Mathematically: PSRN Essential Knowledge for Early Years Practitioners*. Nottingham: DCSF.

DCSF (2009c) *Building Future: Believing in Children – A Focus on Provision for Black Children in the Early Years Foundation Stage*. Nottingham: DCSF Publications.

DCSF (2009d) *Learning, Playing and Interacting – Good Practice in the Early Years Foundation Stage*. Nottingham: DCSF.

DCSF (2009e) *Early Education Pilot for Two-Year-Old Children: Evaluation*. Nottingham: DCSF.

DCSF (2009f) *Independent Review of Mathematics Teaching in Early Years Settings and Primary Schools (Williams Review)*. Nottingham: DCSF.

DCSF (2009g) *Numbers and Patterns: Laying Foundations in Mathematics*. Nottingham: DCSF.

DCSF (2010a) *Finding and Exploring Young Children's Fascinations*. Nottingham: DCSF.

DCSF (2010b) *Challenging Practice to Further Improve Learning and Playing and Interacting in the Early Years Foundation Stage*. Nottingham: DCSF.

DCSF (2010c) *Select Committee Report for Children's Centres*. London: DCSF.

Denham, S.A., Blair, K.A., DeMulder, E., Levitas, J., Sawyer, K., Averbach-Major, S. *et al.* (2003) Preschool emotional competence: pathway to social competence. *Child Development*, 74: 238–256.

DES (1975) *The Bullock Report: 'A Language for Life'*. London: HMSO.

DfE (2004) *Choice for Parents, the Best Start for Children: A Ten Year Strategy*. London: DFE.

DfE (2005) *A Study of Transition from the Foundation Stage to Key Stage 1*. London: HMSO publications.

DfE (2010a) *Sure Start Children's Centres: Statutory Guidance*. London: DfE.

DfE (2010b) *Sure Start Childrens Centre Statuory Guidance*. March Ref. DFE_00020_2011.

DfE (2011a) *The Early Years: Foundations for Life, Health and Learning*. An Independent Report on the Early Years Foundation Stage to her Majesty's Government. Dame Clare Tickell. London: DfE.

DfE (2011b) *The Early Years Foundation Stage Review: Report on the Evidence*. London: DfE.

DfE (2011c) *Families in the Foundation Years*. London: DfE

DfES (1975) *The Bullock Report, A Language for Life*. London: HMSO.

DfES (1989) *The Education of Children under Five*. London: DfES.

DfES (2004) *Choice for Parents, the Best Start for Children: A Ten-year Strategy for Children*. Department for Education and Skills.

DfES (2007a) *National Standards for the Leaders of Sure Start Children's Centres*. London: DfES.

DfES (2007b) *Standards for Leaders of Sure Start Children's Centres*. London: DfES.

DfES and Department of Health (2006) *Sure Start Children's Centres Practice Guidance*. Nottingham: DES.

Dickinson, D. K. and Tabors, P. O. (2002) 'Fostering Language and Literacy in Classrooms and Homes'. *Young Children*, 57: 10–18.

Donaldson, M. (1986) *Children's Minds*. London: Harper Collins.

Donaldson, J. (2002) *Room on the Broom*. London: Macmillan.

Duffy, B. (1998) *Supporting Creativity and Imagination in the Early Years*. Buckingham: Open University Press.

Edwards, E. and Redfern, A. (1998) *At Home in School*. London: Routledge.

Elfer, P., Goldschmied, E. and Selleck, D. (2002) *Key Persons in Nurseries: Building Relationships for Quality Provision*. London: National Early Years Network.

Ellis, S. (2010) University of Strathclyde reported in *The Guardian*, July 2007.

Evangelou, M. and Sylva, K. (2008) *Supporting Parents in Promoting Early Learning: The Evaluation of the Early Learning Partnership Project*. Oxford: Department of Education, University of Oxford and Department of Social Policy and work, University of Oxford.

Evangelou, M., Sylva, K., Kyriacou, M., Department of Education, University of Oxford. Wild, M., and Glenny, G., Westminster Institute of Education, Oxford Brookes University. (2009) *Early Years Learning and Development Literature Review*. Oxford: University of Oxford.

Feldman, M. A., Sparks, B. and Call, L. (1993) The effectiveness of home-based early intervention on the language development of children of mothers with mental disabilities. *Research in Development Disabilities*, 14, 387–408.

Field, F. (2010) *The Foundation Years: Preventing Poor Children Becoming Poor Adults. The Report of the Independent Review on Poverty and Life Chances*. London: DfE.

Friedman, M. (2005) *Trying Hard is not Good Enough*. Available online at: www.trafford.com.

Gardener, H. (1998) Complementary perspectives on Reggio Emilia, in Edwards, E. *et al.* (1998) *The Hundred Languages of Children*. London: Able Publishing.

Goleman, D. (1999) *Working with Emotional Intelligence*. London: Bloomsbury Publishing PLC.

Gordon, M. (1996) *Roots of Empathy*. Available online at: www.rootsofempathy.org.

Goswami, U. and Bryant, P. (1990) *Phonological Skills and Learning to Read*. Hove: Psychological Press Ltd.

Gross, M. (2010) *So Why Can't They Read*. London: Centre for Policy Studies.

Hanson, K. and Joshi, H. (2007) *Millennium Cohort Study Second Survey: A Users Guide to Initial Findings*. London: University of London, Centre for Longitudinal Studies.

Harris, J. (2000) *The Work of the Imagination*. Oxford: Blackwell.

Hart, B. and Risley, T. (1995) *Meaningful Differences in the Everyday Experience of Young American Children*. Baltimore, MD: Paul H. Brookes.

Her Majesty's Inspector of Schools (2004) *Transition from Reception to Year 1*. London: HMIS.

Her Majesty's Stationery Office (1969) *Our Young Children*. London: HMSO.

Johnston, R. and Watson, J. (2005) *Insight 17: A Seven Year Study of the Effects of Synthetic Phonics Teaching on Reading and Spelling Attainment*. Available online at www.scotland.gov.uk/publication/2005/02/20682/52383.

Kennedy, I. (2010) *Getting it Right for Children and Young People*. Overcoming Cultural Barriers in the NHS so as to meet their needs.

Law, J. and Harris, F. (2001) *Sure Start Promoting Speech and Language Development*. London: City University.

Lindon, J. (1998) *Understanding Child Development*. London: Thomson Learning.

Lindsay, G. *et al.* (2010) *Evaluation of the Parenting Early Intervention Programme: First Interim Report*. Warwick: CEDAR, University of Warwick.

Marmot, M. (2010) *Fair Society, Healthy Lives: The Marmot Review*. Available online at: www.ucl.ac.uk/marmotreview.

Mathews, J. *Helping Children to Draw and Paint in Early Childhood (0–8 Years)*. London: Hodder and Stoughton.

Maude, P. (1996) 'How can I do this better?' From movement education into early years physical education', in Whitebread, D. (2006) *Teaching and Learning in the Early Years*. London: Routledge.

Maynard, T. (2007) Forest Schools in Great Britain: initial exploration. *Contemporary Issues in Early Childhood*, 8(4), 320–331.

McCrink, K. and Wynn, K. (2004) Large number addition and subtraction by 9 month old infants. *Psycho. Sci.*, 15(11), 776–781.

McGuinness, D. (1998) *Why Children Can't Read*. London: Penguin.

Meadows, S. and Cashdan, A. (1988) *Helping Children Learn*. London: David Fulton Publishers.

Melhuish, E. and NESS Team (2008) *Findings from the National Evaluation of Sure Start*. London, Birkbeck: University of London.

Melhuish, E. *et al.* (2008) *The Impact of Sure Start Local Programmes on Five Year Olds and their Families*. London: DfE.

Melhuish, E. *et al.* (2010) *The Impact of Sure Start Local Programmes on Five Year Olds and their Families*. London: DfE.

Mickleburgh, J. (2010) *Early Years Foundation Stage Forum*. Available online at: www.foundation-stage. info/news.

Mix, K. S. (2002) The Construction of Number Concepts. *Cognitive Development* 17(3–4): 1345–1363.

Montessori, M. (1986) *Discovery of the Child*. London: Random House (Ballantine).

Moyles, J. *et al.* (2002) *SPEEL Study of Pedagogical Effectiveness in Early Learning (SPEEL)*. London: DCSF.

National Centre for Social Research (2009) *The Early Education Programme for Two Year Old Children*. London: University of London.

Nutbrown, C. and Hannon, P. (1997) *Preparing for Early Literacy with Parents: A Professional Development Manual*. Nottingham: NES Arnold.

O'Brien, L. and Murray, R. (2007) Forest school and its impact on young children: case studies in Britain. *Urban Forestry and Urban Greenery*, 6(4): 249–265.

Ofsted (2001) *Guidance to the National Standards: Full Day Care*. London: DfES September.

Ofsted (2007) *The Foundation Stage: A Survey of 144 Settings*. London: Ofsted.

Ofsted (2008) *Early Years Leading to Excellence: A Review of Childcare and Early Education 2005–2008 with a Focus on Organisation, Leadership and Management*. London: Ofsted.

Ofsted (2009) *The Impact of Integrated Services on Children and their Families in Sure Start Children's Centres*. London: Ofsted.

Ofsted (2010) *Using the Early Years Evaluation Schedule*. London: Ofsted.

Ofsted (2011) *The Impact of the Early Years Foundation Stage*. London: Ofsted.

Piaget, J. (1969) *The Psychology of the Child*. New York: Basic Books.

Piaget, J. (1983) *The Psychology of the Child*. New York: Basic Books.

Ramesh, R. (2011) '60% of poorest children fail to reach good level of behaviour says study'. *The Guardian* (February 11). Available online at: www.guardian.co.uk/society.

Rice, M. and Wilcox, K. A. (eds) (1995) *Building a Language-focused Curriculum for the Preschool Classroom: Volume 1: A Foundation for Lifelong Communication*. Baltimore: Paul H. Brookes Publishing Co.

Rodd, J. (2002) *Learning to Learn in Schools*. Phase 1 Project Report. London: Campaign for Learning.

Rodger, R. (1998) 'Using structured play to promote Language development in the early years', in Halsall, R. (ed.) (1998) *Teacher Research and School Improvement*. Buckingham: Open University Press.

Rodger, R. (1999) *Planning an Appropriate Curriculum for the Under Fives*. London: David Fulton Publishers.

Rodger, R. (2003) *Planning an Appropriate Curriculum for the Under Fives*. London: David Fulton Publishers.

Rogoff, B. (2003) *The Cultural Nature of Human Development*. Oxford: Oxford University Press.

Sanders, D., White, G., Eames, A., Mceune, R. and Grayson, H. (2005) NFER. *A Study of the Transition from the Foundation Stage to Key Stage 1*. DfES: London

Sarnecka, B. W. and Carey, S. (2008) 'How counting represents number: what children must learn and when they learn it'. *Cognition*, 108: 662–674.

Scott, K. (2007) 'Sounds Incredible'. *The Guardian*, July 10 2007

Siraj-Blatchford, I., Sylva, K., Muttock, S., Gilden, R. and Bell, D. (2002) *Researching Effective Pedagogy in the Early Years*. London: Institute of Education.

Siraj-Blatchford, I., Sylva, K., Taggart, B., Sammons, P. and Melhuish, E. (2003) *The EPPE Case Studies Technical Paper 10*. London: University of London, Institute of Education/DfE.

Siraj-Blatchford, I. and Manni, L. (2007) *Effective Leadership in the Early Years Sector: The ELEYS Study Issues in Practice Series*. London: Institute of Education, University of London.

Smith, R. *et al.* (2009) *Early Education Pilot for Two-Year-Old Children Evaluation (DCSF-RR134)*. London: DCSF. Available online at: www.dcsf.gov.uk/reserach/.

Smith, T. (1980) *Parents and Preschool*. London: Grant McIntyre.

Sylva, K., Melhuish, E., Dammons, P., Siraj-Blatchford, I., Taggart, B. (2004) *The Effective Provision of Pre-School Education (EPPE) Project: Final Report*. London: The Institute of Education.

Thomas, V. (2009) *Winnie's Flying Carpet*. Oxford: OUP.

Thompson, I. (2008) *Teaching and Learning Early Numbers*. Buckingham: Open University Press.

Urban Leadership Centre Ltd (2009) *The Children's Centre Leadership Model: Bringing Children's Centre Leadership into the 21st Century*. ULC

Van Der Eyken, W. (1982) *Home-Start: A Four Year Evaluation*. SSRC: Leicester. (2008) Victoria Curriculum and Assessment Authority. Australia Analysis of Curriculum' Learning Frameworks.

Vygotsky, L. S. (1978) *Mind in Society: The Development of Higher Psychological Process*. Cambridge, Mass.: Harvard University Press.

Wasik, B. A., Bond, M. A. and Hindman, A. (2006) 'The effects of a language and literacy intervention on head start children and teachers'. *Journal of Educational Psychology* 98, 63–7.

Whitehead, M. R. (2004) *Language and Literacy in the Early Years*. London: Sage.

Index

Note: The following abbreviations have been used – f = figure; t = table